BLOOD &
Retribution

VAN HOOGSTRATEN
BLOOD &
Retribution

DON JORDAN AND
MIKE WALSH

JOHN BLAKE

Published by John Blake Publishing Ltd,
3, Bramber Court, 2 Bramber Road,
London W14 9PB, England

www.blake.co.uk

First published in paperback in 2004

ISBN: 978 1 84454 017 4

British Library Cataloguing-in-Publication Data:

A catalogue record for this book is available from the British Library.

Design by www.envydesign.co.uk

Printed in Great Britain by CPI Bookmarque, Croydon, CR0 4TD

3 5 7 9 10 8 6 4 2

Papers used by John Blake Publishing are natural, recyclable products made from
wood
grown in sustainable forests. The manufacturing processes conform to the
environmental regulations of the country of origin.

Pictures reproduced by kind permission of ITV News and Priscilla Coleman, Press
Association, Mirrorpix, Brighton Evening Argus, Photo News, John Connor Press
Associates, Rex Features and Katz Pictures. Every attempt has been made to contact
the relevant copyright-holders, but some were unobtainable. We would be grateful
if the appropriate people could contact us.

Dedication

For Diane

ACKNOWLEDGEMENTS

Among the many who helped us prepare this book,
we would like to thank in particular Tony Browne, David Millward,
current and former members of the Metropolitan police
team in South London and Granada Television.

CONTENTS

DEDICATION   v

ACKNOWLEDGEMENTS   vi

PROLOGUE   ix

1 BOY TYCOON   1

2 KING MOD   17

3 BOMBER   33

4 BANGED UP   51

5 SETTLING ACCOUNTS   65

6 THE DREAM PALACE   73

7 VAN HOOGSTRATEN'S WOMEN   83

8 THE DEAL   97

9 SCUMBAGS   113

10 NOTORIOUS   139

11 BUILDING AN EMPIRE   153

12 AT THE COURT OF KING NICK   171

13 FIRE!   185

14 A THORN IN THE SIDE   195

15 VOICE FROM THE GRAVE   207

16 THE CHICKENS COME HOME TO ROOST   225

17 THE RECKONING   245

18 FREEDOM   267

EPILOGUE   275

PROLOGUE

The girl was in bed in her hotel room when her lover rang to say he was coming up.

'I'd already opened the door and got back into bed and he just came to the bed shouting. He grabbed me by the hair and slapped me a couple of times and some big clumps came off in his hand. Then he took off his slipper and started hitting me across the face with it. It broke and he got one of his shoes. He hit me above the eye screaming, "You fucking bitch I know you've been with another man." Then he left the room. Later on I went to my friend and she took me to the police station. And it just started from there, really, at the police station.'

Tanaka Sali was eighteen, tall, black, curvaceous, with the face of an angel. The man who beat her up was white, three times her age and one of the richest men in England.

He was also about to go on trial at the Old Bailey, accused of ordering a contract killing. At the police station the girl he had just assaulted agreed to give evidence against him – the perfect revenge. But Tanaka Sali would soon be in fear of her own life, terrified of telling anyone what she knew.

This book is the story of her lover, his vast fortune, his crimes and his downfall. His name is Nicholas van Hoogstraten.

1

BOY TYCOON

In the mid-1950s the husband of a teacher at a Roman Catholic school in Shoreham-by-Sea developed a fatal cancer. Somehow one of the pupils learned about the illness and took to going to the dying man's house to read to him every night. The pupil was Nicholas van Hoogstraten. It is one of the few favourable anecdotes about Van Hoogstraten, man or boy, that people tell. Van Hoogstraten, or Mr H as his henchmen call him, has spent a lifetime embroidering the evil that he's done. If there is a good side to him he has gone out of his way to bury it.

His reward is a reputation for arrogance, ruthlessness and brutal violence. It is a reputation that for decades intimidated almost everyone who got in his way and helped make him one of the richest men in Britain. That same reputation was almost Nicolas van Hoogstraten's downfall. It was a crucial factor in persuading a jury to convict him of the killing of a business rival. Newspaper headline writers applauded when, in the autumn of 2002, van Hoogstraten was sentenced to ten years in jail and his career seemed to be over.

'On a scale of evil of one to ten, he scores at least eleven', pronounced the *Daily Mail*. The *Evening Standard* said that his life had been, 'dedicated to violence, fear, intimidation and hatred.'

Yet there are women who have loved Van Hoogstraten and still do. And there are one or two men who say they, too, love him.

What explains this man who made a vast fortune and in the process went persistently out of his way to make himself hated?

Part of it is that Nicholas van Hoogstraten is an actor and a fantasist. He has been making up things about himself – good and bad – all his life: his family was rich and built the Indian railways; his father was a shipping agent; he made his first fortune from a land deal in the Bahamas; he is a friend of pop stars and prime ministers; he is so dangerous that if you cross him you might find your balls chopped off.

Some of it appears to be utter fabrication, but, like all the best lies, some of it is true.

On 27 February 1945 the Second World War was coming to an end. That morning American tanks smashed across the River Ruhr to come within sight of the ancient Rhineland city of Cologne. That afternoon US Marines recaptured Manila from the Japanese. That night Berlin was blitzed by six hundred RAF Mosquito bombers. And, in the Sussex town of Shoreham-by-Sea, Nicholas van Hoogstraten was born.

The weather in Shoreham was calm and surprisingly warm for the time of year. Temperatures rose above fifty degrees Fahrenheit that day.

At the local Odeon they were showing I Love a Soldier, starring Charlie Chaplin's wife, Paulette Goddard. The Dome was showing I Walked with a Zombie. The Plaza had Bulldog Drummond Strikes Back, with Ronald Colman.

On the BBC Home Service it was announced that HRH Princess Elizabeth had mumps.

The local paper, the Worthing Gazette, reported a High Court ruling that 'the omission of Mr before a gentleman's name in a newspaper report is not defamatory'.

Baby's Nicholas's birth was registered on 13 March. He was christened Nicholas Marcel Hoogstraten. He would add the 'van' twenty-two years later. The Hoogstraten family were from old Flemish stock and were wanderers. His grandfather settled in India, where his father Charles Marcel Joseph Hoogstraten was born. As a young man Charles made his home in Paris, working in the wine trade. He arrived in England on the outbreak of the Second World War and found a job in a munitions factory in Bognor. There he met a local girl, Edna Brookes, and married her. Then he joined the British army.

It is unlikely that Charles was there to see Edna give birth to little Nick. At the time he was a trooper with the Royal Armoured Corps, then battling its way through Holland for the final assault on Germany. In the midst of war a private soldier only qualified for compassionate leave to see someone at home being buried, not to see a baby being born.

When he came back from the war, Private Hoogstraten settled the family in Rustington, on the eastern edge of Littlehampton. A mile and a half from the sea, Rustington was described in post-war guidebooks as a 'pretty little village' that maintained a happy balance of old and new. Today it is another featureless suburb characterised by ugly concrete shops and street after street of semi-detached houses with narrow, forty-foot-long back gardens.

In the late 1930s the place had expanded rapidly to take families from Wales and the north of England. They had come south looking for jobs in nearby Southampton and Portsmouth. But with the outbreak of war this stretch of the Sussex coast was thought to be the place where the Germans might invade, and Rustington began to empty. The nightly

Luftwaffe blitzing of the two nearby ports hastened the retreat. When the Hoogstratens came looking for a home in Rustington there were plenty to choose from.

The house that Charles and Edna picked was at the end of a cul-de-sac of tiny, pebble-dashed semis called Conbar Avenue. Today, through a collapsed back fence, you can see the window of young Nick's cramped bedroom at the rear of the house.

The bits and bobs about his childhood which Van Hoogstraten has let slip over the years suggest a violent, dominating father absent from home for long periods, a downtrodden, distant mother and an increasingly resentful child.

His father landed a job after the war as a senior wine steward for the Royal Mail shipping line. His ship was the SS Andes, the 'Queen of the South Seas' according to the brochures. She plied the Southampton – Buenos Aires route, which accounts for the long stretches Charles spent away from home. Thanks to the war, he can't have seen much of his son in the first six months of Nick's life, and his job on the Andes meant that he didn't see much more of him later either. The next-door neighbour, Louis Yaxley, believes that Charles's prolonged absences were disastrous for Nick, who eventually began to run out of control.

Nick disliked his father. In a 1998 interview, he said: 'I didn't get on with my father. He always saw me as a rival...'

He liked his mother Edna even less. 'My mother was not nice to me. I never had any affection.' He viewed her 'as an object that I had inherited, someone to do the work. My father treated her like that and I'm the same.' Almost up to her death he would refer to his mother as a 'whining cow'.

Two other children were born to the Hoogstratens, both girls and younger than Nick. They were called Betty and Rita. Neither of them figures in anything Van Hoogstraten has said publicly about his childhood. But one in particular is close to him and later featured as a director of one of his companies. Neither sister ever talks about him.

Snobbishness, jingoism and Roman Catholicism would seem to have marked the Hoogstraten household and Nick especially.

His mother once told him to walk the long way to school to avoid passing through a council estate. He didn't question the instruction. 'She was right,' he recalled. 'They were dirty kids who smelled bad.' He retained a disdain for the British working classes and would grow to hate Labour Party politicians and the trade unions associated with them.

The British royal family was revered by the Hoogstratens and it still is by Van Hoogstraten. After Princess Diana was killed in Paris in 1997 he confessed himself pleased. The reason, he explained, was the 'damage' that the Princess had done to the monarchy.

The Hoogstratens were all regular attenders of Mass at St Joseph's, the Roman Catholic church in Rustington. Nick, however, would soon throw off Catholicism. 'Religion and politics are used to pervert and control ignorant people,' he says. 'If you've got a brain for yourself you know what's right and wrong.'

His march to fabulous riches began at the age of seven. Other small boys in those pre-computer days played marbles in the playground, Five Stones, Cowboys and Indians and the tag game It. Nick studied postage stamps.

His father gave him his own stamp collection. In the early 1950s postage stamps were a window on the world, with their tiny coloured etchings of palm trees, exotic foreign rulers in turbans or military uniform and unfamiliar currencies. They were today's TV travel programmes. The gift from Charles Hoogstraten sparked in Nick a lifelong interest in philately, foreign parts – and in making money.

At nine years old Nick began buying and selling stamps in the playground. He told later how he traded the best stamps from other boys' collections. By the time he was twelve he was trading with professional dealers. At first his newspaper delivery round provided the capital. He'd make up whole albums of stamps which he lodged on a fifty-fifty, sale-or-return basis with shops in Littlehampton.

He also began dealing by post with the big operators in the stamp business, like the Stanley Gibbons organisation, who advertised in the philatelic journals. They had no idea this new player was barely into his teens. 'They don't realise they are dealing with a twelve-year-old kid. I had a nominee name even then.'

The profits didn't go on sweets or comics. The money was saved. By the time he was thirteen Nick had already amassed 'a few thousand pounds' in a bank account which his mother had opened for him. Soon it would be tens of thousands of pounds. What grated with him, it seems, was that neither parent took his astonishing success seriously enough. 'My mother wouldn't invest in me,' he complained. His father called what he was doing 'playing with stamps'.

He was clearly a very difficult teenager. At school he was a barrack-room lawyer accused by teachers of undermining them. 'I started organising things at school like telling them they didn't have to carry milk crates from the front entrance into the classroom.' It was a Jesuit school partly staffed by nuns. One of them 'tried to whack me with a chair leg once. I grabbed it and hit her and she never tried again.'

Thanks to his money and a tough-guy personality, Nick had his gang at school. He had a regular girl, too, for three years. She was called Yolande. But at heart he was and remained a loner. 'I had no close friends,' he told one journalist.

The Hoogstratens' neighbour Louis Yaxley recalls one incident that points up the loneliness of the teenage Nick. And his self-righteousness. 'It was 5 November time and everybody round here had fireworks and bonfires. We had all gone to bed and suddenly we were woken up. It was about two or three o'clock in the morning, and we heard "bang, bang, bang" outside. I said: "It's that bloody Nicky." I looked out of the window and there he was chucking fireworks about. I came down the stairs in me nightclothes and put me coat on and went outside into the garden. I shouted at him and he looked at me and then got hold of a firework. Then he lit it and he threw it at me.'

Yaxley lost his temper. 'It made me mad. There was a milk bottle out on the step. I picked it up. I'm going to throw it at his head and he just jogs round the corner of the house out of sight. The bottle I threw smashed on the corner of the house.'

Nick didn't reappear that night. Yaxley went back to bed. A few days later he was astonished to get a solicitor's letter. It accused him of assaulting 'my client'. The client was Nicholas Hoogstraten, aged about twelve and still in short trousers. Nothing developed. Yaxley says that young Nick gave him a wide berth after that.

Within the Hoogstraten home Edna was bullied by her son. She didn't tell her friend next door. Appearances had to be kept up. But one windy day Mrs Yaxley got a glimpse of Nick's temper. Edna Hoogstraten was in her back garden hanging up the family washing on the clothes line. She had left the back door open. Inside, Nick was sitting at the kitchen table sorting through his stamps. A gust of wind blew some of the stamps on to the floor. Furious, he slammed the back door and locked it. 'He left his mother out there in the garden. He wouldn't let her in,' Mrs Yaxley told her husband later. All afternoon Edna Hoogstraten was made to stand in the garden by her angry son.

Next Nick took to hitting Edna. 'With my father away I was the man of the house. My mother used to get a clip round the ear from me when she asked for it.' And when his mother complained about him to his father 'he would hit her too'. The sight of his father beating his mother would stay with him for ever. It might help explain his lifelong disdain for women and his own violence.

Soon young Nick began to break the law. In 1957 he seems to have persuaded another boy to break into their school for him and steal a typewriter. It was found in Nick's bedroom. He needed it to correspond with dealers for his stamp business. The theft marked him out as being different from other boys. In the fifties other twelve-year-olds stole sweets for immediate gratification; this one stole with a long-term purpose.

It was Nick's first offence. And, as with the others that were to come, he got someone else to do his dirty work. He got off with a warning.

By now, Nick was developing the characteristics that would mark out his life and career – resentfulness, dislike of authority, contempt for others, a reliance on his own abilities and a knack for manipulating others.

The boy tycoon's stamp business continued to expand. By the time he was fourteen Nick was so full of himself that he took to flouting the school's uniform rules by attending lessons in a three-piece business suit. While his school mates read the Wizard and Eagle, he took the Financial Times. He refused to attend certain classes, insisting on sitting alone in empty classrooms preoccupied with his business.

At fifteen Nick had a stamp collection worth £30,000, but he had a police record too. According to his father, the teenager set up younger lads to steal stamps for him from local stamp shops. Two of them were caught in the act. Nick's role was uncovered and he was given probation. His father decided that he had to do something. In the time-honoured British fashion for dealing with errant sons he took Nick off to sea in the Andes.

Looking back, Van Hoogstraten would talk of his time in 'the navy'. Journalists digging for background facts after he became well known would be told that his father was a purser who got him a job as a steward on his ship. A shipmate remembers his father as deputy head wine waiter and Nick as a bellboy.

'I'm not really sure why I allowed myself to go in the first place,' Van Hoogstraten told the Observer in 1988. 'I suppose it's the difference between being 15 and 16. When you're 15 you do as you're told. When you're 16 you don't... I suppose my father saw his position being usurped so he got rid of me.'

The Andes was the stuff of a schoolboy's dreams. She was the Royal Mail line's flagship. She had been launched just before the Second World War when she was the last word in speed and luxury. Converted to a troop ship in 1939, she had taken Allied troops to almost every theatre of war and had survived submarine-infested waters totally unscathed. Her final wartime job was to take three thousand Australian and New Zealand airmen home across the Atlantic and through the Panama Canal. Most of the population of Southampton seems to have turned out to see them go, Royal Marine bands playing, flags flying, RAF escort squadrons screaming overhead. Black-and-white newsreel cameras captured the scene for every cinema in the country. The cameras were back two months later for the ship's return trip too, because on the way back, via India and the Suez Canal, she had broken the speed record for circumnavigating the world.

In 1947 the Andes was reconverted to a luxury liner for use on the South Atlantic route. On her first stop at Buenos Aires the Argentinian President, Juan Perón, and his glamorous wife, Eva, came on board to a reception. Again the cameras whirred. For the boy from the Conbar Avenue semi the opulence of the ship must have been an eye-opener. She was a floating luxury hotel with swimming pools, mahogany-panelled cocktail lounges, marble statues and cinemas. The saloons glittered with crystal chandeliers. Each cabin had its own en-suite bathroom – a real luxury in those days. She was advertised as being 'a class apart'.

The Andes carried four hundred passengers, and the new bellboy did very well out of them. His former shipmate remembers Nick well. 'Like his father, he was very, very smart. Always well turned out. The uniform was a white tunic with blue edgings... He used to make a lot from tips, a lot. What he'd do is grizzle in front of passengers when he was operating the lifts and they'd ask him what was the matter. He'd tell them how terribly homesick he was. Of course the passengers would feel sorry for the lad, especially the women passengers, and they'd give him a big tip.'

According to the shipmate, the snivelling bellboy also played on the good nature of his fellow crew members. 'He went round the crew's quarters asking people for a sixpence or a threepenny bit so he could buy stamps to write a letter home.'

He also made money by covering for his shipmates' boozing and philandering. He'd happily fill in for them if they made it worth his while.

What the teenager saw on the Andes changed his life. 'The wealth was incredible. That's when I started to see what was going on in the world. I put it all to good advantage.' He also saw what happened below decks and in the galley, which might explain some of the peculiarities he exhibited later on in life. One was his preference for baked potatoes. He explained that he could peel a baked potato and throw the peel away knowing that 'no one has pissed on or spat on' what he was consuming.

Nick spent twelve months on the Andes. There was a three-week cruise in the Mediterranean, followed by a quick trip north to the Baltic and then, for the rest of the year, there were lazy, month-long cruises round the Caribbean and Florida.

One of the regular ports of call was Nassau, capital of New

Providence Island in the Bahamas. It was here that Nick spotted an opportunity and made his fortune. Or he says he did.

Nassau was still an old colonial port in 1960. On the hill overlooking the bay loomed the battlements of Fort Charlotte, built by slaves in the eighteenth century. Down below, black policemen in white helmets and khaki shorts patrolled the bustling harbour. Horse-drawn surreys trotted through narrow passageways with names like Goat Alley and Burial Ground Corner. Here and there along the shore an elegant pastel-coloured mansion peeped out from behind a wall of bougainvillea or hibiscus. Expatriate white men chatted in their clubs. Black children hailed incoming yachts, offering to dive for pennies. Bahamian women tramped the marketplace and the shantytown of wooden huts 'over the hill', balancing impossible parcels on their heads.

But Nassau was changing. There were more and more Cadillacs and offices on Bay Street, the commercial hub of the town. There were more and more men with briefcases. The port was about to develop fast, and property prices were about to explode.

When Nick first arrived land prices had already been shooting up for several years. The rise was fuelled by the increasing numbers of the super-rich opting for a hideaway on the powder-soft sand of a Bahamian cove. It wasn't a new phenomenon. The first rich Britons and Americans to spot the Bahamas as a perfect bolthole had arrived as long ago as the 1880s. There had been no big influx of the rich, however, until after the Second World War. Then, in the fifties, British aristocrats like Colin Tennant and Sir Victor Sassoon fetched up there, and more followed. At the end of the decade some land prices had trebled. That was nothing to what was coming.

Two men had visions for the island of New Providence that would help to send the Bahamian land values through the roof.

One of them was an American tycoon called Huntingdon Hartford. In 1959 he had paid £3 million to buy a plot of six thousand acres on an islet across the bay from Nassau called Hog Island. It was an enormous sum in those days. Hartford announced that he planned to build a 'resort of taste and refinement' there, though he was looking for a 'more appealing' name for the island. He found one. In 1962 the colonial authorities gave permission for Hog to become Paradise Island. The news of the American millionaire's plan prompted a scramble among entrepreneurs to snaffle up every acre of the Bahamian shoreline that they could.

The second man's vision would have an even more dramatic impact on the islands. Meyer Lansky was the American Mafia's financial wizard, but in 1959 he and his even more notorious partner, Lucky Luciano, lost their lucrative gambling outlet in Havana. Fidel Castro's left-wing revolutionaries overthrew the corrupt regime of Fulgencio Batista, then promptly closed the Havana casinos and kicked the Mafia out. To Lansky and Luciano, dreamy little Nassau was an ideal replacement for Havana. Their predecessors had once used the islands. During prohibition in the 1920s American bootleggers had made the Bahamas one of their main staging posts for running hooch into the USA. But its real attraction to Lansky and Luciano was that the authorities there were likely to be a pushover. There was no income tax in the islands. Currency controls were minimal. The colonial administration didn't much care who set up shop there as long as they weren't communists. And the place was almost as near to the USA – and so almost as close to US gamblers – as the Mob's old base in Cuba was.

Lansky and Luciano quietly moved in on the Bahamas. Later they would open their own Mafia-controlled bank there and own two of the smaller islands. Gambling and drug running would take off. The impact on land prices would be massive. In a couple of years prices would quadruple, then quadruple and quadruple again.

The *Andes* docked just as all this was beginning to happen. Van Hoogstraten, speaking to one of the authors in 2001, described what followed. 'The executors of Sir Harry Oakes were selling his estate. They had this idea of splitting it up and selling ten-year options on each little parcel. I had some money and bought as many options as I could... I took out hundreds, no, thousands.'

Sir Harry Oakes was a fabulous character from another age. In 1917 he had made the second-biggest gold strike ever in the Western Hemisphere. It brought him so much money that he was reckoned to be the richest man on earth. In the 1930s he purchased the huge Westbourne estate outside Nassau and settled there. But in 1943 he was murdered in his Westbourne mansion, apparently the victim of a Voodoo ritual. His only house guest found his body lying face-up on the bed. It was tarred and feathered and was smouldering as if the corpse had been set on fire. Oakes's playboy son-in-law, whom he had openly disliked, was arrested and charged with the murder. But after a sensational trial he was acquitted. Nearly sixty years later the killing remains a mystery.

Van Hoogstraten never explained how he heard that the Oakes estate was being sold and how he then got in ahead of all the others who were scrabbling for prime sites in Nassau. Whatever the explanation, he managed to buy up 'hundreds of acres' without putting up anything other than minimum 'option money... Peanuts.'

Then he quit the 'navy', as he called it, and waited. He didn't have to wait for long.

Within two years he was rich. 'I saw land that I had bought for nothing, £300 an acre, go for six, eight, ten thousand an acre. It was colossal money in those days.' He didn't gamble on prices going any higher but sold everything. 'I pulled the whole lot out and put the money in Switzerland.'

'Where I was clever or lucky was when I got out,' he later told the Observer. 'All markets go in cycles. You can't always get in at the bottom and out at the top. As long as you get in and get out you make money. I always had an instinct for knowing when enough's enough.'

How much did he make? He claims that he went 'from being worth £30,000 [his stamp collection] to a few hundred thousand'.

Later he would invest the Swiss money in mining, land and gold in the USA and Africa. It was these investments which eventually made him super-rich, he claimed in an interview with Business Age.

Inevitably, journalists and others have wondered about the story of the launching pad for his wealth – that inspired piece of land speculation in the Bahamas. But investigative reporters who have dug for details have come up with nothing. Enquiries to the land registry there have produced no records of anyone called Nicholas Hoogstraten. Real-estate operators who were active in the islands in the 1960s profess not to know the name, but then this is a rich man's paradise and so it is a place of secrets.

Is the Oakes land story a fiction? Does it seek to cover up a much more sinister explanation for Hoogstraten's sudden wealth? There is no evidence of any wrongdoing, but the enormous amount of money he claims to have made – together with his later criminal activities – has fuelled continual speculation.

One friendship which he says he forged there was with Sir Lynden Pindling, the first black prime minister of the Bahamas. When Nick was striking gold with the land deal, Pindling, a lawyer, was leading the fight for independence from British colonial rule. He was known by his followers as the 'black Moses'. Van Hoogstraten says that he was introduced by a girlfriend to the charismatic Pindling and that they became friends. He is a compulsive namedropper. One or two meetings with a famous person and, in his mind, he or she becomes a friend. Mick Jagger, the Rhodesian Prime Minister Ian Smith and Janet Street-Porter are just a few examples. If Pindling was indeed a friend, he was a friend with dangerous connections. As Prime Minister of the Bahamas, he was to become totally dependent on the Mafia. His regime was supported by drug money. He was finally forced from power in the 1970s because of corruption, and because those Mafia connections had become an international scandal. At that time ninety per cent of all the cocaine consumed in the USA was being routed through the Bahamas.

However Nicholas Hoogstraten made his first fortune, he never forgot the Caribbean as giving him the opportunity to change his life. He'd return there time after time. He'd try to live there. He'd name his companies – and his family – after towns there. He'd go there to celebrate his greatest triumphs and his greatest escapes. And he'd find a beautiful woman there who fell in love with him and might have kept him on the straight and narrow if only he had stuck with her.

2

KING MOD

A triumphant Nicholas Hoogstraten packed in his job as a bellboy on the Andes and went back to the Caribbean. He was in the Bahamas on that day in November 1963 when US President John F. Kennedy was assassinated. He remembered that he felt glad at the news as it came through from Dallas. 'Kennedy was on an ego trip,' he later explained. The young Englishman had no time for other people's egos. He was about to embark on an extensive ego trip of his own. Before he was twenty-three it would land him in jail, sentenced to nine years.

But up to that moment life would seem very, very good.

He was, in his own eyes, very rich and he was about to get very much richer very quickly.

At eighteen he'd take the first step to becoming a property tycoon.

At twenty he'd open his own boutique and have his own pop clubs.

At twenty-two he would be able to call himself Britain's 'youngest self-made millionaire'.

Later – after he was released from jail – he'd get richer still. First he would call himself a 'multi-millionaire', then a 'multi-multi-millionaire'. He would visibly relish hearing himself stress the words 'multi-multi'.

He'd also relish reeling off the goodies his ever-growing pile of money was buying: first the Rolls-Royce and the Cadillac, then the jewels and the Persian carpets, then the two Turners, the Holbein and the Boucher, then the 'finest collection of antique French furniture in private hands' and finally the palace, a real one – 'the biggest private dwelling built in this country in more than a hundred years'.

But he found out very early on that there was one thing that money couldn't buy: social acceptability. He was made to learn that as he dreamed his teenage dreams in the Caribbean. Nick had decided that, having struck it rich there, he would try to make a go of living there, just like so many rich or aristocratic Brits. Colin Tennant, Princess Margaret's friend, had made a home on Mustique, Noël Coward in Jamaica, Nicholas Hoogstraten would make his home in Bermuda. Or that was the plan.

He set his heart on living in Hamilton, the capital. 'Hamilton was one of the few places that I visited when I was younger that I fell in love with... I purchased a hotel there, on Langton Hill. It had thirty bedrooms. I bought it to live in, as my home. But in those days I was only a kid – I was only eighteen – and I didn't know much. When I moved in I was uncomfortable. I felt like a fish out of water. I only stayed there one night and it was my own hotel.'

It seems that his face didn't fit in the exclusive clubs and chic hotel bars of the British expatriate elites. Blacks weren't made very welcome in such places. Nor, evidently, was a smart-arse kid from Sussex with a lot of money and the wrong accent. He was an outsider, a parvenu, and he was made to know it.

His bile at the memory of how he was treated suggests the humiliation ran deep. It must have hit that ego very hard indeed. He made no white friends on the islands. Of the whites whom he did come across there he says: 'they were riff raff … sickos, the lot of them'. He didn't like them and they didn't like him. The way that the whites in Nassau and Hamilton reacted to him seeded in Hoogstraten an intense dislike for British expatriates that he would show again and again in later years.

At the same time the arrogance of the whites stirred in him a fellow feeling for blacks that would temper his whole life, especially his sex life. He must have felt more at home in the black shebeens 'over the hill' in Nassau than he did among the blazers and old school ties in the Porcupine Club, where the Duke of Windsor had held court during the war when he was governor of the Bahamas.

Nick sold the Bermuda hotel – 'I had an offer from a Yank that I couldn't refuse' – and decided to go home to England.

Did Charles and Edna Hoogstraten welcome the prodigal son with open arms? Initially, perhaps they did. He had lots of money, he lent them some of it and he was ready to buckle down to a normal career.

Aged eighteen, he landed a job in the business he loved – cataloguing stamps with the Stanley Gibbons organisation. Over the next two years he travelled up and down from Shoreham to the company's headquarters in London. If he was full of himself and lippy, to the outside observer he must have seemed to be just another young commuter on the Victoria run.

The job at Gibbons didn't stop him trading in stamps on his own account. He had kept that lucrative sideline going on the Andes and during his sojourns in the Caribbean, and he would continue with it always. Then the firm discovered that some of its employees had been pilfering, creaming off stamps for themselves. A young colleague of Nick's was accused. He claimed that Nick was behind it. There was no proof. Nick denied it, but he was out on his ear. He was twenty.

By this time he had already dipped his toes into the world in which he would eventually become a national hate figure in England – property. Many years later he described how his first move into the field came about. It was in 1963. He was driving down St Magdalene Street, in Brighton, with a girlfriend. She pointed out a terrace of five houses all with 'For Sale' boards outside. On enquiring about them Nick found that they were to be auctioned, and the guide prices amazed him: 'They were going for nothing.' The reason – they had sitting tenants. He went to the auction and bought all five properties. 'They were a bargain. I thieved them.' By 'thieving' he meant buying something for less than half what it's worth. That was to become Nick's guiding star.

In 1988 Charles Hoogstraten gave one of the authors his alternative version of his son's first venture into property. He said that he and his wife had their savings sunk into a little property business of their own. He claimed that because young Nicky was so good at figures they asked him to do the paperwork. Nicky obliged them, but later they claimed they found that the deeds were transferred into his own name.

Van Hoogstraten claims that he actually lent his parents money to buy a better house and then put some of his assets in his mother's name because he was still a minor.

Whatever the truth is, Nick had found his niche for life. Playing the property market astutely, he bought and sold and bought again quickly. Two years after the Brighton purchases, he bought his first properties in London – a house in Chelsea, then several in Notting Hill. They were followed by more properties in Brighton and Hove. Showing the same eye for a bargain that he had displayed in the Bahamas, he was on his way to his first million.

At home relations appear to have plummeted. Charles Hoogstraten had sour memories about his son. Nick was equally bitter about his father, who, he said, resented him. 'He objected to me ruling the roost.' The bad blood would fester until almost the end of Charles and Edna Hoogstraten's lives.

Nick decided to leave Rustington for Brighton. The raffish seaside town and its genteel neighbour, Hove, would be his centre of operations from now on.

He carried with him lessons of a resentful, lonely boyhood, fractious teens, a violent father and, if there is a dishonesty gene, he took that too. He was cocky, handsome, hard-working, and he was charming when he wanted to be, especially to women. He trusted no one and he seemed to care for no one either, except perhaps his sisters.

To the rest of the country Brighton was the place where teenagers rioted. It was the era of Mods and Rockers, and Brighton's Marine Parade was their battleground. Every weekend and Bank Holiday they converged from all over the south-east of England. The Mods, with their neat haircuts, short Italian jackets, cutaway collars and slip-on shoes, came on scooters laden with lights and other decoration. The Rockers, with their long hair and regulation studded leather jackets and jeans, came on powerful motorbikes. Fights between the two groups were endemic. Sometimes hundreds of Mods and Rockers were involved. Deckchairs were smashed and used as weapons. Holidaymakers scattered. Police launched baton charges to break the groups apart. The battles on Brighton's beaches made the headlines week after week.

Violence had a fascination for Nick Hoogstraten. He became the friend of a tough character called Andrew Emmanuel. Of Greek-Cypriot origin, Emmanuel was known as 'Mr Wimpy' because he had a Wimpy Bar concession in the town. Emmanuel had reputedly been a professional wrestler and was a notorious fighter. Aggressive teenage boys, knowing his reputation, often made the journey to his Wimpy bar just to show their mettle by picking a fight with him. Van Hoogstraten would recall how he was there every afternoon, watching approvingly as Emmanuel wiped the floor with the latest young upstart.

Years later he would concede that he was a violent man himself. 'I'm probably ruthless and I'm probably violent,' he told the television programme World in Action in 1988. Whether that trait developed at school, or was a reflection of a violent father, is unknowable. But the mature Van Hoogstraten talked with relish about the impact a single ferocious individual can have if he dives in without worrying about the consequences. He told one of the authors that a small man could rip two large men apart 'if he lets himself lose it completely'.

To Nick, Brighton was a place which held out limitless opportunities to make money. It was the hippest spot on the south coast. There were beat clubs everywhere – the Cad-Lac Club, the Bar, the Box, the Mo Club, the Electricity Club and scores more. Even the nineteenth-century Aquarium, where one main attraction used to be the sight of its resident chimps having tea, was now a stage for local pop groups. Teenagers and twenty-somethings flocked to Brighton from miles around to hear the newest sounds. They also came to shop in the trendy new boutiques and dress shops that sprang up in the famous Lanes behind the two piers.

Nick got into the music business himself. He started by opening a 'teen club' in Portsmouth, then he opened a similar club in Brighton and, later, one in Bristol.

His expanding property business proved handy to him in his role as a club owner. One of the great problems in the pop business at the time was that many of the groups – a lot of them Purple Heart poppers – were so unreliable that they would often fail to materialise for the next night's gig. Nick ensured that this wouldn't happen to his clubs. The groups he booked were lodged not in some hotel but in the latest flats in the Hoogstraten property business to fall empty. There he could keep an eye on them. He reminisced about it during a penetrating interview with the journalist Duncan Campbell for the Observer in 1988: 'There were others around who booked their artistes into a club and beat them up if they didn't turn up. That was their way of doing things till I came on the scene. The Moody Blues and Small Faces used to come and stay in my apartments in Brighton.'

Some performers still caused him problems. 'That skinny geezer, wears tight trousers, what's his name? Rod Stewart. We had him at our club in Bristol. He was trying to dispute the gate money he was being paid. I said: "Look, you little runt, if you think I'm the sort of person who would get my people to click the clicker wrong, I suggest you make a phone call." We nearly had to thump him.'

Nick was a Mod. Not just that, he had to be King Mod. He took to touring the clubs to spot the Mod with the sharpest, newest gear. He would make detailed notes on any really outstanding outfit and take them that night to his personal tailor. The tailor had a day to turn out something on the same lines but better. Nick would wear it the following night at the club or coffee bar or pub in which he'd spotted the outfit that inspired it.

It was a camp decade, the first in a century and a half when fashionable men could be peacocks wearing silk and satin, and have their hair long and curled. Nick posed and pouted and camped it up with the best of them. There is a whole series of carefully staged photographs of him in his way-out gear looking as arrogant and decorous as Beau Brummel. In some of these shots he exhibits that youthful gawkiness of young men just grown into adulthood, his walk a little ungainly, arms loosely dangled by his side. He decided to cure this. What he required was a role model. He chose Napoleon Bonaparte.

Napoleon had no doubt stood at a mirror before coming up with that famous pose, right hand inside his coat just about level with his breastbone. This appealed to the young man from Sussex. But he did not want to be seen to copy Napoleon, so he experimented. His great hero, Adolf Hitler, had done the same, hiring a photographer to take pictures of him as he struck different poses.

Nick came up with a neat solution. He adapted Napoleon's business with the hand and made it his own. He put his right hand into his jacket at a lower point, approximately across his abdomen. It looked original and allowed him to show off his rings made of gold sovereigns, which he wore like a gilded knuckleduster across his fingers.

He remained a camp figure long after the sixties were over. In the seventies he took to wearing all-black outfits and tasteful diamond or amethyst rings. In the eighties he had a passion for ankle-length white mink coats.

Many wondered about Nick's sexuality – and not just because of his campness. In his twenties he was to establish very close friendships with two tough, handsome young men. People who saw the chemistry between them suspected there was a sexual side to it. His attitude to women added to the suspicions. He was spectacularly misogynistic. Women were 'filth', he said, and he treated them accordingly. He slapped them around, just as his father had slapped his mother. He spat on some of them – literally. But they flocked around him. He would go on to have strikingly beautiful mistresses. If there was a gay side to Nick Hoogstraten there was a straight side too.

For all his trendiness he must have been an odd man out on the sixties music scene, with its dope and acid, booze and heroin. He was a rarity among the pill-popping Mods. He was and is a near teetotaller, he hates smoking and he has always displayed an apparently genuine abhorrence of drugs.

Maybe it was this that explains what he subsequently admitted was a glorious opportunity missed. It was offered to him during a meeting at Victoria Station with someone from the music business. Nick was asked if he wanted to manage a pop group – the Rolling Stones. He turned the offer down. The Stones at this time were being savaged by the establishment as the standard-bearers of teenage debauchery. This followed a highly publicised drugs bust at Keith Richards's Tudor mansion in West Sussex early in 1967.

Many years later, when explaining why he spurned the offer to manage the Stones, Van Hoogstraten didn't mention drugs. He said that all the percentages and all the paperwork had been sorted out, but when he met the group he changed his mind and pulled out of the deal. 'They were scruffy buggers... The only reasonable one of the lot was Charlie Watts – the only one you could sit and talk to... I didn't realise that Mick Jagger was intelligent and worth dealing with... I subsequently found out that Jagger was completely articulate, very straight and very intelligent. It was just an act... It was one of the only mistakes I made.'

Music was only one of Nick's ventures. He opened a boutique, Deb, in Brighton's modish Regency Parade and he sank money into the rag trade. For the boutique's champagne launch he hired Jimmy Saville, one of the best-known disc jockeys of the day.

Saville pulled in the crowds. According to the Brighton Evening Argus, 'wave after wave' of fans 'pushed through the portals to claim his scribbled autograph'. But it was Nick, not the disc jockey with his long, flaxen hair, who grabbed the attention of the paper's reporter: 'Looking on at the punishment his establishment's decor was taking was the owner Nicholas Hoogstraten of Furzecroft, Hove – in many ways as remarkable a man as his colourful guest-of-honour. At the age of 21 he is in the tycoon bracket. Deb Boutique is just the latest of a long line of successful business ventures – property dealing companies, interior decorating, a successful teenage club in Portsmouth, a clothing manufacturers... "You name it and I seem to have a controlling interest in it," said Nicholas.'

'And he isn't boasting,' the report added, detailing how the Hoogstraten fortune began with a boy's interest in stamps. 'I haven't really looked back since,' the young tycoon was quoted as saying.

By 1966 Nicholas Hoogstraten was a familiar figure in Brighton. Everyone in the Lanes and the beat clubs knew 'Nick' with his terrific clothes and his stamps. A contemporary recalls him regularly commandeering a table in a Brighton coffee bar, an intense figure sorting through files of cellophane-wrapped stamps day after day.

But he was not a friendly figure to strangers. 'People kept back when he was walking through to his table. There was something about him.' The air of menace given off by the older Van Hoogstraten was evident to some people even then.

While Nick's clubs and his boutique attracted a lot of attention, for the moment he kept a much lower profile about his ventures into property.

Private landlords had an evil reputation in the early sixties. That was due especially to one man, the former London estate agent Peter Rachman.

Rachman had become a millionaire by exploiting a lax law and the desperation of black immigrants as they tried to find accommodation in the capital. Rules that had protected tenants' rights had been largely swept away by the Housing Act of 1957. Meanwhile, to attract cheap labour to run Britain's public services, the Conservative government encouraged tens of thousands of West Indians to come to Britain. The newsreels pictured them arriving in huge numbers at Waterloo Station looking lost but hopeful. What the cameras didn't show was that when the new immigrants went knocking on doors around London for rooms, many white landlords didn't want to know. There was no Race Relations Act then. Until that moment no one had seen the need for one.

Rachman spied an opportunity. He began buying up old tenanted houses and mansion blocks in run-down parts of Notting Hill and North Kensington. Then he made life so unpleasant for the sitting tenants that they moved out. After undergoing a cheap conversion, which carved the old houses and flats into as many single rooms as possible, the properties were filled with West Indian immigrants. They were charged sky-high rents.

What made Rachman's name notorious was his methods of getting rid of old tenants and of getting much higher rents from their replacements. Old ladies who had lived quietly in Powis Square or Lisson Grove for decades suddenly found home life had become a nightmare, with the electricity cut off, or a brick through the bedroom window, or the lavatory blocked and overflowing or holes in the bathroom ceiling, or a new neighbour who partied all night – or all of these.

On rent days the new tenants were confronted by intimidating toughs. One was called Serge, like Rachman a Pole. He went knocking on tenants' doors accompanied by a snarling Alsatian on a leash. The dog was called Demon. It was always kept hungry. The new tenants always paid.

Van Hoogstraten once implied that he'd had dealings with Rachman. It seems unlikely that he saw him often. Rachman died in 1962, a year before the younger man first got into the property business. But there appears to have been one very powerful personal link between them in the shape of a character just as bizarre as Rachman or Hoogstraten. His name was William Bagot.

Bill Bagot was the slum millionaire the press never found out about. He was to become Hoogstraten's mentor. But, according to one of Hoogstraten's former confidantes, he'd also been Rachman's secret mentor. He'd put up the money for the Polish landlord to buy property.

Unlike the high living, womanising Rachman or the elegant Hoogstraten, Bagot kept himself in the shadows. He was a Fagin-like figure who built one of London's biggest bed-sit empires. He was a large Irishman who looked like a down and out. Many knew him as their eccentric landlord who personally collected the rent. Few would have imagined that around Notting Hill and Paddington alone he had 400 houses and was collecting rent from thousands. A council official who investigated him and Hoogstraten in the 1980s saw him at property auctions. 'He shambled in, never seemed to do any bidding and didn't seem to talk with anyone. He was dressed like a tramp'.

Hoogstraten's ex-architect, Tony Browne, recalls his first sight of Bagot. 'He was in a shiny old black frock coat and a red waistcoat. He had a gold watch chain across his chest ... and as well as the gold I saw a line of something on the waistcoat that looked like silver. When I came closer I could see what it was. The man was running with silver fish. He was filthy.'

Bagot was a classic miser. He endlessly tramped the streets collecting rents from each tenant rather than pay a rent collector. It was the same with repairs – broken windows, blocked lavatories, leaking pipes – Bagot invariably tried to fix them himself. Hoogstraten, who is so mean that he reuses teabags and relies on 'bucket-shop' bargain flights to take him round his world-wide property empire, found Bagot's stinginess incredible. 'You know he tarmac-ed his own roofs. He was always covered in the stuff'.

Bagot had another characteristic of the classic miser, too. He buried his wealth – literally. A fortune in notes and gold coins is thought to have been stashed under floorboards, and behind secret panels and in the gardens of the houses where he lived. As we will see, following Bagot's death many years later, Van Hoogstraten mounted a frenzied treasure hunt to unearth the old man's secret hordes.

Bagot was a batchelor with no family. He lived in Ledbury Road, now the epitome of Notting Hill chic, but in the 1960s a flaking row of stuccoed Victoriana. He would become the pivotal figure in the vast network or property dealing and money lending that Nick Hoogstraten would create. Bagot taught the budding tycoon everything he knew and was soon to be outshone by his hungry pupil. After his death, 30 years later, Hoogstraten cried and described him as his father figure.

The young Hoogstraten made many of his early London purchases in Bagot country – in places like North Kensington and Paddington. At the time his growing property empire created no waves, no publicity.

An even more lucrative line was developing still more secretly, and stayed a secret during the years and years in which he was in the headlines. He became a moneylender. He didn't exact ruinously high interest rates like a conventional loan shark – though some called him just that, a loan shark. His tactic was to lend at relatively modest rates on any venture, however dubious, so long as he was given rock-solid security, and a lot of it.

People whom every other lender had turned down could expect to get a loan from Nick Hoogstraten provided that the value of the stock or the deeds or whatever security they gave him was higher, much higher, than the loan they wanted. Gradually the word spread that although other lenders may say 'no', it would be a 'yes' from Nick. He called himself 'the lender of last resort'.

Other moneylenders did not want their borrowers to default. Nick counted on them defaulting. When it happened he 'sequestrated' the asset they had lodged as security in a flash. There were no delays, no renegotiation, no extra period of grace. 'I became rich by others going skint,' he boasted.

And his riches were flaunted. In the mid-sixties he began to wear expensive rings, he started to buy silverware and he acquired a Rolls-Royce. Louis Yaxley, his parents' neighbour in Rustington, remembers seeing the Rolls parked outside their home next door. 'He'd drive up here every Monday. He was bringing his dirty washing for his mother to do.'

Nick had a black Jaguar as well. Just after midnight one October night in 1966 he was driving home in it from his teen club in

Portsmouth, when a police patrol car started to follow him. He was clocked at 46mph in a 30mph zone. When he spotted the police car in the mirror he took evasive action, turning off the main drag into side-streets before re-emerging on to the main road. But the police car was waiting and it followed him. When Nick stopped, the police car stopped. Nick waited for the police driver to get out, then roared off.

With the police car now in full pursuit, its lights flashing, its bell ringing, Nick finally came to a halt and, like so many people when they are pulled up for speeding, he lost his temper. He stormed up to the now stationary police car screaming obscenities. It took two policemen to arrest him. He was taken to Portsmouth police station, where, it seems, officers had to forcibly restrain him. He later complained that a valuable ring was snatched from his finger and that his watch strap was broken during the struggle. The magistrates were not sympathetic. He was fined £2 for using obscene language. It was his first offence as an adult.

Not for the last time, Nick, always self-righteous, appealed against the conviction. 'I appealed on a matter of principle,' he said later. 'I got a QC, it was in the High Court. It cost me something like £600. My QC said: "You've been a policeman all your life. Has no one ever said 'fuck off' to you before?" He [the policeman] said it wasn't what was said, it was the way he said it.' The appeal was turned down.

But everything else was going wonderfully for him. In the summer of 1967 Nick announced to the world that he was a millionaire.

In fact at twenty-two he was 'Britain's youngest self-made millionaire'. He celebrated by adding an aristocratic flourish to his name. Nicholas Hoogstraten became Nicholas van Hoogstraten.

The press took notice. Sub-editors carefully added 'self-proclaimed' to the 'youngest self-made millionaire' sobriquet. But their news editors took him seriously. Nicholas van Hoogstraten was a figure worth watching, still small beer on the national stage but with news potential.

The Sunday Mirror sent its reporter Carolyn Martin to interview Brighton's youthful tycoon. Always studiously polite and with a way of looking piercingly into your face, he seems to have captivated her. The headline to her piece read: 'Nicky makes a million pounds ... at 22'. The article described a diamond ring on Van Hoogstraten's hand and his 'staggering' confidence. 'When he talks of business he sounds an experienced City gent much more than his 22 years but there is an incongruous childish chuckle and a shy grin when he has made someone laugh. His attitude to the City gents is honest. "They can't afford to treat me as an impudent long-haired kid because they know I could buy and sell them just like that. My real dislikes are fakes – people, antiques, even mongrel dogs..."'

He was soon being spoken of as part of a new breed of successful young tycoons who, typical of the sixties, didn't abide by the old rules. Social historian David Gladstone got to know some of them, Van Hoogstraten included. 'They tended to be anti-establishment and anti-professional,' he says. 'They were iconoclasts and consciously against the status quo. They had become very successful not through the help of professionals but by their own efforts. Their view on life was that they'd got where they were unaided, and that was how the world should operate.' This new breed had no time for people who fell by the wayside. Victorian self-help was their credo. They were pre-Thatcher Thatcherites.

In August 1967 Van Hoogstraten posed for a Daily Mirror photographer. The picture that the paper published showed him cuddling his stamp collection as he took it to lodge in a bank safety deposit. 'A fortune in his arms', the headline read. The story underneath reported that the stamp collection was now worth £380,000.

Van Hoogstraten basked in all the publicity. He was rich, successful, and on the verge of becoming a national celebrity. Everything was wonderful. He began throwing outrageous parties. There was always a spectacular mini-skirted girl on his arm. He hired planes to take him to Paris so that he didn't have to sit with 'the peasants'. He called this period 'my King's Road days'.

They were about to come to an abrupt end.

Behind the glitz and the music the young businessman with the staggering confidence was secretly making connections with the underworld. After London, the Brighton of the sixties was the most corrupt town in the south of England. It was the main clearing house for stolen goods, had a thriving drug trade and was the favourite hang-out for half the gangsters south of the Thames. It also had a notoriously bent police force. It was the place to meet very bad people if that's what you wanted. Nicholas van Hoogstraten met up with one of the most dangerous gang leaders in the country. That connection, plus his greed and his big mouth, were about to land him in deep trouble – and in jail.

3

BOMBER

Success didn't change Van Hoogstraten. The bile and the violence which, as a teenager, he had displayed in his treatment of his mother were still there. Shortly before his twenty-third birthday, they came bursting to the surface.

The target this time was a friend called David Braunstein who had become his business partner. Van Hoogstraten, ever watchful for betrayal, became convinced that his pal was ripping him off.

They had met in 1963 on the train from Brighton to Victoria. Braunstein, a young man with huge Buddy Holly spectacles, could not have looked more different to the fashionably coiffeured Hoogstraten. But he was the same age, eighteen, and they began commuting together regularly. Maybe, as the train rattled through the Sussex and Surrey countryside towards the dingy London suburbs, David talked about his tough East End uncle who knew the Kray twins. That would have fascinated Nick. Maybe Nick, in turn, fascinated David with his plans for making money and with his cockiness.

They got on so well that Nick began calling in at the

Braunstein house for supper. David's father, Bernard, was the cantor at a local synagogue. He and his wife, Sylvia, took to the handsome young go-getter with his tales of the Bahamas. Sylvia would later tell a court that she regarded him as 'one of the family'.

Nick's relationship with David was cemented in 1966 when the two friends set up a joint company, Demaria Textiles. The deal between them was that Nick would put in several thousand pounds to fund the operation and Braunstein would do all the work. Nick liked bankrolling his friends or making friends of those whom he bankrolled. He found that the more you discovered about people – especially their weaknesses – the more surely you could dominate them. He was learning to use friendship to acquire information, and thus to acquire power.

'Yes, I'm a control freak,' he says. 'Isn't every self-made man?'

Demaria Textiles folded after less than two years' trading. Van Hoogstraten reckoned that he had lost £3000 in the venture. He turned on David Braunstein, who accepted the blame. Braunstein hastily put his name to a document that Van Hoogstraten presented to him in which he agreed that he owed him £2000. However, he said he could only afford to repay £6 a week. Van Hoogstraten declared that he was 'not much enchanted' with that idea and the arguments began.

The climax was a screaming row between the two former friends in the boutique in Brighton that Jimmy Saville had opened only a few months earlier. Van Hoogstraten accused Braunstein of stealing nearly four hundred dresses from the firm's stockroom. He warned him that unless he made good the loss he would be in big trouble. A wholesale supplier who was in the shop heard him shout: 'If I don't get the money from you I'll get it from your father; he's got plenty. If I don't get it I'll do you and your father and the synagogue.'

Braunstein's sister Hannah remembers Van Hoogstraten arriving at their house in Chatsworth Road, Brighton, spitting fury. He demanded the money from her father and threatened the entire family. Then he warned that any one of the Braunsteins might be walking in the street and something could happen to them.

Van Hoogstraten would claim in court that the only threat he made to the Braunsteins was to go to the police about David unless he paid up.

Later that day Van Hoogstraten returned to the Braunsteins' home. According to David's father, he made more threats. He called himself a fascist and a Nazi and said he could have a stick of gelignite thrown into the house. He also allegedly said that he had enough money to pay to have every Jew in Brighton killed.

He followed that up with threatening phone calls saying Jews were 'the scum of the earth' who 'breed like rabbits ... a cancer on the community'.

What might have been dismissed as the empty threats of a hysterical bully became more ominous the next day. Two men the Braunsteins had never seen before arrived at the house and threatened them. A phone call from Van Hoogstraten followed shortly after this visit: 'When am I going to get my effin' money? The two blokes who called tonight – that's just an example of what you are going to get.'

Braunstein senior said he was given a deadline by Van Hoogstraten. Half his money – £1000 – by Saturday – 'or else'.

A night or two later a brick was thrown through the front window of the Braunsteins' house. A threatening note, composed of letters clipped out of newspaper headlines, was found in the garden.

The bizarre part of it was that Van Hoogstraten wasn't responsible. David Braunstein was. He had composed the note and thrown the brick. He confessed later that a relative had suggested this idea as a way of getting the police involved.

The ploy worked. The following afternoon Van Hoogstraten was interviewed by two police constables. He denied all knowledge of the brick and insisted he hadn't called himself a Nazi. But when one of the police remarked to him that it would take a lot of money to kill every Jew in Brighton, Van Hoogstraten's black humour got the better of him: 'I could get the money and it is not such a bad idea after all.'

The police posted a guard on the Braunsteins' house; he was rostered to stand outside each night until the early hours of the morning.

On 12 November 1966 the guard quit for the night at one o'clock. A few minutes later a hand grenade was thrown through a downstairs window. It exploded and wrecked the sitting room. Luckily, everyone was asleep upstairs and no one was injured.

Van Hoogstraten, accompanied by his solicitor, was brought in for questioning. 'We are appalled,' said the solicitor.

Immediately, Van Hoogstraten contradicted him: 'I am not appalled. I think it's marvellous. The bastard owes me money.'

The outburst was an early example of what was to become a trademark of the man. Others might keep their lip buttoned. Not Nicholas van Hoogstraten. Even in a tight spot he would never be able to resist saying exactly what he thought. He developed a taste for saying the unpardonable. Eventually there was almost nothing he wouldn't dare to say, no one he wouldn't dare to shock, nothing he wouldn't criticise – except money.

He was arrested and charged with causing the explosion. There was no concrete evidence, only his own threats, and his big mouth. However, it would later emerge that the Braunsteins weren't the only witnesses against him.

Police quickly discounted the idea of Van Hoogstraten himself throwing the grenade. It was assumed that he had paid someone else. But who?

The track led towards one of the most dangerous armed criminals in the country, Anthony 'Little Legs' Lawrence.

Lawrence was a fitness fanatic. He was notionally a scrap-metal dealer, but in fact he led a gang of criminals operating in south London. At the age of thirty-two he already had a dozen convictions. During one stretch in jail he had to be sent to Rampton, the special hospital where the country's most psychotically violent prisoners are held. It was thought that Little Legs provided the grenade for the Chatsworth Road attack and maybe provided the grenade thrower too.

Earlier that year he obtained a quantity of stolen explosives, grenades and firearms from a Coldstream Guardsman who had stolen them from the armoury at Chelsea Barracks. One of the grenades was thrown at a pub associated with a rival gang. Some of the stolen explosives were used to make a radio-detonated bomb for an attack on the same gang.

Police discovered that Van Hoogstraten and Lawrence knew each other, and they suspected that the Brighton grenade was from the Chelsea Barracks consignment. But there was no proof. Police were still looking for something to link the two men when Van Hoogstraten was committed for trial for the Braunstein attack.

The committal proceedings were due to start in Brighton magistrates court on 14 December 1967.

With such a serous event hanging over him a wise man would have kept his head down. Van Hoogstraten did the opposite. He got caught up in an episode that thirty-five years later looks almost surreal: a phony jewel robbery that was obviously a set-up.

It happened nine days before the committal proceedings opened.

Van Hoogstraten had his heart set on one particularly spectacular emerald ring in London's Hatton Garden. The nineteen-carat stone was priced at £15,000 – a huge amount in those days. He contracted with the jeweller, Raymond Taghioff, to buy it. They arranged to carry out the transaction at the Grosvenor Hotel at Victoria Station. Van Hoogstraten, accompanied by his secretary, Piers Dunkley, was supposed to bring the £15,000 in cash ('I always pay cash') and the dealer was to hand over the ring.

The other men arrived at the station before Van Hoogstraten. Raymond Taghioff carried a case with the emerald in it. He was accompanied by a man called Harry Loeb, who acted as minder. Piers Dunkley carried a 'safety case' supposedly containing the cash. Van Hoogstraten didn't appear at a prearranged meeting point on the station concourse. So the three other men trooped up to a room that had been booked in the hotel. They were inside for only a minute when there was a knock at the door. Loeb opened it expecting to see Van Hoogstraten. Three armed men burst in waving pistols that looked as if they were fitted with silencers. Dunkley and Loeb were both knocked to the ground. Taghioff, who for a moment thought it was all a joke, was told that he would be shot if he did 'anything funny'. The three men, none of them masked, grabbed the money case and the emerald case and took off.

Afterwards Van Hoogstraten refused to comment. 'I can't say anything,' he told reporters.

Two days later a twenty-one-year-old man from Camberwell called Michael George Blackmore was stopped in his car by police in south London because his car had no lights. Blackmore claimed to be an antique dealer. He was in fact a villain. Police found a bullet in his car. That led them to raid his home, where they discovered two guns and the two cases from the Grosvenor Hotel jewel robbery.

Pointing to the 'safety case' which was supposed to have contained Van Hoogstraten's money, Blackmore said that there was no money in the case: 'You can take it from me ... it only had a pile of papers.' Asked if he meant someone connected with the sale was concerned with the robbery, he answered: 'Of course

I do, but I daren't say anything about that now, I have my wife to think of.'

Try as they might, the police couldn't get him to talk. Or anyone else. They questioned everyone – including Van Hoogstraten – and got nowhere. In the end they had evidence enough only to charge Blackmore and another man called Terry Belding with armed robbery. Belding was acquitted. Blackmore was sentenced to five years in prison.

But it was clearly an inside job, and just as clearly a phony robbery. The brazen cheek of it was stunning.

It is probable that the man whom Michael Blackmore was so frightened of was Tony Lawrence, one of whose specialities was terrifying witnesses. Shortly before the Grosvenor Hotel job Little Legs had put out a contract to kill a man in an unrelated case for refusing to perjure himself in a trial. A small-time hood called Terry 'Ba Ba' Elgar took his money but bottled out of the killing. Instead of shooting Lawrence's appointed victim, Elgar warned him to get out of London and to lie low. Little Legs found out what had happened, and Ba Ba, the would-be hit man, ended up dead himself.

The committal proceedings against Van Hoogstraten for the grenade attack opened at Brighton magistrates' court on 14 December 1967. They were supposed to take a week and be over by Christmas. Instead they stretched out over three months, and then the full trial was postponed. The case wouldn't be finally completed until the following summer.

The charges against Van Hoogstraten were grave. There were five of them. The first was of maliciously damaging part of the Braunsteins' home. The second was of conspiring with person or persons unknown to blow up the house. There were also three charges of demanding money with menaces. Van Hoogstraten pleaded not guilty to all of them.

Outwardly, he was his usual cock-sure self. He had his

personal tailor working frantically. As the case proceeded the press gleefully detailed the different clothes that the dandy in the dock was wearing each day: 'After the hearing Mr Van Hoogstraten, who wore a purple and blue striped suit...' 'Van Hoogstraten ... wore an off-white silk brocade jacket, bright blue frilled shirt and a navy blue overcoat thrown around his shoulders like a cape...' 'Van Hoogstraten wore ... green tinted gold spectacles and on his fingers were four heavy gold rings.' 'He stepped into the dock today wearing a Regency-style brown suit with a brown velvet collar and a purple tie.' 'Van Hoogstraten, wearing an olive-coloured Regency style jacket, and bottle-green trousers, was ordered to surrender his passport.' 'The accused ... stood between two police officers with a patterned jacket of oyster brocade with velvet trimmings and white trousers.'

But underneath the brashness the twenty-two-year-old was very worried. This is evident from an astonishing move. The committal stage had barely begun when a reconciliation with the Braunsteins was attempted. It took place far away from Brighton – in the Dorchester Hotel in London. Both the Braunsteins, father and son, were there. So were Van Hoogstraten and two other men. It appears to have been a relatively relaxed – and revelatory – encounter. No voices were raised. Anyone walking into the Dorchester lounge from a wintry Park Lane might have glimpsed the group talking earnestly over coffee and drinks, but, apart from Van Hoogstraten, they looked like just another bunch of politely haggling businessmen.

In fact it was confession time. Van Hoogstraten insisted that he'd had nothing to do with the first attack on the Braunstein home, the brick thrown through the window. David Braunstein admitted that he had thrown it. He had also left the threatening note found in the garden. The idea, he said, was to galvanise the police into providing his family with protection.

According to the Braunsteins, Van Hoogstraten also owned up. Yes, the responsibility for the grenade should be placed at his door. But, no, he hadn't thrown it himself. In the plush quiet of one of London's most exclusive hotels, he then came up with a proposition so audacious that it must have taken the Braunsteins' breath away, if indeed he really did say what they claim.

Van Hoogstraten suggested that the police be told that David faked the first attack on the Braunsteins' home. This would confuse the whole issue and cause the entire case against him to be thrown out. Van Hoogstraten would then sue the police for damages. If he was awarded enough money, he promised to forget the £2000 which he still claimed David Braunstein owed him. 'He said that if the damages came to more than £10,000 he would not claim the £2000,' Bernard Braunstein said later.

According to him, another threat accompanied the proposal. Van Hoogstraten warned him and his son that if he went to jail the whole Braunstein family would be 'shot up'. He added that he would have six or seven men with machine guns surrounding their home.

The meeting broke up and the participants wandered out into Park Lane. Van Hoogstraten offered his former friend a lift home. David Braunstein accepted. This abrupt switch from threat to friendliness was to characterise Van Hoogstraten. People would later remark on his chameleon-like behaviour: venomous rage one moment, a smile and a handshake the next. His mercurial character was constantly on display. Others might try to hide their feelings from moment to moment. Not him. As the years went on he learned to use these mood changes as a weapon to gain control over others. Again and again people would find it impossible to gauge the man or know what was coming next.

Van Hoogstraten and David Braunstein were driven back to Brighton in Van Hoogstraten's Rolls-Royce. On arriving there in the early hours of the morning Braunstein asked Van

Hoogstraten not to drop him in sight of his home just in case the police were watching. He didn't think it a good idea to be seen with the man he was accusing of bombing his family.

The deal proposed by Van Hoogstraten got nowhere. Someone – presumably from the Braunstein camp – immediately told the police what had happened in the London hotel. The committal proceedings were suspended. But only briefly.

The hearings resumed. The whole story of the failed company, the missing dresses, the storming rows and the two attacks on the Braunsteins' home – the brick and then the bomb – was laid before the magistrates. They had no doubt there was a case to answer. Van Hoogstraten was duly committed for trial at Sussex Assizes, in Lewes, in May.

The prospect of the trial might have daunted anyone. But this was only one of the trials Van Hoogstraten was to face that summer. While the Brighton magistrates had been feeling their way through the committal evidence in the Braunstein case, he was, amazingly, getting himself into even deeper water with the law.

He already had the swanky cars. He wore amazing clothes. He was buying antique French furniture. But he wanted more of the trappings of great wealth. He wanted to be a collector of rare objects, including jewels and silver, and he didn't much care how he got them.

In January 1968, just as the Braunstein case was beginning, country houses in Surrey and Sussex were hit by a series of break-ins. The burglar or burglars were after jewellery and antique silver – tea sets, dinner services, trays, goblets.

The first burglary was at a chartered accountant's house in Lewes. The accountant was awakened in the middle of the night. Having seen the outline of a man's figure creeping across his bedroom, he quietly dialled 999 and eventually switched on the light. The intruder was still there. He took off down the stairs and escaped. When police arrived they discovered that silverware worth £1000 had gone. The accountant described the figure he had seen fleeing from his bedroom as lithe, between twenty and thirty years of age and athletic-looking.

A few days later a house in Wentworth, Surrey, twenty-five miles away, was burgled. Among missing items was silverware worth more than £2000. Some of the stolen pieces were rare, including a jewelled elephant goblet. Over the next two months eight or nine houses were hit.

What brought Van Hoogstraten into the frame was the jewelled elephant goblet. Along with other stolen items its description was circulated to police stations in February 1968. It also featured on the ITV crime programme Police 5.

As luck would have it, a Metropolitan Police detective had seen a jewelled elephant goblet among antiques displayed at Van Hoogstraten's flat in Kingsway Court, Hove. The detective had gone there to look for evidence of a link between Van Hoogstraten and the grenades stolen from Chelsea Barracks. The detective connected the goblet in Van Hoogstraten's flat with the one reported missing. On 15 March the flat was raided.

No jewelled elephant goblet was found there. A friend of Van Hoogstraten had seen Police 5 and warned him to get rid of it. Van Hoogstraten said later that the goblet had been dumped and was 'probably at the bottom of the Thames'. But in the kitchen of his flat detectives found a large suitcase stuffed with silver. Attempts had obviously just been made to erase identifying marks on the different items.

Van Hoogstraten admitted nothing to the police. When questioned about the cache of silver found in his kitchen, he tried bluster. He hadn't yet learned how to keep his head under pressure and to lie with conviction.

He claimed that the silver in the suitcase was all his. 'Yes, I collect silver. I have one of the finest collections in the country.'

Asked where he had got the items in the suitcase, he said that his friends and associates bought them on his behalf at auctions. He admitted that he had indeed been trying to erase identifying marks on some items. It was a common practice, he explained. He was only trying to remove unsightly marks because he wanted to display the silver.

He insisted that he did have receipts for all the items, but not at the moment. 'I will have them later.'

As for the jewelled elephant goblet, he said: 'I have never had one.'

The police took away more than a hundred items of silver from Van Hoogstraten's flat after the raid. More than half would be identified as coming from the recent spate of burglaries.

A few days later Van Hoogstraten produced the promised receipts. They were on the headed paper of a local 'antique dealer' called Jack Swaysland. In fact, Swaysland was one of Brighton's notorious 'knockers', the men who comb the country knocking on the doors of the unsuspecting in an attempt to con them out of any valuables and antiques they have. Van Hoogstraten said that, as far as he knew, Swaysland was reputable. He was helping him build up his antique silver collection by spotting items at auctions and buying for him. He'd been doing this for a year.

The police weren't convinced. Swaysland's signature was on the receipts. Yet when he was taken to Hove police station and shown a hundred or more items of silver laid out in rows, he didn't seem to recognise any of the items. He looked 'amazed' when he saw all that silver, said Ted Mantell, the detective inspector in charge. What also weighed with Mantell was that Swaysland had a police record. He was not the reputable dealer that Van Hoogstraten claimed he was.

Swaysland was questioned closely. He stuck to his story. He insisted that he had sold the stuff to Van Hoogstraten. It seemed that Van Hoogstraten was in the clear. Or was he?

The police wouldn't let the jewelled elephant goblet case go. In later years the Hove force in particular would be subject to all kinds of rumours about pay-offs and corruption because of Van Hoogstraten's seeming immunity from the law. But at the start of his career, in 1968, both the Hove police and the Met pulled out all the stops to nail him.

Pressure was put on Van Hoogstraten. On 28 March he was hauled in to Fulham police station, in west London, for questioning. The police account suggests he was in turn boastful, petulant and jocular. He appears to have dropped all pretence at innocence and tried to browbeat his interrogator.

Detective Superintendent Alfred Moody conducted the Fulham interview. Unknown to Van Hoogstraten, the superintendent was tape-recording everything. His transcript – which was later challenged – has Van Hoogstraten admitting to having possessed the jewelled elephant goblet and then crowing about being untouchable: 'You'll never pin anything on me... I can get off anything you can charge me with... You will not touch me. My business associates will see to that. I'm too valuable to them... Anyone can be bought so long as you have the right money and I have got it. Twenty, thirty, fifty thousand, you name it and I will pay it.'

The bluster didn't work. That same day Van Hoogstraten was charged with six cases of receiving. Later he would also be charged with burglary.

His hope, of course, lay with Swaysland. If the knocker stuck to his story that he'd sold the silver and Van Hoogstraten had bought the pieces in all innocence, then the case against Van Hoogstraten would be wafer thin. For the moment Swaysland did stick to the story.

The police pressed on with the case against Van Hoogstraten, but without much confidence.

What they didn't know was that Swaysland was a very

frightened man. A friend of Van Hoogstraten was forcing him to shoulder the blame for the silver. The friend was no other than the terrifying Tony Lawrence. This finally emerged when the Hove detective Ted Mantell asked Swaysland why he was agreeing to be Van Hoogstraten's fall guy. According to Mantell's notebook, Swaysland said: 'I will tell you what, Ted. When Tony Lawrence is convicted and put away come and see me again.'

Little Legs was about to be tried himself on explosives charges. His trial was to be at the Old Bailey in May. If he went down Swaysland would talk.

It was Easter 1968. Van Hoogstraten's future depended on three juries – two that would try him and the one that would try Tony Lawrence.

The first trial was of Van Hoogstraten himself on the grenade charges. It opened in Lewes on 23 May 1968. The headlines were riveting: 'House blast: the youngest millionaire in court today'... '£3000 bail for "youngest millionaire" on bomb charge'... 'Millionaire accused of causing bomb blast'... 'Grenade damaged the rabbi's home'... 'I had enough money to have every Jew in Brighton killed'.

The jury listened for five days as Van Hoogstraten and the Braunsteins gave their conflicting versions of the escalating rows and the threats that preceded the attacks. Van Hoogstraten claimed that his only threats were that he'd go to the police about David. He'd never threatened any physical harm to the Braunsteins or anyone else. 'I'm not the violent type.'

The words 'Nazi' and 'fascist' had first been used by the Braunsteins, not by him, he insisted. And he certainly hadn't organised the attacks on their house.

The accused did himself no favours in court. His attitude visibly upset his own expensive defence counsel, Victor Durand QC. At one point Durand even threatened to walk out on him. It happened when the barrister was cross-examining Leon,

David's seventeen-year-old brother. Leon Braunstein was recalling an evening when he listened to a telephone conversation between his father and Van Hoogstraten. As Durand questioned him, Leon began to smile.

The QC rebuked him: 'I don't think this is funny, do you?'

The judge intervened, saying to Durand: 'I don't think you could have seen what happened because the dock is behind you.'

When Durand turned round he saw Van Hoogstraten grinning at the witness.

The barrister was not amused. After apologising to Leon Braunstein he turned to Van Hoogstraten and said in open court, so that everyone could hear: 'Either you behave yourself or I shall have to leave this case. You must control yourself, please. I mean that.'

The case hung on Van Hoogstraten's threats and whether they were serious. Had the Braunsteins been the only witnesses to them there might have been doubts in the jury's minds. If David Braunstein had thrown the brick, couldn't he have thrown the grenade too? But there were two other witnesses against Van Hoogstraten unconnected to the Braunsteins.

One was the wholesale buyer who had witnessed the first eruption in Van Hoogstraten's Deb boutique. The other was a Jewish businessman called Jack Mazzier. He was a passenger travelling on the Brighton – Victoria train shortly before the grenade attack. He told the court that he had overheard a 'frightening' conversation between two other passengers in his first-class compartment. One was Van Hoogstraten, who was complaining about someone who owed him money. Mazzier recalled him saying that he would have the man 'done up for £50 and then said something about having a bomb thrown'. He also testified that Van Hoogstraten said: 'They are Jews and they can afford to pay.'

Mazzier was scared of getting entangled with Van Hoogstraten and so had not come forward immediately after the grenade attack. He'd been persuaded to do so by a Jewish friend.

The jury of ten men and two women believed him and the Braunsteins. It took them just eighty minutes to find Van Hoogstraten guilty of maliciously damaging the Braunsteins' house and of demanding £2000 with menaces.

In later years Van Hoogstraten would admit a measure of responsibility for the grenade attack. The affair was 'the most seriously silly thing' of his life, he told us. 'All my later troubles go back to that.'

The judge told him at the time: 'You seem to have a most exaggerated sense of your own importance and take the view that other people ought to do what you wish ... you are an arrogant and evil young man and a bully.'

He gave him four years.

Trial number two, of Anthony Lawrence, opened the same week as the grenade trial. At the end of it Lawrence was found guilty, and put away for fourteen years. The next day Jack Swaysland gave a new statement to the police. He had indeed been lying about the silver found at Van Hoogstraten's flat. He'd never seen any of the items before. Van Hoogstraten hadn't got them from him. His testimony would make all the difference at the third trial.

It opened two months later when a prison van brought Van Hoogstraten from Wormwood Scrubs prison, in west London, down to the same court in Lewes to face charges of burglary and receiving. In the Braunstein case his own big mouth had brought him down. This time the cause of his downfall would be his ceaseless desire to get everything on the cheap or, better still, get it for nothing – in this case silver.

He even tried to get himself defended for nothing. In a move that took many people's breath away Britain's youngest self-made millionaire applied for legal aid. He told the East Sussex quarter sessions that he couldn't access his considerable assets. For tax purposes they were arranged in such a way that he could only get at them if he could 'attend to the business of his companies in person', which he couldn't, of course, because he was in jail.

The court asked the police about his finances. For a moment it appeared that the world might get a tantalising glimpse into what Van Hoogstraten's wealth amounted to. But no. All that the police could offer was the accused's own talk of a cache of gold bars, 'a large quantity of Scottish banknotes', his stamps and 'property in the UK and the Bahamas'. The Crown called his plea for legal aid 'ludicrous', and the court thought likewise. The legal aid application was rejected.

Van Hoogstraten decided that he would defend himself. It wasn't because his wealth was a myth and that he couldn't afford another barrister. As subsequent events were to show, he did indeed have huge assets. The reason he gave at the time was the truth: he had 'somewhat lost faith in British justice' after the Braunstein verdict. What he meant was that he thought that he could do a better job defending himself than a QC would.

But the jewelled elephant goblet trial turned out no better for him than the Braunstein trial. The only plus for him was that the charges of burglary were dropped for lack of evidence.

Otherwise it was downhill all the way. Fifty items of silverware found in his flat were displayed before the jury and identified by their rightful owners. Swaysland was brought in to the witness box to swear that he had lied the first time about selling Van Hoogstraten the silver. Then the police related Van Hoogstraten's alleged attempts to bribe them.

His defence was that it was all a fit-up and that the police had been looking for a 'deal' in which both the silver and the grenade charges would be dropped in return for a £25,000 bribe.

For the second time in as many months a jury didn't believe

him. They found him guilty on eight charges of receiving. Before passing sentence on Van Hoogstraten the chairman of the quarter sessions told him: 'It is quite clear that ... Brighton is a centre for stolen goods and we are quite satisfied that you have been playing a substantial part in that centre.'

The sentence was five years, to run consecutively with the four years that he had already been given for the grenade attack. It could hardly have been worse.

4

BANGED UP

Nicholas van Hoogstraten, aged twenty-three, began his nine-year sentence at Wormwood Scrubs in the summer of 1968. With typical braggadocio he'd say that the prison experience made him 'five times richer, a hundred times more intelligent and a thousand times more powerful and dangerous' than before.

There was some truth in that verbal V-sign to the world. Van Hoogstraten proved a much more slippery customer when he emerged from his first long stretch in jail. He seemed to have learned from a master con man how to manipulate British company law and the tax laws of a dozen countries.

He showed that he had learned how to exact 'retribution' from those he considered his enemies without being caught himself. He'd be especially unforgiving of anyone suspected of ripping off his property.

In his early days in the Scrubs he was full of chutzpah; he even petitioned the Home Secretary to be allowed to run his businesses from his prison cell. When the request was refused he tried to do it anyway, bribing a hard-up warder to help and storing up a lot of trouble ahead for both of them.

Life behind bars was harder for him than most, though his mother, Edna, told her neighbour Mrs Yaxley how her Nicky was buckling down to it. He had landed a quiet job in the prison library, she said. In reality Van Hoogstraten was proving such a handful that he had to be disciplined several times. He spent three weeks in solitary confinement.

Eventually he learned to keep his head down in jail. He stayed out of trouble with other prisoners by lending them tobacco, the main currency in jail. 'Anyone could borrow from me without paying interest. It wasn't an ounce at the beginning of the week and an ounce and a half back. It was an ounce at the beginning and an ounce at the end. I wasn't making any money out of it. I just believed in keeping the whole place ticking over nicely. Keep all your fellow associates happy and you don't get any aggravation.' The authorities knew what was going on, he claimed. They turned a blind eye. His deal with them was that there would be no drugs.

He made friends inside with another wealthy prisoner, a restaurateur who called himself Baron von Benno, an extrovert, over-the-top character. Reminiscing about those days, Van Hoogstraten described Benno, a vodka drinker, smuggling bottles of the stuff into the Scrubs and drunkenly throwing the empties down at warders from an upper walkway.

Von Benno was Jewish, and Van Hoogstraten claimed that their friendship showed that he wasn't anti-semitic. The Braunstein grenade affair had been about money. 'A lot of people think that I'm anti-semitic. I'm not... I'm more anti-Irish than anything.'

In the Scrubs he nursed his grudges. All his life he blamed others for his problems, and rationalised every mean thing that he had done, reasoning that they were all down to someone else. David

Braunstein was never forgiven. Thirty years later Van Hoogstraten would still be blaming him for the whole affair and musing over the punishment his former partner supposedly deserved. Reflecting on the grenade attack, he told a TV reporter in 1999: 'When somebody robs you, sticks their hand in your pocket, they deserve everything that's coming to them.' Braunstein, he said, should have had had 'his bollocks chopped off'.

The differences with his parents festered too. They appear to have come to a head during his time in jail. They sprang from disputes over who owned what during his teens. He claimed that his assets were put in his mother's name because he was under-age and that he had to go to the High Court to get them transferred to his own name. His father claimed that he ripped him and Edna off – and not just over properties. He later told the Daily Star that his son 'obtained' antiques, gold, jewellery and a Jaguar car from him and his wife, worth around £40,000 at 1960s prices, a fortune in those days.

Van Hoogstraten absolutely denied it, and it has to be said that there is nothing known about his parents' lifestyle at the time to suggest that they had managed to accumulate any kind of wealth. They lived modestly and Charles's job was as a wine waiter. The only remotely ostentatious thing the neighbours remember of the Hoogstratens was the amount of booze in the house at Christmas time, no doubt from the Andes. True they had a car, but it was a modest one.

This resentment towards his parents led to one of Van Hoogstraten's nastier moves. While inside he decided to 'repossess' furniture from his old home which he said belonged to him. He set up a raid on the Rustington house. It was stripped of curtains, carpets and furniture.

There was other business to attend to in prison, and Van Hoogstraten put his personal attractiveness to good use. He struck up a friendship in Wormwood Scrubs with a fifty-two-year-old Catholic priest called Robert Gates. Father Gates had just become a chaplain at the prison when Nick arrived there. With his Catholic upbringing the handsome young tycoon was automatically on the list for a chat with the new chaplain.

The priest was charmed by Van Hoogstraten. He would later write that the young prisoner was a victim of 'unscrupulous parasites who exploit his ordinary human needs to get what they can out of him without caring where they leave him emotionally as well as physically'.

Father Gates became Van Hoogstraten's confidant and began to help him with his business and his personal affairs, ultimately acting as a conduit with the world outside. He was persuaded that the problems with Charles and Edna were down to their son being in jail, no more. Gates bought the line that relations between parents and son had been fine up until Van Hoogstraten's imprisonment. According to Van Hoogstraten's account, Gates became his bridge with his parents and went down to Rustington on his behalf to see them. There Gates handed over a suitcase full of Van Hoogstraten's cash in exchange for properties that were in his parents' name.

However, the young prisoner's greatest use of the chaplain was as an enthusiastic advocate in his attempts to get his long sentence reduced.

An appeal for a cut in the sentence was heard in 1970, two years into the nine-year term. Gates spoke up for Van Hoogstraten. He told the authorities that he was basically harmless, more a fantasist than a thug. He had 'created a myth of wickedness about himself'.

The appeal court judges concurred. Echoing the chaplain's assessment, Lord Justice Winn suggested Van Hoogstraten had created a world of make-believe. 'He built up a picture of himself as a sinister international figure, of treasure buried here and there, of houses, indeed palaces, all over the world... He wanted to acquire beautiful things, to possess them and gloat over them so that they could pander to his vanity in the same way as it is said that eccentric millionaires might acquire great masters and keep them at lock-up store rooms in their ranches.'

He was, the judge went on, 'a sort of self-imagined devil. He thinks he is an emissary of Beelzebub.' It was a characterisation that would be recycled in almost every subsequent pen portrait of Van Hoogstraten.

Their lordships accepted another argument also put on Van Hoogstraten's behalf: that if he had been tried at the same time for both his crimes – the grenade and the silver – he would have been sentenced to far less than nine years.

The court cut his overall sentence to five years.

Lord Justice Winn was optimistic about Van Hoogstraten's future. He believed that he just needed to mature, and was like 'a child, a Walter Mitty character who will grow out of all this nonsense'.

A High Court judge has seldom been proved more wrong.

Meanwhile Van Hoogstraten had to get through his sentence. He was a good-looking youngster in a jail containing more than a thousand sexually frustrated men. He would have needed a tough friend to protect him.

Tony Lawrence would have been ideal. He had been banged up just a few weeks before Van Hoogstraten, for causing explosions. But he wasn't in the Scrubs. Van Hoogstraten's psychotic friend, who had protected him in the past, was reckoned to be too dangerous to be held there. He was thirty miles away in the high-security wing of Chelmsford prison. A couple of years later someone smuggled out photographs of Lawrence doing press-ups and weightlifting in his cell.

But Van Hoogstraten did find in jail two men who were tough and dangerous enough to defend him against anyone. He never talked much about the friends he made while he was there but he forged relationships with these two that were closer than anything else in his life.

Rodney Markworth was one of these two new friends.

These days Rodney Markworth is a nondescript, stocky man of medium height. He sports a mutton-chop moustache and looks like a grumpy French farmer. But his appearance couldn't be more deceptive. His is a record of explosive, uncontrollable violence.

When he and Van Hoogstraten met he was a good-looking twenty-year-old serving four years for beating a motorist unconscious. That was the beginning of a record of repeated violence that would range from running down a traffic warden in a Rolls-Royce to attempting to assault a judge in his own court. He leaped out of the defendant's box in an attempt to reach the judge before he was stopped by court officials.

Van Hoogstraten took to Markworth at first sight and Markworth to him. There is no doubt that there was a special affinity between Van Hoogstraten and Markworth.

Markworth came out of jail as Van Hoogstraten's close confidant and protector, and played this role for over a quarter of a century. He was a Van Hoogstraten 'Kapo', sometimes his front man, sometimes his business partner, and always one of his top heavies. Using a variety of different pseudonyms, he would pop up regularly as a director of companies that Van Hoogstraten was believed to control. But it was for his capacity as an intimidator that Van Hoogstraten seemed most to value him. Sometimes calling himself Markworth, sometimes Lombard, sometimes Hamilton, he surfaced again and again in the violent episodes that have made Van Hoogstraten's name so feared over the past three decades.

The so-called 'Battle of Brighton' in the spring of 1973 was a Rodney Markworth operation. It involved the eviction of a family that was carried out so brutally that Markworth, Van Hoogstraten and another of his violent henchmen, Leon Moscrop, ended up in the dock together at the Old Bailey.

A still more notorious event involving Markworth was the 'siege' of an old people's home in Framfield, East Sussex. In the late seventies Van Hoogstraten laid claim to the place and sent Markworth and others in to terrorise the occupants. It made national headlines when a social services rescue van sent by the local council had to ferry a dozen old people across fields after a gang led by Markworth had blocked all entrances to the place and invaded the home itself.

With occasional breaks, Markworth continued as a close associate of Van Hoogstraten for many years. At one point Markworth vanished for a while. His disappearance coincided with a police probe into his affairs and Van Hoogstraten fanned a rumour that Markworth was dead. He implied that his henchman had been murdered, and that his body was under a motorway somewhere or under the Brighton Marina. 'He wasn't the cleverest of blokes. I think he stepped out of line and was dealt with,' he told a reporter. A newspaper headline at the time read: 'The henchman who vanished.'

In reality Markworth was very much alive, as Van Hoogstraten well knew. In the 1980s the tycoon employed him as a ganger organising the students and dole cheats who maintained his properties on the south coast. Markworth continued to work for his friend well into the nineties. He and his family were lodged on Van Hoogstraten's country estate in what the owner called a 'grace and favour' cottage.

Markworth sank from sight in the late nineties. But in the spring and summer of 2002 he was back again, silently rooting for Van Hoogstraten when his mentor stood trial for murder. He was spotted in the public gallery at the Old Bailey in London, watching as Van Hoogstraten fought for his freedom. Journalists attending the trial were advised for their own safety not even to try talking to Markworth, and none of them did.

The other man whom Van Hoogstraten met in jail in the early seventies was an even heavier character than Markworth, and would one day appear in the Old Bailey alongside Van Hoogstraten in that murder trial. His name is Robert Knapp.

Six foot three tall and with piercing blue eyes, Knapp was a striking figure. He is remembered by a childhood friend, the journalist Janet Street-Porter, as 'a stunner ... highly intelligent and very attractive'. Acquaintances of his later in life, when he was making big money out of bank robberies, talk of his 'big hats', 'fat cigars' and 'his white Cadillac convertible'. But above all they talk of his unpredictable ferocity.

Fulham-born Knapp was beginning his first stretch after a botched armed robbery when he and Van Hoogstraten first met, around 1969. He went to work for Van Hoogstraten almost immediately after his release from prison in 1978. To outsiders Van Hoogstraten introduced him as 'my lieutenant', while among friends he usually called him 'Uncle Bob'. Years later, in a boastful slip that would help pave the way to his, and Knapp's, eventual downfall, Van Hoogstraten called him something else. 'He's one of my hit men,' he whispered to a girlfriend.

'Bob Knapp was like a typhoon,' says Van Hoogstraten's former architect, Tony Browne. 'He carried an air of menace that was tangible but you didn't know what would happen ... whether he'd throw up all over you, or crack a joke or shoot you, you never knew.'

Browne, who began working for Van Hoogstraten in 1982, recalls an early encounter with the latter's lieutenant. Knowing no better at that point, he demanded an interview with Van Hoogstraten over some money that hadn't been paid to him. He made an appointment by telephone and went into his employer's office breathing fire. Van Hoogstraten was seated behind his vast baroque desk. Browne recalls: 'Standing on Nick's right at his shoulder was "Uncle Bob". Big and dressed in black. He was just looking at me and getting more and more agitated at what I was saying. And then he suddenly just moved out from behind Nick's chair – put himself between me and Nick – and physically he turned me round and suggested that I leave the room with him. I didn't argue with him, I'm glad to say now.'

Knapp was 'the persuader', says Browne. When bothersome tenants had to be dealt with, Knapp dealt with them. Just the sight of him usually proved sufficient. One typical instance in the eighties was recalled by a former rent collector for Van Hoogstraten. It involved Knapp putting in an appearance at a mansion in Third Avenue, Hove, which Van Hoogstraten had just bought. The property was split into twelve or so furnished rooms and flats, mostly occupied by elderly tenants. 'Nick decided the furniture they had was too good for them. He was going to replace most of it with old rubbish – wardrobes, tables chairs... When some of us came in to shift the old stuff out and move the rubbishy stuff in, Bob appeared and just innocently stood there in case there were any complaints. There weren't any. They were mostly old people. No one said anything. He was so big and intense...'

Like Van Hoogstraten himself and like so many of his associates, Robert Knapp used more than one name. Robert Pierson and Robert Bradshaw were two of his pseudonyms. When Colin Adamson, a journalist on the Brighton Evening Argus, went to interview Van Hoogstraten for a colour piece in March 1979, he was introduced to his 'new henchman Bob Pierson'. Adamson quoted Pierson/Knapp as saying: 'There's nothing I wouldn't do to protect Mr Van Hoogstraten. I'd stop a bullet for him and do anything he asked of me. So be careful.'

Janet Street-Porter met Van Hoogstraten and Knapp in 1978

when she went to interview him in Hove for a television programme. Twenty-four years later she recalled it in an article for the paper she was now editing, the Independent: 'Robert Knapp, clad entirely in black, with black dyed hair and a leather coat, answered the door. He was Van Hoogstraten's right-hand man... Like Robert, Van Hoogstraten was clad entirely in black, wearing a tight Edwardian-style suit and rectangular dark glasses; a menacing, rather camp mod.

Is there a gay side to Van Hoogstraten? If we are to believe the man himself, the answer is a resounding no. Publicly he is scathing about homosexuality. 'Disgusting poofters' is one of his favourite terms. Yet there undoubtedly is a big feminine ingredient in this vain, complex man, with his built-up shoes and penchant for dramatic clothes. Tony Browne certainly thought so when he first met Van Hoogstraten in 1980. At the time Browne was a student who was looking for lodgings in the Brighton area. Together with some fellow students he arranged a meeting with a man who was said to specialise in cheap rooms.

'We rang the doorbell ... to be greeted by a very strange-looking individual who opened the door. He was wearing – in the middle of the day – a cream dressing gown that was slightly open. He had on a pair of purple underpants and a pair of purple slippers. And his face seemed to be caked in what looked like foundation ... a bit strange.'

Van Hoogstraten came up for parole in 1971, and the support of Father Gates again proved more than helpful. In a probation report the chaplain enthused over the prisoner's motives for turning down a pre-release employment scheme that meant living in a bail hostel for a short time. 'He told me that much as he would like the chance to get out of prison he could not see, in his circumstances, that the hostel would be of much practical use to him. He did not want to take a place which might be better used by someone else, and he felt he ought to make his views known before people were put to the trouble of interviewing him and writing lengthy reports.'

Father Gates quoted this as 'a tangible indication of Van Hoogstraten's growing awareness of his responsibilities to others.' A number of people, said the priest, had commented on a 'change for the better in his attitude and behaviour' and had noted 'the very marked and encouraging progress he has made'.

He concluded: 'In my opinion and I think in that of everyone who knows him well, Van Hoogstraten presents no public risk.'

Van Hoogstraten was released in January 1972. But it didn't mean freedom. A witness said that as the freed man walked out through the prison gates he looked astonished as two police officers jumped out of a car and grabbed him. They told him he was under arrest on suspicion of bribing a prison officer.

It was alleged that Van Hoogstraten had been making pay-offs to one of his jailers since 1969. At that time he had petitioned the Home Office to be allowed facilities to run his businesses from jail. He had been turned down but he had still attempted to do so.

A hard-up warder gave him the opportunity. He told Van Hoogstraten that his car had broken down on the M1 and he didn't have the money to repair it. Van Hoogstraten promised the man cash if he would take business documents out for him to a woman at an address in Chelsea. The warder agreed to act as his 'postman'. When the warder met the woman she handed him £100 in cash. It happened several times. And when he returned to the jail he had supplies of soap, deodorants and scent for the young dandy.

This time Van Hoogstraten got bail. The trial date was set for October. He did not appear to have worried that much about the outcome. He hadn't made any secret of the fact that he was trying to run his business empire from his cell or that letters were being taken out for him. He claimed that the prison governor knew about his arrangement with the warder and had not objected. So at his trial in October 1972 he pleaded guilty, assuming a nominal penalty. He was stunned at what happened then. The judge, noting Van Hoogstraten's 'bad record', said that he had used his riches to 'seduce' a prison officer and 'you must pay for it'. He sentenced him to fifteen months in jail and the warder to nine months.

Van Hoogstraten was sent to Wandsworth Prison. He was outraged at the disparity in the two sentences and immediately appealed. Once again he turned to his friend Father Gates. The appeal court heard from the priest about a transformed and beguiling Van Hoogstraten.

The two had spent time together regularly – several hours a week – over the last nine months while Van Hoogstraten was on bail awaiting trial. And Father Gates would be only too happy to continue seeing him when he was ultimately released. 'It would not just be a matter of social duty. Van Hoogstraten can be a pleasant companion and while I think it essential to broaden his horizons and widen his acquaintance with the right kind of people, including those of his own age, it is no burden to spend time in his company.'

Gates reported that all was now well between Van Hoogstraten and his parents. Problems had arisen but that often happened when a lad went to jail, and anyway bridges had been mended and his parents were ready to let bygones be bygones. Van Hoogstraten was on good terms with his married sister. While out on bail he had visited her regularly. She had a little baby and he was proud to be an uncle. On top of that, since his release he'd worked hard at his businesses, 'which no one has ever doubted … have been built up honestly and by his own hard work'.

The appeal succeeded, and Van Hoogstraten was finally

released in January 1973. Lord Justice Roskill suggested that he would benefit hugely if he agreed to seek voluntary prison aftercare 'although that might be a blow to his pride'.

Van Hoogstraten agreed – no aftercare.

Father Gates had hoped to provide that aftercare. The priest had persuaded himself that his young protégé was now a different animal who would allow himself to be guided. He set it all out in a memorandum which weighed heavily in securing Van Hoogstraten's final release. He drew a picture of the young man regularly visiting the vicarage, being introduced to Gates's friends, and being entertained at Gates's mother's house in Walmer, East Sussex. Van Hoogstraten would even 'take part in parish life' in Fulham. After all, Brighton was only an hour from London by train.

Father Gates was, alas, a lousy judge of character.

Prison had neither softened nor reformed Van Hoogstraten. He came out vengeful and threatening. He was more of a vindictive outsider than ever. Gone was the sixties dandy. Dressed from now on entirely in black, he radiated malevolence. Tenants were his special hate. 'Scum' was just one of his words for them. But he would prove just as venomous about anyone who got in his way. He had been called a 'self-imagined' devil by a senior judge. Free again, he seemed to be determined to demonstrate that it wasn't self-imagined, he was the real thing.

Some of it was, of course, play-acting for a gullible press. But by no means all. Now almost twenty-eight, Nicholas van Hoogstraten was a very dangerous man.

5

SETTLING ACCOUNTS

Van Hoogstraten's first priority as a free man was to sort out his holdings in Switzerland. He flew to Geneva. He claimed later that he'd forgotten where he had put £2 million in cash. He spent two days walking the streets before he recognised the bank and worked out what the account number was. Then he turned his attention to revenge for what had happened to his money while he was inside.

Paranoia was a Van Hoogstraten trait. Everyone was suspect … after a piece of him … trying to defraud him … trying to 'thieve' his property … 'taking the piss'. On his release he went through the books and decided that his accountant David Harris, who had once been found guilty of fraud, owed him £14,000. Harris was later to agree that he owed Van Hoogstraten some money but only a fraction of the sum that Van Hoogstraten claimed.

Van Hoogstraten decided to take over Harris's businesses and then make the accountant work off his 'debt' by doing his company accounts free of charge for two years.

He kidnapped the accountant. It happened as Harris was leaving a bank in North Street, one of Brighton's busiest roads. Van Hoogstraten, Markworth and another man grabbed him. They bundled him into his own Rolls-Royce and drove him off to the Newhaven – Dieppe ferry, then to Paris. Harris, a pinched little man with a damp handshake, was told that he was there to work off his debt and he'd have to stay until he'd done it.

In Paris, he was first lodged in a hotel, then a flat. On one occasion Van Hoogstraten arrived and said that he was dissatisfied with Harris's progress. 'He thrashed me within an inch of my life,' said the little accountant, who claimed he couldn't walk for the next two weeks.

It is probable that he wasn't there just to work on Van Hoogstraten's books. There was another good reason for him being out of the country. Harris was bankrupt, and no doubt Van Hoogstraten didn't want his former accountant's financial affairs – and therefore his own as well – to be opened up for scrutiny in a bankruptcy hearing. So Harris was spirited out of England – and kept out.

Why didn't he try to escape or alert the authorities? He later told the authors: 'I was told that I'd be killed if I returned. Or a member of my family would be.'

What happened to Harris's family became known as the 'Battle of Brighton'. It was an affair that would land Van Hoogstraten in the High Court once again.

The battleground was a house in Vere Road. The accountant's sister, Sue Williams, her husband Jack and their two young children lived in the upper floors, and Harris's sixty-five-year-old mother, Winifred Harris, was the tenant of the ground-floor flat. The property was one of the hundreds that Van Hoogstraten companies owned in the Brighton area.

In February 1973 the Williams family were suddenly told that the house had changed hands and the new owners, a building firm headed by a Mr Markworth and a Mr Moscrop, wanted all of them out. They heard nothing more for several months. One day Mrs Harris and her daughter returned home to find thugs throwing their furniture into the garden. Windows in the upper storeys were missing. Rodney Markworth and Leon Moscrop were inside the house changing the locks.

Susan Williams tried to intervene as Moscrop wrenched off an internal lock: 'I rushed up and told him to stop... As soon as I got near he flung me off and threatened me. He told me: "You stand in my way and I'll slash you to pieces."' The local council's harassment officer appeared. 'Fuck off,' shouted Moscrop at the official, who had protested as a mattress thumped down on to the pavement.

The same short shrift was given to the tenant's solicitor when he appeared after being phoned by a frantic Mrs Williams. A police constable who asked what Van Hoogstraten's men were doing was told to 'fuck off' too.

Eventually more police arrived. They had to break down the door to arrest Markworth and Moscrop. By that time the house was uninhabitable. Water, phones, electricity had all been cut off, every lock was gone. So were window frames. The garden was a pile of furniture.

All this time a Rolls-Royce was cruising up and down Vere Road. In it was Van Hoogstraten.

Later that day he, Moscrop and Markworth were spotted in a nearby restaurant by a freelance journalist. He asked them if they were afraid of the consequences of what they were doing. According to the freelancer, Van Hoogstraten replied: 'I could not care a toss about what anyone tries to do. I don't live here any more officially anyway. I live in Switzerland and I'll be going back on Monday.'

Van Hoogstraten also told him: 'It was a real blitz operation... It's the best bit of fun we have had for some time.'

Police dug into the background of the Williamses' eviction and tracked the ownership of the house. There was the usual bewildering web of sales and transfers to mask where the real ownership lay, but the finger pointed at Van Hoogstraten. Inconveniently for him, the police also uncovered an alleged fraud over his acquisition of the building.

Back to jail went Van Hoogstraten. He was remanded in custody charged with causing criminal damage, unlawful eviction and conspiracy to defraud. He spent five more months behind bars before a court finally granted him bail – of £100,000.

The hearings in the 'Battle of Brighton' case were to last for most of 1974. Van Hoogstraten's defence was that he wasn't involved. Markworth and Moscrop's defence was that the Williams family had no right to be in the house. At the end of it – after a stream of national headlines about the 'tycoon' and 'his thugs' – the exhausted parties reached a deal of some kind. Van Hoogstraten, Markworth and Moscrop changed their pleas to guilty on the three charges over the eviction, while the fraud charges were dropped. A benevolent-sounding judge wagged his finger at Van Hoogstraten and fined him just £2500 plus £1000 costs. Peanuts for Britain's youngest self-made millionaire.

It was altogether a good result for Van Hoogstraten.

He didn't let on that this was part of the vendetta against the accountant who he thought had betrayed him. It suited him that the outside world should think this was just another example of Brighton's answer to Peter Rachman beating up some tenants.

'This is nothing compared to what we did at 10 Albion Street, Portslade,' he told a reporter. 'We ripped out everything. Yet the family are still living there. The roof will have to come off next.'

Thus encouraged, the press duly descended on Portslade to find a family called the Johnsons at 10 Albion Street, or what was left of it. Their plight seemed outrageous. They had five young children. To get them out of their home, Van

Hoogstraten's men had bashed in the front door with sledgehammers, ripped out the windows and interior doors and smashed through walls. The roof was badly damaged too. When reporters found them, the Johnsons had evacuated the first floor and nailed polythene across the gaping window spaces.

Van Hoogstraten, however, hadn't pointed this out to the press to show how bad he really was, but as a warning to other tenants. It emerged that he had been allowing the Johnsons to live in the house without paying rent. Quite a number of people had rooms or flats at low or no rent in Van Hoogstraten properties. The tycoon wanted someone in residence because empty buildings deteriorate. The quid pro quo he expected was that they'd get out immediately when he decided that it was time to sell the building. The Johnsons had said no. So he'd sent in the heavies.

He told reporters that he'd warned the Johnsons that if they didn't get out he would demolish the place: 'If people get in my way I'm going to steamroller all over them... I say what I'll do and I do it... People know what I'm like. No one has to do business with me. If they do, they know what they're taking on...'

The Johnson and Williams cases were the first of many that would build Van Hoogstraten's reputation in the press as an extremely tough landlord. If the newspapers had found out what he was up to privately, his reputation might have been still worse. It was a period when he was giving full vent to his juvenile paranoia and threatening everyone who had crossed him or, in his view, betrayed him.

Lawyer Michael Dring, who had represented Van Hoogstraten in the 'Battle of Brighton' case fell into that category. Van Hoogstraten accused him of having 'stolen' £1500 from him. The tycoon learned that Dring and his wife were on the boat train to Paris and decided to meet them. As the Drings left the train Van Hoogstraten walked up to the unsuspecting lawyer and, in his own words, 'gobbed full into his face'.

Two days later Mr and Mrs Dring caught the 10.45 am boat train back to England. Van Hoogstraten was also on board. He went to the lavatory, excreted into some paper, entered Dring's compartment and squashed the excrement in his face.

Twenty-five years later Michael Dring still won't talk about it.

There is an immaturity about this escapade: skulking on trains, the delight in the use of excrement, savouring the revenge. But the childishness does not make it any less harrowing for the target. The resort to violent assault is a sign of being unable to draw a line. A more mature man might shrug and walk away. But never Van Hoogstraten. The persistence that has enabled him to amass a fortune, when allied to that love of violence carried over from his childhood, drives him to persecute his enemies. The dreadful thing is that his intimidation works. And that is why he is so dangerous.

Two weeks later various people were circulated with a two-page note on Van Hoogstraten-headed paper signed by his secretary. It described in minute detail the two incidents in Paris. They were, it said, meant to serve as a warning: 'Whereas people like Dring are relatively safe among their corrupt "local clique" such safety does not extend to areas now controlled by my principal. Such incidents will be repeated in future against all such persons who have defiled their position in order to "attack" my principal.'

Half a dozen men and women were named in the note. The list included two solicitors – one female and described as 'butch', the other male and described as a 'crook' – and a judge who was labelled 'kinky'. The note ended: 'War has been declared. And in due course just retributions [sic] will be taken as further opportunities arise.'

Another former friend who was to experience Van

Hoogstraten's vengeance was the priest to whom he owed so much, Robert Gates.

Father Gates had remained close to Van Hoogstraten after his release from prison. He had learned about the kidnapping of David Harris. Several times he visited the accountant in Paris. There he heard about the threats that Harris would be 'disposed of'. At first he didn't take them seriously. He evidently still believed that his young protégé was basically harmless. But finally he became very alarmed at what he might be planning. He remonstrated with him and then appears to have advised Harris to seek police protection. Van Hoogstraten blamed the priest when he learned that Harris had wired Scotland Yard and returned home, from where he was taken into protective custody.

Van Hoogstraten never forgave Gates, and began a campaign to discredit him. A memorandum accusing Gates of misusing his position as a prison chaplain and having homosexual relations with prisoners was sent to Cardinal Heenan, the Catholic Primate of England.

Then, in 1976, Van Hoogstraten's man Rodney Markworth launched a civil damages claim in which Gates was a witness. It gave Markworth the opportunity to launch into the kind of lurid sex allegations about the priest that newspapers adore.

He suggested in open court that Gates had had affairs with two prisoners and had written a 'love letter' to Van Hoogstraten. Father Gates denied the accusations but the damage was done. A press headline read: 'Priest denies love letter to Van Hoogstraten'.

This was not the end of it. Van Hoogstraten hadn't finished with Gates.

One Sunday morning the priest was saying Mass at the Holy Cross Church, Fulham, when three men advanced down the aisle, each clasping a banana. They were the emissaries of Van Hoogstraten come to humiliate the cleric in front of his flock. The bananas were presented to the helpless Gates, and the men filed back through the stunned congregation handing out sheets of paper describing in lascivious detail what their priest had allegedly got up to with male prisoners when he was a prison chaplain.

Gates denied everything and did nothing. He told a court later that he thought the allegations against him were childish. The Cardinal backed him.

Van Hoogstraten had the last laugh – a subtler, and ultimately more effective, way of wounding his erstwhile friend. He set up a new property management company in Hove. It would become the most notorious on the south coast for its treatment of tenants and its venomous attitude to council officials and solicitors or indeed to anyone who intervened on a tenant's behalf. One of its ways of responding to a letter of complaint was to return the letter with the word 'bollocks' scrawled across it. Those complaining in person would have a bucket of urine poured on their heads from a first-floor window as they left. The name Van Hoogstraten gave the management company was 'Robert Gates and Co'.

6

THE DREAM PALACE

A chance encounter in a dry cleaner's in the East Sussex town of Uckfield started it. Van Hoogstraten was in a hurry. His car was parked on a double yellow line. As he made to leave the shop another customer said she just had to speak to him. For some reason Van Hoogstraten stopped and listened. It changed his life. The woman was an Irish clairvoyant who said she could tell him his fate. A session was arranged. He emerged from it claiming to be psychic and calling himself 'a child of the Sun'. He was destined, he told friends, to live in a white marble palace on a hill.

So began a dream that would lead to ridicule and one of the most outrageous follies of his career. It would also cost him a good slice of his fortune.

He first set eyes on High Cross House in 1972, just after his release from prison.

The nineteenth-century neo-Gothic timbered mansion was set in over forty acres of East Sussex countryside. Hidden away down a country lane just twelve miles from the coast, it was picture-book old England. The terrace looked out on parkland and woods, complete with lake, horses and the South Downs rolling away into the distance.

If this sight sparked a dream in Van Hoogstraten at the time, he didn't show it. He was there to find out what had happened to his money. He had discovered that David Harris, the accountant whom he would later kidnap, had used some of his money to help a south London publican buy High Cross.

The publican, Cyril Newton Green, was a tough, middle-aged man with underworld connections. He'd run a hotel in Streatham frequented by the most-feared gang in south London, the Richardsons. In the late 1960s he decided to quit London and try his hand at something different – opening an upmarket nursing home in the country. After weeks touring the Home Counties he finally lighted on the High Cross estate, near the village of Framfield. His wife Shirley, who was crazy about dogs, fell in love with the place. So did his stepdaughter, Leslie, who was equally besotted by horses.

Their idea was to operate a riding stables as well as a nursing home.

To buy the place Newton Green raised a mortgage with the National Westminster Bank. But he didn't have enough to fit out the kind of exclusive money-spinning establishment he planned.

David Harris appears to have arranged to fill the finance gap. Harris had invested in High Cross either by making a loan or buying in as a partner. On his release from jail in 1972 Van Hoogstraten started to dig through Harris's transactions, and what he found about High Cross had him rushing to see Newton Green at the house.

Peter Couldridge, a Newton Green employee since the Streatham days, remembers Van Hoogstraten's arrival. 'He came storming in with three or four men and said: "This is my place."'

An accommodation of some kind was reached. Newton Green accepted that he owed Van Hoogstraten nearly £100,000. He apparently signed a mortgage document for that amount with one of Van Hoogstraten's companies, Getherwell Finance Ltd.

While Van Hoogstraten was putting the pressure on Newton Green he was displaying a very different side to the man's wife, Shirley. The young tycoon, with his Rolls-Royce, dark, inquisitive eyes and talk of investments round the world, made a play for her.

He took Shirley to dinner, and arranged trips to the coast in the Rolls for her and her twenty-one-year-old daughter Leslie. He even took Shirley to his clairvoyant. Leslie remembers a day at High Cross when her stepfather was ill in hospital. 'Nick came in with this huge emerald ring. He put it on my mother's finger and she couldn't get it off. He said: "Now you're going to have to run away with me and marry me."'

Shirley, twenty years older than her suitor, was smitten. 'I really do think he fancies me,' she told a disgusted Peter Couldridge.

'You could tell, you know, that he was stringing her along,' says Couldridge. 'He put on the charm. All the women loved it. It was David Niven stuff. And Shirley, she just fell for it hook, line and sinker.'

Daughter Leslie, who, after all these years, still appears to have a soft spot for Van Hoogstraten, bridles at the idea that he and her mother became lovers. She was mortified at a television programme that claimed the two had an affair. However, she recalls that her mother was attached enough to Van Hoogstraten to offer to put up bail for him of £25,000 when he was next up in court, facing a bribery charge.

Van Hoogstraten wasn't the Newton Greens' only creditor. Cyril had also gone to moneylenders in his old Streatham stamping ground. No sooner did Van Hoogstraten appear at High Cross than the moneylenders from south London dispatched some heavies to the mansion apparently wanting a piece of the action. Cyril asked Van Hoogstraten for help. The tycoon is believed to have called on associates of his old gangster friend Little Legs Lawrence, who was in jail. 'We went down there with banjo cases and saw them off,' is how he later described what happened. His four years in jail had left him better connected than ever.

Newton Green was now a very sick man. When he died, Shirley inherited Purlville, the company that owned High Cross. She decided to hang on to the estate she loved by running a more modest operation – a rest home rather than a nursing home. To prepare for the changeover she closed the place down for a while.

At this time Van Hoogstraten was living almost permanently abroad. He seemed to have homes in Switzerland, Liechtenstein and France. Nevertheless he kept in touch with Shirley. He even sent air tickets to Paris so she could fly in for a romantic weekend with him there. The tryst doesn't seem to have been a success. Afterwards the relationship began to cool and Shirley found a new man.

She also – fatally – began to fall behind with repayments of the loan to Van Hoogstraten's Getherwell Finance Ltd. Van Hoogstraten, far away in Switzerland, pounced. Shirley was informed that Getherwell was seeking a possession order for High Cross. However, the company told Shirley, she could stay, they didn't want her out.

The deal was that Getherwell would pay off her mortgage to NatWest. In return Shirley would pay rent of £1600 a quarter and not oppose the possession order. Shirley consulted her lawyers. The legal advice was that she'd have only a fifty-fifty chance of overturning the possession order and that, knowing Van Hoogstraten, it would be a long, costly battle.

So she agreed to the Getherwell deal. Now renamed Parklands

Rest Home, High Cross was reprieved. Shirley could return to her animals and the new man in her life, Paul Hales.

In 1976 she discovered the NatWest mortgage hadn't been discharged. Getherwell had reneged on their side of the deal. Her lawyers advised her to stop paying rent. Shirley stopped and wrote to Van Hoogstraten telling him why. She was, she made clear, challenging the possession order.

After a month or two's silence, warning letters began to arrive from Van Hoogstraten and Getherwell. Knowing the man's reputation, Shirley and Paul Hales tried to outflank him. They asked the NatWest, as the main mortgagor, to repossess the High Cross estate. They calculated that the bank would then sell it on the open market, realising enough through the sale to take what it was owed, give Van Hoogstraten what he was owed and still leave Shirley with a tidy sum.

But once Van Hoogstraten has his claws in a property he doesn't easily let go. On 26 April 1978 his secretary wrote to Shirley: 'I write to give you formal warning that pending the obtaining of a Possession Order against your company you are not entitled to "quiet enjoyment" of the Estate.'

One of the spots which the High Cross estate overlooks is called Tarble Down, named after a bloody battle fought there 750 years ago between Simon de Montfort and King Henry III. A new battle was about to be fought at High Cross.

Some of Van Hoogstraten's men, led by the formidable young Rodney Markworth, now occupied the gatehouse flanking the estate's entrance. Among them was Leon Moscrop, who, with Markworth, had gone to jail after the notorious 'Battle of Brighton' three years earlier.

One morning soon after Markworth and Moscrop moved in, staff at the rest home arrived at work to find that they couldn't get in – and the residents couldn't get out. The gates were chained and padlocked. Paul Hales cut the chain. The next morning the chain was back. That night Hales cut it again.

In the big house, which had twelve residents, all over eighty, the phones began to ring incessantly. When staff answered, there was either a stream of threats or, even more worryingly, silence.

One morning Shirley took a call and a gruff male voice said: 'We've been taken for cunts long enough. We're going to start putting poison down for the horses and the dogs.'

Shirley called in Securicor. They were to patrol the grounds at night.

The gate-locking saga continued. It was an astute tactic. Visitors coming to see their relatives couldn't do so and wanted to know why. More worryingly, in an emergency it would be impossible to get ambulances or fire engines up to the house. If the siege went on, Parklands Rest Home would have to close down.

On 4 May the first violence occurred. Paul Hales decided to remove the front gates altogether. In the early hours, as he set to work, Rodney Markworth suddenly appeared. Hales claims that Van Hoogstraten's hard man went for him. But Hales, who had brought along a wrench for protection, got the first blows in. He laid out Markworth, who was taken to hospital with a gash in the head that needed fifty-eight stitches. Later Hales pleaded guilty to causing grievous bodily harm. The judge proved very lenient, letting him off with a caution and a £50 fine.

Over the next month Shirley and her elderly residents learned what the 'quiet enjoyment' letter meant.

The anonymous calls multiplied. Hales says they averaged some two hundred a day.

Outside, Van Hoogstraten's men circled the house in an old car 'from dawn to dusk', revving the engine and smashing into fences and through the garden.

The climax came on 16 June. That day Shirley and Hales were

due in London to seek a High Court injunction to stop the harassment. It was also the eighty-fourth birthday of one of the residents. A party with a cake was being laid on for her in the main dining room.

The house awoke to find the electricity had been cut off and the phone lines severed by a hacksaw. Both exits were impassable. The main drive was blocked by a twelve-foot-high barricade of felled trees, piles of gravel and tarmac topped with barbed wire. A five-foot-deep trench had been dug overnight across the only other way in, the tradesman's entrance.

Social workers turned up from the county council. They were unable to get past the main gate. Markworth told them that he was taking possession of the estate on behalf of Getherwell. Residents' relatives were advised by the police not to try to get in.

The daughter of one resident told a reporter: 'My mother is in there and she can't get out. I'm hoping the social services and the police are going to do something.' She was too scared to be identified. 'I don't want to give my name because it might be traced back to my mother.'

Eventually a Social Services mini-van was driven through a gap in the fence at the far end of the estate and across fields to the house. Press cameras clicked as the bewildered residents were helped into it.

On the advice of the police, the remaining staff at the home trooped off after the old people. It wasn't safe for them to remain. Markworth and company wouldn't let them take their belongings. So they left them, and the birthday cake.

An hour later Shirley returned from the High Court with an injunction ordering Getherwell to withdraw. But it was too late. Everyone was gone except Van Hoogstraten's men.

All that was left were Shirley's four dogs. She found them in her Daimler parked down the drive. Acid had been thrown over the car. The dogs were all bleeding. One had to be put down immediately. One lost an eye, another an ear. Police manning the perimeter suggested the dogs had been fighting. A vet later stated that the wounds had all been caused by a sharp instrument, maybe a knife.

Van Hoogstraten, far away in Paris, was only too happy to take responsibility for what the press called the 'Sussex siege'. The day after the evacuation he phoned the Evening Argus to put his side of it. As always, he was convinced that right was on his side. 'We have £150,000 tied up in this property. The tenants are £8000 in arrears although they're drawing £800 a week from the residents.'

'Don't think these people have been unjustly treated,' he added. He had been seeking possession for months. 'I stalled off doing anything drastic or morally wrong, if you like, until the old folks had been removed. But we have had considerable trouble with East Sussex Social Services in moving them out.'

Asked about Shirley Newton Green's injunction, he said: 'They know where they can stick their court order... If they arrest any of my employees I will just employ more.'

The News of the World headline read: 'Stick your court orders says the siege thug tycoon'.

For once Van Hoogstraten didn't want to be presented as wholly heartless. In another phone call to the Evening Argus he announced that he was offering Leslie Newton Green a flat. 'We have no argument with this twenty-one-year-old girl.'

But everyone else beware. A few days later copies of the following notice were nailed to some two hundred trees fringing the estate:

'TAKE NOTICE that this company as (a) Landlords (b) Mortgagees are now in possession of the High Cross estate and all goods thereon.

'AND TAKE FURTHER NOTICE that any adult person other

than police officers or other persons duly authorised by this Company in writing who enters any part of the Estate is liable to be shot at and/or attacked by our guard dogs.

'BY ORDER – DIRECTOR OF GETHERWELL FINANCE LTD.'

No one from Parklands Rest Home – members of staff or old folk – set foot on the High Cross estate again.

A year later Van Hoogstraten took a journalist on a tour of the battlefield. He talked of 'the great fun' that he'd had over the siege. He pointed to the battered Daimler, still where it had been left by Shirley a year before, indicating the bloodstains on the back seat. 'That's where I ordered the dogs to be slaughtered.' At the nearby stables he said: 'That's where we poisoned the horses.'

He had no special plans for High Cross at the time. It was just another piece of real estate whose value would accumulate and could one day be sold at a huge profit. 'We are not proposing to do anything with the property. What does one do with these places?' It would, he said, simply be secured and made safe from fire hazards.

He had it boarded up, and for a time the mansion was forgotten. It would hit the headlines again – involved in a colossal tax claim against the tycoon. Then it would mysteriously burn down. Many years later the white marble palace Van Hoogstraten was destined for would arise from its ashes.

7

VAN HOOGSTRATEN'S WOMEN

Late evening in a hotel suite in Brighton. Tanaka Sali, a pretty seventeen-year-old not long arrived in Britain from Zimbabwe, is watching The Jerry Springer Show on television. Van Hoogstraten comes in. He says he is going to bed and asks the girl to join him. She says she wants to stay up to watch the show.

Van Hoogstraten goes through to the bedroom and prepares for bed. After a while he reappears in the sitting room. He grabs the remote control and turns the volume down. He then stalks back to bed. Tanaka turns the volume up. The millionaire reappears and turns the television off. Tanaka turns it back on.

Van Hoogstraten unplugs the television and carries it towards the bedroom. The teenager tries to grab it from him. Van Hoogstraten lets go of the television and slaps her hard across the face. She pushes him against the wall. Her lover's face contorts into an evil mask. The transition is so violent it's almost unreal.

Tanaka has seen this before. 'His face changes and it's a different person. It's weird. I can't explain it to you if you haven't seen it. He's got two personalities.'

The couple begin hitting each other. He calls her a fucking bitch. A fucking cunt. She screams back, obscenities, mutual abuse – they've done this before. Finally Tanaka grabs her handbag and leaves.

Van Hoogstraten heads downstairs, the terrifying mask sliding back into its usual shape. On his way past the dining room, he finds a blob of jam on a doorknob. Spotting a member of his staff nearby, he tut-tuts: 'One can't be having this, can one?'

These scenes of the bedroom and the public arena provide a condensed portrait of the two sides of Nicholas van Hoogstraten. He conducts a stormy relationship with his young mistress while keeping a steady eye on business. Two opposing forces are at work here, in an uneasy balance.

Tanaka Sali could give as good as she got and was well used to her lover's tantrums. She was, after all, a teenager who wanted to go out with people her own age and have fun. Her middle-aged lover would indulge her up to a point, giving her pocket money to go to clubs with a female friend. But he was careful not to indulge her too much.

'If I wanted to go out, he'd give me twenty quid, that's all,' she recalled. 'That's five pounds for a taxi going to the club, five pounds for a cab coming back, five pounds to get into the club and five pounds for a couple of lemonades, because I wasn't allowed to drink any alcohol.' She used to save her money up until she had enough 'to get wrecked'.

When she first met Van Hoogstraten, in Harare towards the end of 1999, Tanaka thought of him as 'an elder' who was respectable and nice. But after she had lived as his mistress for some time, his violent mood changes began to scare the young woman.

'Since I started going out with Nick, I noticed I started being suicidal. When I had a fight with him one time, I cut my wrist because I wanted to kill myself and then I passed out on the bathroom floor. That's how mad he used to drive me.'

For his part, Van Hoogstraten always said he was only trying to control the headstrong teenager. His paternal attempts to get her to obey him and take direction were for her own good. Their rows were therefore about her drinking, smoking, staying out overnight clubbing, not getting up in the morning and, ultimately, seeing a younger man. Like those young women in 1960s Brighton, she was – horror of horrors – frivolous. If only that Van Hoogstraten ideal could be attained: sexiness without frivolity. Sex on tap, on demand, but switched on and off by him. A fantasy shared by more than one or two males.

Despite it all, despite the lectures, the reproofs, the tirades, the hammerings, Tanaka Sali still likes him. Women do like him.

When Van Hoogstraten appears on television it has an odd effect on hundreds of women. They watch transfixed as this self-assured, well-groomed man lays down the law according to Nick. There is a touch of the celebrity bad boy about him. With his immaculate hair, his growling, screen-gangster voice and his certainty that he is right, he appeals to a band of women who immediately fall for him. Or maybe it's just the money that's in his trousers. And in the bank. And in his international investments and his houses.

Whatever it is, after every appearance he gets fan mail. The letters are mostly declarations of love, or lust, and more often than not they propose marriage. The aphrodisiac of a hundred million or so acts like musk to these doe-eyed, spellbound women. Van Hoogstraten is, of course, hugely amused by the letters, but also flattered. Who would not be?

If it were just the money, it would be too simple. There is something else about Nicholas van Hoogstraten.

He is, when you see him, right there, in a deliberate, self-made sense. You feel he wants you to experience him. The problem is, how exactly? He says everyone, the media especially, gets him wrong. It's no wonder. He is difficult to read.

These days he is quieter than he was, less in-yer-face than he used to be. He is still far from self-effacing, but quietly assured and not quite so full of himself. He can play the bashful schoolboy, dipping his head, giving a short laugh, half turning his upper body away, lowering his gaze, before glancing up to see what effect he has had. He is more reflective. He can appear – odd though it is to say it – almost vulnerable. It is a clever act that appeals to female sensibilities.

The Courtlands Hotel clientele includes a large smattering of the wives of Brighton's business elite. They gather here for Inner Wheel meetings and other social functions. These middle-aged and elderly genteel ladies seem comfortable in the hotel owned by the unobtrusive man dressed in black. At one of these gatherings an elderly widow whose husband once owned the hotel remarked when introduced to Van Hoogstraten: 'Do you know, you are almost charming!' It was probably only that old English disease, snobbery, that prevented her from admitting that he really was charming.

His good looks no doubt help with the women. A strong forehead, straight nose, angular jaw, not jutting but turning around and then up to a longish, masculine face with cheek bones a model would starve for. He has hair any movie star would be proud of. It sweeps back off the temples in a Mach 3 swerve and at the forehead it describes a great aerodynamic thrust before blowing effortlessly over the crown to a finely etched line of closure just above the collar. The collar is on the high side, stiff, as white as any detergent commercial. And the hands. Perfect manicured nails and a gold signet ring set with a huge purple amethyst.

Then there's the eyes, of course. But first, the mouth. It has a fluid nature. Hard, but soft. His top lip declines in the middle like the centre, the apex, of a jet wing, moving down in the

Previous page and this page: Nicholas Van Hoogstraten as a young man.

With his beloved stamp collection.

Top: The Braunstein family.

Bottom left: Residents from the old peoples' home in the High Cross estate being taken away by the local council.

Bottom right: 11 Palmeira Avenue where an arsonist caused five deaths.

Top: The original house at High Cross, which mysteriously burned to the ground soon after Van Hoogstraten took control of the estate.

Centre right: In his mausoleum, which he plans to decorate in the Egyptian style.

Bottom left and right: With the construction plans for the new palace.

Top: Former wife Agnes and their son, Orrie, Hoogstraten's fifth child.

Bottom: Agnes in Cannes, where she now lives.

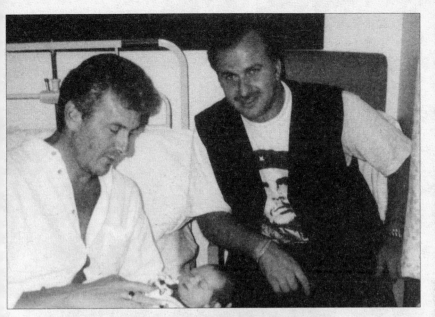

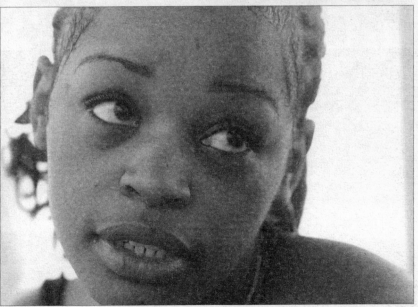

Top: Van Hoogstraten and his then friend and business associate, Michaal Abou Hamden, a Lebanese property developer, with newly born Orrie.

Bottom: Tanaka Sali, Hoogstraten's 18-year-old girlfriend, whom he boasted was 'given' to him by her Botswanan father.

Looking composed
on his way to court.

middle and upwards to either side. When he smiles, he pulls this central V down further while the cheek muscles pull the edges of his lips naturally up. The effect is a vulpine look at once comical and sinister.

And this is the problem with Van Hoogstraten. The very heart of the matter of describing him and getting close to his nature. He is at this fleeting moment, with the grin, almost a pantomime villain. But a closer look tells you that he is owed much more respect. He is, perhaps, an evil bastard. Or somewhere between the two. Or perhaps both – a protean, fluid personality, seesawing from one to the other. Just what is he?

And that takes us back to the women wooed by him through the cathode-ray tube. Do they realise that marriage to Van Hoogstraten might not be a bed of roses? Maybe they do and they don't mind. Maybe they want the thorns. These fans could be made from the same pattern as those women who go on daytime television shows to explain why they married the man who killed his first wife for her money, who shot his best friend when a drug deal went sour, who is doing twenty-five years in Category A or Broadmoor. Maybe they are the same women.

What do they see when they look through the TV screen into his eyes? The eyes appear at first to be dark brown. But there are moments when they change. A transformation takes place when he is annoyed or angry. As if by some alchemy, he seems to be able to alter the pigment in his irises, which turn from brown to black. It is truly remarkable to watch as his eyes take on an impenetrable, coal-black stare. They become opaque and no light permeates them. He has only done this trick once on television, on World in Action in 1988. So those who fall for him could be excused for not realising just what lurks within.

During these moments of tension the mouth hardens into a vulpine V. The line from the thin bottom lip to the tip of the jaw lengthens, and the rock-black eyes swivel towards you to capture your returning gaze. They turn to darkest stone and leave you disconcertingly shut out of any of that human response we all expect. In this state he can – and has – ranted and raved, threatened and turned to violence. This is what Tanaka Sali saw, and it made her shudder. There is more than just a touch of Heathcliff about him.

No psychologist or psychiatrist is needed to tell you that you are faced with an uncanny act. The names that should be put upon such behaviour are those both of pop psychology and old religious superstition. Is he a psychopath? A sociopath? A cold-hearted shit? An agent of the devil? Possessed? An actor, for God's sake? For those who have seen him change, obliterate one self for another in the time the rest of us might smooth a strand of wayward hair, there is little option but to wonder if what medical science calls a psychopath and the religious call evil could be applied to the personality of Nicholas van Hoogstraten.

So this is the complex and dangerous man that so many women find attractive.

His first girlfriend was called Yolande. She was a childhood crush. He went with her from when he was eleven until he left school and joined his father on his cruise liner. When he returned from the sea, he lost his virginity. He was seventeen. He has not said who the girl was.

In his youth, he was as obsessed by his looks as any other teenager. His membership of the Mods, that style-obsessed cult of the early sixties, allowed him to wear foppish clothes. Always the individualist, he was not so keen on the anoraks and scooters much liked by other Mods along the English south coast. He wore brocade and silk and ruffled shirts.

It was an androgynous age and his apparent sexual ambiguity would not have put off the chicks. But the skinny white girls hanging around the pop and fashion scene of Brighton in the sixties in their mini-skirts still lacked something for the young

Van Hoogstraten's taste. They were just not as sexy as he had hoped. He was an intense young man. These girls were frivolous. Sex, like everything else, was a serious business for the tyro. It was not until he was living in exile in Liechtenstein in the mid-seventies that he discovered his true desire for women.

The moment came on a train from Zurich to Paris. He spotted a beautiful black African girl. Right away he knew that this was it. He was immediately attracted to her. This girl was his first black conquest. The experience did not disappoint.

'What do I see in black women?' he has exclaimed. 'Sex appeal!' The fuller, more pronounced African figure, allied to a less inhibited manner, appealed in a way the Twiggy lookalikes of England had not. They did not twitter and simper and behave in so girly a fashion. To this young man they had more, well, more bottom. In their flush of youth, they seemed to him already more complete, more earthy in a D.H. Lawrence kind of way. Just recast the tale of Lady Chatterley's Lover, and here was his lordship and these forces of nature, so avid, uncomplicated, up for it.

Where the girl on the train first went, many others were to follow. From then on Van Hoogstraten was always to have a good-looking black girl as a companion. He says he did have one white girlfriend, with whom he had a relationship lasting several years in the seventies, but all the rest have been black. Some of them were to fall for him, some were just passing in the night. Those who did fall in love were to find to their cost that he loved only one person, and it wasn't the one inside their black skin – it was the person inside his own.

Perhaps the cost of broken relationships has not always been carried by the women. Those who know Van Hoogstraten recall one young woman who might, just might, have been the one to make a different man of the ruthless young millionaire. Her name was Myrtle and she was from the Caribbean island of St Lucia.

Myrtle was not only very beautiful, she was also a kind, intelligent young woman. 'Beautiful outside, beautiful inside,' as Tony Browne put it. The tycoon's architect was introduced to Myrtle in 1988 by Van Hoogstraten. The two men and another friend had flown to St Lucia to celebrate after Van Hoogstraten had won his court case against Westminster City Council. Myrtle had met Van Hoogstraten some ten years before. It was obvious, says Browne, that she was still in love with him. If he had stuck with her, who knows what he might have become.

But it was too much for Van Hoogstraten. He could never have been expected to commit himself to one woman, even one like Myrtle. Her goodness and kindness would have disturbed, even frightened him. How would he have been supposed to respond? Would she have put up with him the way that he was? Would he have been expected to change, to alter his ways? It would have been like asking a lion to become a vegetarian. Myrtle finally gave up waiting for her charming, wayward lover and married a German dentist.

At the time of the visit to St Lucia, Van Hoogstraten had another girl on the go. She was a remarkable young woman from Ethiopia. Her name was Zaki, and she was five foot six and very attractive. When only thirteen or fourteen she had escaped from drought and starvation with her little brother. Together they walked hundreds of miles out of Ethiopia into Kenya. From there she made it to Europe and finally to the south of England, where she met Van Hoogstraten.

The school of hard knocks was to take its toll and Zaki suffered from depression. She lost her looks, went to seed and her hair fell out. Van Hoogstraten took pity on her. She still lives in a flat on the High Cross estate, where she has security and has become a member of the odd family on the 'funny farm', that gathering of retainers, acquaintances, old friends and hangers-on who make up the court of King Nick. A friend once saw Zaki standing in the middle of a road near the estate, holding a doll, looking lost.

Van Hoogstraten became a father for the first time around 1983, with the birth of a son, Rhett Maximillion. The Maximillion was his father's little joke – maxi-million. Hardly surprisingly, the boy's mother prefers Rhett, a romantic name familiar to anyone who has read Gone with the Wind, Margaret Mitchell's epic novel of the American Civil War, or seen the film staring Vivien Leigh as Scarlett O'Hara and Clark Gable as Rhett Butler.

Van Hoogstraten doted on the boy. In the late eighties he told the authors with pride how he had taught five-year-old Max – as he then called him – to flip over the edge of a silk rug with the toe of his shoe in order to count the number of knots per square inch and so judge its quality.

Rhett's mother is Rosemary Prouse, an English girl with a white father and a black mother. Her father lived in a good Van Hoogstraten flat in Hove. Rosemary herself used to hang out in the eighties with another one of Van Hoogstraten's tenants, Caroline Williams. The millionaire landlord was often chatty to his tenants and, as long as they were not complainers, he would be quite friendly towards them. He was very friendly to Caroline and they had been lovers since the seventies.

When Van Hoogstraten met Rosemary, she was a party girl – lots of lipstick, and clothes that showed off her excellent figure. She knew what she wanted and Van Hoogstraten took a shine to her. They had a second child, Eugenie, several years later, after Van Hoogstraten had fathered two other children by another woman. That other woman just happened to be Caroline Williams.

Rosemary was hurt by the renewed attention received by Caroline. What also rankled in later years was the way that Van Hoogstraten at first ignored their daughter and always favoured his son, taking him out for rides in his Rolls-Royce. But in time he began to take an interest in Eugenie, and father and daughter formed a good relationship.

However, it is hard not to see in the father's initial dismissal of his daughter something of the man's view of women in general. For Van Hoogstraten, women are inferior to men. Among the pictures in his collection is a Victorian watercolour of an African slave girl. The girl, probably in her early teens, is depicted bare-breasted, staring unabashed directly at the viewer. Van Hoogstraten is especially fond of the picture.

Van Hoogstraten moved from collecting stamps and coins to furniture and women. He expends considerable time and effort in wooing women, though once he has won them, proven to himself that his charisma remains uncracked, and paraded his latest conquest for a while, he can lose interest. The object of his attentions is left wondering what mistake she made to be no longer in favour. The answer seems more usually to lie with him rather than with her. He is not the first powerful man to behave like this.

He says that his private life is 'very boring' as he has always had a string of monogamous relationships with different women. But he has a habit of not quite severing links with some of his past lovers – or maybe they just won't let him go. Either way, things are more interesting and the girls – past or present – are kept on their toes. The artist Pablo Picasso liked his sexual arrangements complicated. It was more fun that way. Similarly, there is always a buzz of sexual tension around the Sussex tycoon.

Van Hoogstraten chooses not to live with any of his women, saying that to do so would be to lose his independence. They would always want to know where he was. His life would not be his own. He calls his women his bitches, his property. He may feel he owns them – and he certainly can be good to them – but he does not always like paying for his responsibilities.

Rosemary decided Van Hoogstraten was not pulling his

financial weight towards their children. She took him to the Family Division court, claiming £2 million in maintenance for the children. He was furious. He settled before the court hearing, reputedly for £1 million.

According to Van Hoogstraten, the relationship with Rosemary ended 'when she clicked that I thought more of Rhett than of her'. He says the same has happened with the other women by whom he has had children. Amazingly, he and Rosemary have since settled their differences. She now lives in a small but pleasant mews house that he has renovated for her. Generosity with Van Hoogstraten sometimes only requires a little persuasion.

The woman Van Hoogstraten was seeing while he was continuing his relationship with Rosemary Prouse is perhaps the most interesting of all his women. Caroline Williams is a handsome Nigerian with a degree in philosophy. She is shrewd, worldly and intelligent.

For many years Caroline has handled a great many of Van Hoogstraten's affairs. She is a director of several of his companies and keeps an office at the Courtlands Hotel. They met in the seventies when Van Hoogstraten came round to her flat to collect the rent. Caroline remembers her first impression of the young landlord, dressed ostentatiously in a full-length fur coat.

'I thought, who the fuck does he think he is?' she said on a BBC documentary many years later. She was filmed in the Courtlands Hotel, standing beside Van Hoogstraten, who was seated at a table, looking slightly embarrassed.

'Why did you split up?' the reporter asked her.

'I don't know,' Caroline replied. Then she looked at Van Hoogstraten. 'Why did we split up?' she asked.

Van Hoogstraten appeared even more uncomfortable. 'I don't know,' he said.

Caroline was clearly still mad about him.

When they first met, Caroline was young and pretty, with good legs which she showed off to their best advantage with short skirts and thigh-high leather boots.

She and Van Hoogstraten have two children, both boys. The younger child, now about eleven, is called Louis, after Louis XIV, the Sun King, whose masterpiece was the Palace of Versailles. The older one is named Seti, after the ancient Egyptian king remembered for his work on the great colonnaded hall at Karnak begun by his father, Rameses I, and his astonishing galleried tomb in the Valley of the Kings. It is worth remembering that Seti was also a keen gold miner.

Those who know how Van Hoogstraten runs his business affairs see Caroline as the person who can be trusted always to do what is best for him. During his murder trial at the Old Bailey in 2002, she showed her solidarity by sitting in the public gallery on many occasions throughout the long proceedings. She was always beautifully turned out, wearing expensive clothes and much gold jewellery.

There have been many other women, including one called Jennifer, a beautiful, petite woman with an hour-glass figure, who also showed her support at the court. And recently there has been the fiery teenager Tanaka Sali, who dared to defy him.

Tanaka arrived in Britain from Zimbabwe at the end of 2000, her airfare paid by Van Hoogstraten. She was sixteen or seventeen and the experience blew her mind. She had been a frequent guest at the millionaire's Zimbabwean estates, but her new life with a room in the Courtlands Hotel was her real introduction to a life of luxury and ease. She was still a student and continued at college in Brighton, studying for her GCSEs. But at night the student turned into a millionaire's mistress.

Tanaka was not the first woman with whom Van Hoogstraten had a stormy relationship. He met Agnes Gnoumou, yet another African beauty, in the flat of one of his tenants on the French Riviera. Agnes was born in the Ivory Coast in 1965. She was bright but left school when she was twelve. At the age of seventeen she met a French architect and moved to Paris.

When Van Hoogstraten met her she was living in a tiny flat in Cannes, having fled there in 1990 when her relationship with the architect had foundered. She was working in a dress shop and was trying to rebuild her life. Van Hoogstraten took an instant liking to her looks. The millionaire and the young African beauty were unable to talk much as he had no French and she had only a word or two of English. But it didn't stop Van Hoogstraten. He got one of his tenants to act as translator.

Unknown to Van Hoogstraten, the tenant tried to warn Agnes not to get involved with her attentive new suitor. Soon the beautiful young woman was wearing expensive clothes and jewellery and accompanying the dapper tycoon around the best restaurants and clubs in town. She told a reporter from the Brighton Evening Argus that she liked Van Hoogstraten because he was handsome and looked like Richard Gere, who had recently starred in Pretty Woman.

Soon the rows began. Agnes found Van Hoogstraten would fly into a rage at things she considered minor but which he saw as important, such as how one behaved while walking in public. After their disagreements he always won her round and after a while she moved into his apartment and was given a large allowance. Agnes spent time in England and took English lessons. The relationship had its ups and downs. Agnes says she received telephone calls from Caroline Williams, telling her to stop seeing Van Hoogstraten. When she found she was pregnant, Agnes had an abortion at a clinic in Richmond. Van Hoogstraten did not visit her.

Despite their stormy relationship, they finally got married. The ceremony was held in Las Vegas, a surprising choice by Van Hoogstraten, who so often complained that other people were tacky or acted like 'peasants'. Agnes got pregnant again and this time kept the child. She had a baby boy, whom the couple named Orrie.

Regardless of the child, the relationship continued on its tempestuous course. Occasionally Van Hoogstraten gave Agnes expensive gifts. Almost immediately they would vanish, taken back and put into a vault as part of his collections. For the woman attracted to a wealthy and powerful man, it must be dispiriting to discover that she has married a miser.

According to one of his former business associates, Van Hoogstraten was afraid of Agnes. By 1998 he would not be alone with her. The child was not enough to save the marriage, and by 1999 Agnes found herself struggling to bring up her son on a small allowance from his father. The expensive clothes, jewellery and the car were all gone – taken back by her husband.

Van Hoogstraten often referred to Agnes as 'the mad woman'. He seemed unaware of his own role in precipitating her violent behaviour. After one particularly bad row he told her that he hated all women. She became very bitter about her predicament as the discarded wife. Eventually she lost her child completely to the tycoon. Orrie, now aged seven, lives in England, where he is looked after by another one of Van Hoogstraten's women.

Alone in her tiny flat, all Agnes has left to remind her of her child are a few photographs of a smiling, bright-eyed little boy with curly russet hair. She also has a collection of photos of herself with a good-looking man with well-groomed hair who looks a little like Richard Gere.

8

THE DEAL

To a man like Nicholas van Hoogstraten, wealth is a measure of self-worth. Anyone not motivated by money is likely to think that all individuals should be measured by what is inside them, not what they have in the bank. But to understand why men like Van Hoogstraten feel as they do, one has to understand the mystical allure of 'the deal'.

For those with an entrepreneurial mind, the deal is a religion. Its appeal can only be understood by those initiated into the dark arts of wheeling and dealing. Before any deal can be made, there must be painstaking preparation – forming a plan, researching the strengths and weaknesses of the other side, thinking how to outmanoeuvre them, estimating the risk, the amount of money to be put up against the money to be made, the negotiations, the haggling. All of these are enjoyable, to be sure, but nothing compares with that moment of victory when the deal is clinched, the entrepreneur is sure the thing is his, that he has succeeded, has it in his grasp, and knows in his very soul that he has outwitted the opposition, beaten them, won.

This is the moment of pure joy. The intensity of that ecstatic pleasure is measured by money. The amount of money made in the deal is the measure of the deal maker's abilities, his craft, his craftiness, how smart he is. Money, value, profit are what make the deal into a religion. The intensity of the deal-making experience is what creates the true adept, the truly great man. And he is to be revealed to the rest of us by his wealth.

Van Hoogstraten likes to talk about his deals. When he does, his eyes shine with pleasure at the memories they evoke, a trait shared by other wheeler-dealers. He once boasted to the authors over lunch how he had 'obtained' some property and within an hour had transferred it through eighteen different companies so that its passing through his hands would be hidden for ever. The description of this frantic and complicated activity was intended to show the entrepreneur's cleverness, his ability to outflank his opponents and therefore how successful and wonderful he is as a person. Those not motivated by money will never really grasp this. How could they? They are not believers. It is not their religion.

By the late seventies Van Hoogstraten already considered himself a copper-bottomed success. He said: 'I am ... safer financially than Paul Getty or Howard Hughes ever were. I will never end up like them because I will never fall for the trap that these two incredibly powerful men fell for – that of showing even the slightest compassion or sentiment to other human beings. So in that way I am hard-hearted. I view people as trash, just trash.'

The interview concluded with an observation on the importance of that amassed fortune. 'It has been said that no man is an island. Well, I am. Money gives me the power to get and demand what I want. I want nobody. I need nobody... I ask nothing of anybody other than the right to go on with my life the way I want to lead it not as others would run it for me.'

Van Hoogstraten went to huge lengths to insure against the outside world finding how he was making that money. He developed webs of interlocking companies, whose sole purpose seemed to be buying and selling between themselves. Assets were transferred back and forth bewilderingly. A Van Hoogstraten-controlled company would bid for a property at auction, pay for it with a loan from a second Van Hoogstraten company, then sell to a third Van Hoogstraten company, which in turn would pay for it by raising a mortgage from the first company. The third Van Hoogstraten company might then sell the property on to yet another company in the Van Hoogstraten web – or back to the company which bought it in the first place. It was deliberately confusing, fooling creditors, tax investigators or hacks – as it was meant to do.

Some companies had names which gave them away as Van Hoogstraten operations. Nassau and Hamilton Investments and Hamilton Prior were two. Both were named after his favourite spot in Bermuda. Other company names reflected his macabre sense of humour. One was Tombstone. Others were Ripe Profit and Rarebargain.

Van Hoogstraten sometimes operated personally under a variety of improbable names. Reza Ghadamian was one. Adolf von Hessen was another. In the eighties he changed his name to the latter by deed poll and retained a passport in that name. He also called himself Dr Karl Brunner and Nicholas Hamilton.

Mysterious foreigners popped up time and again as directors of his companies. One was Pierre Mouchin. Van Hoogstraten always said that Mouchin was a Parisian brothel keeper. There were also Africans with postbox addresses in Nigeria, and Europeans – judging by their names – with addresses care of the Turks and Caicos Islands and other tax havens.

What made this web still more difficult to penetrate was that Van Hoogstraten didn't call the tune all the time. In some cases he lent money to an associate for a specific acquisition and let the associate get on with 'turning it round' at a profit. The onus was on the associate. If he couldn't do it and didn't repay Van Hoogstraten the interest rates he charged, the tycoon simply repossessed the property. His victims included his friends.

The odd part of it is that most of these friends remained in the fold. Another property dealer recalled how one, a large, dreadlocked West Indian called 'Karate Frank', had a shop he owned and everything in it 'repossessed' by Van Hoogstraten's men. The dealer says he was invited along by Van Hoogstraten 'to see the fun'. Yet Karate Frank was reportedly back acting as the tycoon's bodyguard in 2002.

After Van Hoogstraten himself, the key figure was the Fagin-like Bill Bagot, the slum landlord from Paddington. He and Van Hoogstraten were partners in all kinds of moneylending and other ventures. The old man with the red waistcoat running with silverfish felt close enough to his younger business associate to make him his heir. Shortly after Van Hoogstraten's release from jail in 1973, Bagot made out a will leaving all but two of his buildings to him. Well before his death twenty years later, a lot of his stock is thought to have already passed into Van Hoogstraten's control.

Occasionally the outside world had a glimpse into some of the workings of the business world inhabited by Hoogstraten and Bagot. In 1977 an investigation showed a Hove-based company called Masterzone Finance was involved in fraud.

The company had applied to the Department of Trade for a moneylender's certificate. It proposed to make loans of between £1000 and £30,000 a time, charging interest rates of up to forty-eight per cent. The documentation with the application showed that the company's seed finance was from a hefty mortgage – 300,000 Swiss francs – with a subsidiary of the Swiss Banking Corporation. Something about that must have smelled, because the Department of Trade decided to track down Masterzone's Swiss funders – and found they didn't exist. The Swiss Banking Corporation had no knowledge of any dealings with Masterzone.

Police homed in on who was behind Masterzone. The pointers could hardly have been stronger. Masterzone shared an address with Van Hoogstraten's company Hamilton Prior. According to Masterzone's books, it had made a loan to another Van Hoogstraten company. Its list of directors included two names known to be used by Van Hoogstraten himself (Reza Ghadamian and Karl Brunner). A third director was Bill Bagot. And the company secretary was Ron Dedman, another long-term associate of Van Hoogstraten.

The police now moved in and interviewed the seventy-one-year-old Bagot. He gave nothing away. No, as far as he knew, Van Hoogstraten had nothing to do with Masterzone. What about the loan to Van Hoogstraten's company? Bagot said he knew nothing about it. When it was made he had been ill in hospital. The police pressed him. He was adamant. Van Hoogstraten was not involved.

Filing false information wasn't a major crime, and the police did not pursue it. However, Masterzone's application for a moneylending certificate was turned down. Van Hoogstraten would not have been happy.

His attitude to the laws of the land in this period was totally cavalier. They were a challenge – to be circumvented, defied and wherever possible mocked. In 1978 creditors moved in on Getherwell Finance Ltd, so Van Hoogstraten decided to bankrupt the company and to claim that his henchmen were its main creditors. It was a farce and Van Hoogstraten made that all too obvious. At one creditors' meeting he nominated Donald Duck as trustee of the bankrupt company. Later, in court, he had Robert Knapp, calling himself Robert Pierson, claim to be a creditor of Getherwell. Knapp nominated Grumpy, Bashful and Sleepy as members of the committee of inspection that the law required to oversee the liquidation.

In other courts Van Hoogstraten's childish brand of humour sometimes gave way to paranoid outbursts. In 1977 he went to court to watch a case involving Robert Knapp. Suddenly he shouted at the police barrister: 'You had better be very careful... People like you are party to the corruption and when it comes to the reckoning it will be people like you who are dealt with.'

Police officers grabbed him and took him off to Hove police station. When he was searched and a four-inch roofing nail was found in his pocket, he said that it was for defence against muggers. At the time he was wearing a two-thousand-year-old Egyptian necklace made of gold and worth 'in excess of £100,000'. He was charged with threatening behaviour and carrying an offensive weapon. In court his counsel argued that his client was well known to be very rich and so was open to attack.

The magistrates were not impressed. Van Hoogstraten was fined £100. Naturally, he appealed.

Much, much worse was about to befall him. What he didn't know was that in the mid-seventies a secret investigation had begun. The Inland Revenue were after him. By 1979 their investigators were ready to pounce. The man who claimed to be more secure financially than the legendary Paul Getty and Howard Hughes was about to be clobbered by the taxman as no one had ever been clobbered before. The outcome would stagger everyone and the size of the payment would put Van Hoogstraten's name in the Guinness Book of Records.

The Revenue told him it wanted £2.9 million he owed in unpaid taxes. He didn't pay. So in August 1980 the Revenue secured a High Court order freezing a huge chunk of his assets, including High Cross, various other properties, a Rolls-Royce and a Cadillac and even his beloved stamp collection. The total value of the seized assets was reckoned to be close to £3 million.

Without a hint of irony Van Hoogstraten subsequently painted himself as financially naive. 'I was living abroad in Liechtenstein and I didn't think I was liable to pay tax on my UK assets but I was.'

He reacted to the blow by trying a favourite dodge – the use of front companies to squirrel property away and thus minimise his assets during the Revenue's investigation. Bill Bagot was the key to the strategy. In the weeks immediately after the seizure of the assets two companies on which Bagot was a director 'bought' £150,000 of Van Hoogstraten properties in the Brighton area.

But Bagot and Van Hoogstraten slipped up. The Revenue discovered that Bagot was a partner in a company selling the properties as well as in those buying them. The sales were a sham.

A vain struggle now began to get to the bottom of Van Hoogstraten's finances. When facing a huge bill he was at his most slippery. The Revenue demanded jail for both him and Bagot for defying a court order banning Van Hoogstraten from getting rid of assets. A judge ruled that out. The taxmen then demanded that both men be made to produce the sale documents. Amazingly, the courts ruled against that too. Van Hoogstraten's counsel successfully claimed privilege on the grounds that his client might incriminate himself. The Revenue couldn't even force the two companies who were supposed to have purchased the properties to produce their receipts.

The taxmen's investigations into Van Hoogstraten's business empire would stretch over four years. While they ferreted he was busy finding ways to reduce his apparent income. Some 150 of his properties had been sequestrated. Although that meant he couldn't dispose of them, he still controlled them.

As many as fifty of the seized properties had no tenants. They had been emptied before the Revenue struck. Van Hoogstraten wasn't going to spend money on maintaining them. Most were boarded up and left to moulder. Some became notorious local eyesores. At various times councillors talked hopefully of compulsorily purchasing them, but it was just talk.

The biggest property of all – High Cross – mysteriously burned down during a rainstorm in the early hours of one morning in April 1983.

An anonymous 999 call alerted the fire brigade shortly after midnight. Flames were already shooting through the timber-framed roof as they arrived. Van Hoogstraten turned up in his Rolls, and watched from beneath an umbrella as forty firemen struggled to contain the blaze. Uncharacteristically, he said nothing. The fire was so fierce the firemen had to withdraw and watch as the roof collapsed. All they could do was prevent it spreading to outbuildings and cottages. The entire house was gutted. The next day Robert Pierson refused to let reporters on to the property.

CID and fire investigators probed the causes of the fire. The ferocity of the flames strongly suggested arson. 'We are treating it as suspicious,' the police announced.

Van Hoogstraten didn't disagree. The fire had been started by 'left-wing anarchists' as part of a vendetta against him, he claimed.

Two others among his sequestrated properties were hit by arson around this time. In one case a gas pipe was deliberately severed and a lighted candle left next to it. Had the gas ignited it would have blown up 'half of Hove', according to the fire brigade.

Again Van Hoogstraten blamed left-wing anarchists.

No one else appears to have taken that idea seriously. The tycoon himself looked a much more credible suspect. Was he after the insurance? That was an obvious possibility. High Cross was reputedly insured for £1 million. That idea was put to Van Hoogstraten, who dealt with it with his usual brio. He replied that claiming that kind of money just wasn't worth the bother.

Very quickly after the High Cross inferno there was an

agreement with the Revenue. Only the broad outlines were ever revealed. No one ever discovered enough to know which side won. But the Revenue seemed to have done very well. Van Hoogstraten was reportedly to pay £5.5 in back tax and interest, half of it immediately, the rest over a period of two years. Against that all his assets – the known assets – were his again, and the charges against him and Bill Bagot were dropped.

Van Hoogstraten claimed to have learned one big lesson, thanks to the Revenue. He explained it to the magazine Business Age: 'It was the Revenue officials who really helped me out by saying you're crazy to put everything in your own name. You'd be much better off, £5.4 million better off, if you transfer assets offshore. So now I own very little. It's all in trusts and tax haven companies that can't be traced back to me.' Years later he would boast that not a single one of his assets was in his own name.

To return to 1983, what was to happen to the ruins of High Cross? Van Hoogstraten says that he was in a quandary. 'After the old place caught fire we were faced with the problem of what would we do with it. Totally abandon it? At one time I was thinking, get rid of it. It's bad news.'

In fact he already knew exactly what he wanted to do with it. He would make the clairvoyant's prediction come true – by building his white-marble palace on the site. He'd call it Hamilton Palace. A search through company records shows that Van Hoogstraten set up a company with that name eleven months before High Cross caught fire.

He kept the idea of building a palace there secret for several years. Then he played it so carefully that a young architect agreed to design the huge structure for almost nothing, believing that he – not Van Hoogstraten – had conceived the idea in the first place.

The architect was Tony Browne. He'd become one of Van Hoogstraten's tenants in 1980, while studying for his degree in architecture at Brighton Polytechnic. Van Hoogstraten started to use him on work that would normally go to a fully qualified professional and would command a professional's high fees. Tony Browne was cheap labour.

His first job for Van Hoogstraten was a tree survey at High Cross. Browne remembers it vividly. He made the mistake of taking a friend to see the estate and the friend was terrified just by the sight of Van Hoogstraten. 'There was a roar of a powerful engine and he was suddenly there in front of us in a black Corvette. He was wearing dark sunglasses and undertaker's clothes, it looked to us. My friend, who had heard of his reputation, took one look at him and disappeared through the hedge.'

Browne, who was made of much sterner stuff, stuck around. He was fascinated by Van Hoogstraten. 'He thought outside the envelope ... if there was a problem he'd come up with a solution no one else would think of. It might be so totally over the top that it was crazy, but sometimes it wasn't.' Browne had more practical reasons, too, for attaching himself to Van Hoogstraten. The tycoon entrusted him with enough work to make any recently qualified architect go green with envy. They included 'major design projects' and, eventually, the management of the Van Hoogstraten properties in Brighton and Hove.

The biggest project of all came his way after Van Hoogstraten learned that Browne had to design a major building for his postgraduate degree. Not a building that would ever be commissioned, but a fictional project. Van Hoogstraten let drop his idea about a palace, and they talked. Why should Browne's postgraduate project be fictional? Why not design Van Hoogstraten's white palace?

Designing a one-off building of any size is an expensive business. A modest three-bedroom house involves a few hundred calculations and five drawings. In the mid-eighties an average architect charged about £3000 for such a job. Van Hoogstraten wanted something bigger, richer than Buckingham Palace, plus fantastical trimmings. It involved some five thousand drawings, plans, drawings and calculations. An established architect would have charged £200,000 for the job. Tony Browne agreed to do it for just his expenses. They came to £2000.

Van Hoogstraten was very happy. He commissioned the project and appointed Browne architect. The idea planted by the clairvoyant was to become reality. Van Hoogstraten said later: 'I didn't make a conscious decision. It just sort of happened.'

Browne was equally happy. He had the kind of commission no other British architect had been given in a century.

Van Hoogstraten went public about the project in February 1986. He was going to build an 'art palace' for his treasures, he told the local paper. It would display his 'massive collection' of French furniture and his paintings, including his Turners and his Holbein.

'I am not going to do anything ridiculous or fanciful,' said the tycoon. 'I am not building anything that looks mad like some fairytale castle.' The finished building would look like the palace of Fontainebleau in France, he explained.

It would be six hundred feet long and be on just two storeys. His collection would be housed in one vast piano nobile, the elevated main floor running the entire length of the building. There would be frescos on the ceiling and tapestries on the walls.

Browne was quoted as saying: 'We are going for a stylish elegance, avoiding all crudity in design.'

Van Hoogstraten was bursting with excitement about the project. Journalists were driven personally by him to Browne's office in Islington, north London, to be shown the model. Van Hoogstraten claimed to have designed most of it himself. It would be the largest private residence built in over a century, he enthused.

The interior was to be of Carrara marble. There was to be a

majestic central staircase and outside a series of waterfalls would lead to a five-acre lake and a boathouse. Across the water would be a bandstand. The walls were to be three and a half feet thick, and the foundations – incredibly – 150 feet deep.

Van Hoogstraten knew what he wanted. He described being inspired by Buckingham Palace. 'I went there when I was in my late teens to collect some items from King George V's stamp collection. When you go in initially it's through what looks like a medieval flagstone courtyard area which extends into the ground floor. Then, when you go up that grand staircase, you are in what I presume is the formal salon and you're hit with what all the money in the world can't buy... I wanted to replicate that impression you get.'

The style he finally settled on was a form of English baroque created by Browne. The house consists of a central block surmounted by a dome with a bronze cupola and two wings with their own smaller cupolas.

Some ridiculed Van Hoogstraten's dream and sneered at the design as a tasteless pastiche. Punch called it a folly. The Daily Star called it 'The Devil's Palace'. An Evening Argus reporter labelled it 'Hoogstraten's Toad Hall'.

But others reserved judgement or were even prepared to be impressed. One of the leading authorities on the English country house, John Martin Robinson, said that what Van Hoogstraten was planning was 'a serious house ... not just interesting ... but pretty staggering'. Interviewed by the Independent, Robinson said the High Cross house was neither a slavish copy nor a pastiche. Would it be a great building? he was asked. 'That's hard to say... I wouldn't have thought so. If you don't get classical detail absolutely right it has a tendency to degenerate into kitsch.' He thought that the best definition might be 'Post-modern classical with a dash of megalomania'.

This was hardly surprising given the client. Tony Browne had great fun presenting Van Hoogstraten with humorous options for the architectural style that might be adopted. One drawing depicted Van Hoogstraten as the Statue of Liberty – entitled 'The Statue of Taking Liberties'. Hoogstraten enjoyed the joke.

There had always, of course, been more than a dash of megalomania about the owner of the estate. At High Cross it would find full expression – and not just in the huge palace Van Hoogstraten was bent on creating.

He began to gather round himself his own version of a court. He took to staying in the lodge on the estate. Later he made it his main home in England. Members of his inner circle – some of them the heavies he employed – were offered homes in cottages in and around the estate. Half a dozen, with their wives and families, moved into 'grace and favour' cottages.

Others on the firm who didn't find a place there – or didn't want one – started calling High Cross 'the funny farm'. Van Hoogstraten appreciated the joke. He guffawed.

Browne had seen Van Hoogstraten in purple underpants. He wore a lot of purple. His most recent girlfriend, Tanaka Sali, told us: 'Yes, he likes purple. He wears a purple ring and a purple armband. He told me it was a royal colour and he regards himself as royalty, and that's why he's building himself a palace.'

It would take several years for work on the palace to begin. Then, after it had begun, Van Hoogstraten decided on a final royal touch. He would have a mausoleum included – not for his family but for him alone.

The mausoleum, built of thick concrete, would be under the palace itself. It would be designed to last two thousand years, he announced. On his death his body would be entombed there, along with some of his priceless works of art. As for the palace, it would be closed up around the mausoleum and left with all its contents.

No one was sure whether to take him seriously. Did he really mean it? Or was this another wind-up in the game that he has been playing with the outside world all his adult life. Or was it something that began as a wind-up but ended in him taking it seriously. It was never clear.

He gave the authors one version in 1997: 'The mausoleum initially started as a joke. I certainly don't want to be cremated and I don't like the idea of being put in someone else's ground where even if you've bought the plot they come along fifty years later and dig you up and chuck you away and turn it over to a housing estate. So I think the safest thing is to be buried on your own land and inside a building that can't be destroyed ... and I like the idea of some kind of memorial.'

Two years later he gave a souped-up version to Martin Bashir of ITV. 'What do you propose to accommodate in here?' the reporter asked him near the steps disappearing down into the mausoleum.

'Well, me for a start, plus certain important personal artifacts... That may be a form of insanity, filling it with priceless works of art and treasures. I suppose really it's the nearest I can get to taking all my wealth with me and ensuring that nobody benefits from it.'

Van Hoogstraten's real wealth is hard to gauge. He likes to give different answers at different times to different people. It is a game he plays. Obfuscation, fantasy and misinformation feed the Van Hoogstraten mystique. In 1988 he told the authors he was worth £100 million. By 2002 he was saying that one of his collections alone was worth £200 million. One former business associate says mischievously that as Van Hoogstraten likes to exaggerate, every number he mentions should be 'divided by ten'.

According to the Sunday Times, which publishes a list of the richest people in Britain, by 1997 he was worth £160 million. The following year, the newspaper put the sum at £200 million. And there it stayed until 2002, when it estimated his wealth to have declined to £185 million.

At lunch with the authors, Van Hoogstraten made fun of the Rich List's estimates. He laughed as he posed the rhetorical question, 'Where did I lose that £15 million?' before answering himself with a snort, 'I've probably lost more than that in Africa alone.'

As Van Hoogstraten has large investments in Africa, one can assume that this rare admission does indeed mean that his fortune has been recently declining. One former friend puts his wealth at a figure as low as £30 million, but the true amount must be higher. There was a time in his glory days when he made more than that in a year.

9

SCUMBAGS

If ever there was a decade for the property speculator it was the 1980s. Thanks largely to government policy, house prices rocketed. Smart dealers like Van Hoogstraten foresaw what was coming and grabbed every property they could lay their hands on before prices really took off. In the space of just two years he bought and sold at least two hundred properties and made an astonishing amount of money – as much as £80 million, according to one source close to him. In the process he displayed a nonchalant ruthlessness that capped his reputation as the heir to Peter Rachman. One newspaper called Van Hoogstraten 'the devil's landlord'.

The price explosion was set off by radical changes in government housing policy following the election of Margaret Thatcher in 1979. A central plank of a revolution which Mrs Thatcher envisaged was the transformation of Britain into a nation of owner-occupiers. Everything would be done to help people buy their own homes. Those who couldn't or wouldn't buy could largely be catered for by private landlords – private landlords freed from rent controls.

It was manna from heaven for the property world. Not only could property dealers anticipate a bonanza from rising house prices but, if rent controls went, there were good times ahead for everyone renting out.

Mrs Thatcher rapidly became the one living politician Van Hoogstraten had time for. Twenty years later he is still an ardent fan.

Step one for the Iron Lady was to sell off council housing, then the bedrock of housing provision. Local councils were forced to offer their houses to their tenants at substantial discounts. Next, building societies were encouraged to provide easy loans. Then, bit by bit, tenants' rights began to be curtailed.

Owner-occupation did rocket, just as the government hoped. But part of the price was a new era of Rachmanism. Ruthless developers grabbed every tenanted building they could get and tried to 'winkle' out their tenants and convert their bedsits into homes for owner-occupiers.

Winkling meant getting the tenant out by fair means or foul – a few thousand pounds in compensation for the lucky, harassment for the rest. A measure of the scale of the winkling is that between 1981 and 1984 the numbers of privately rented properties in London dropped by sixty-eight thousand. Some of that was slum clearance but a great deal was due to rapacious developers.

Whole areas of the capital were 'gentrified' in this way – notably the bedsitlands of Kensington, Camden, Maida Vale and Notting Hill. Even the most God-fearing institutions were tempted by the pickings to be had and stuck their snouts in the trough. In South Kensington one of the big landlords is the Henry Smith Charitable Estate. It was founded three hundred and fifty years ago to help the poor. Come the 1980s, the charity was suddenly revealed to be helping the rich. Its properties in some of London's most upmarket addresses – places like Onslow Square – were being sold to developers who then hustled their tenants out.

Examples reached MPs, who took the issue up on the floor of the House of Commons, but to no avail. Much the same was said to be happening with other respectable landlords. Winklers were reported to have got their hands on Church Commission houses near Regent's Park and Eton College properties in Swiss Cottage.

Tenants' rights groups protested. One produced a pamphlet featuring the story of a blind Irish lady in her seventies, whose home had been in an Edwardian block of flats off Gloucester Road, South Kensington. An ex-hospital cleaner, she had lived there for some twenty years. She learned that the block had a new owner, a developer, who told her she would have to get out. He gave her 'compensation' – £120. With no idea that she might have legal rights to keep her home, she didn't argue. Some weeks later a charity worker found her, dying of pneumonia in a tiny, unheated room with a broken window. A TV reporter working on a story about winkling discovered that the old lady's previous home and the rooms next to it had been converted into one huge apartment. It had become the home of the chairman of the BBC, Marmaduke Hussey, and his wife, a lady-in-waiting to the Queen. They would have known nothing, of course, about the dead Irishwoman whose home was now theirs.

The tenants' protests got nowhere. An all-party committee of MPs pressed the government to investigate but it refused. The winkling and the profit-taking gathered pace. According to a survey conducted by the Greater London Council, in one year alone around sixteen thousand private tenants in London suffered 'significant harassment' at the hands of their landlords.

Van Hoogstraten had to be careful in getting on to this new Rachmanite gravy train. His tax problems with the Inland Revenue hamstrung him. For a long time he needed to minimise his holdings on paper and not be seen to be a buyer. But secretly he and his front men began buying tenanted blocks across London and on the south coast.

The news of his expansion in Brighton and Hove eventually leaked out. In September 1983 every private tenant in the area must have felt a thrill of panic on reading the article the Evening Argus headlined: 'Van Hoogstraten's buying spree'. The report underneath revealed that Brighton's most notorious landlord was planning to buy as much tenanted property as he could. By now Van Hoogstraten had settled with the Inland Revenue and so could admit he was a big buyer. He told the reporter that the only constraint on how much he'd buy was availability. In Hove there just wasn't enough property on estate agents' books.

For once Van Hoogstraten tried to sound reassuring. He explained to the Argus that his reputation was undeserved. It was based on allegations made against him in the past. There were hundreds of tenants of his in Brighton and Hove who lived peacefully without any talk of harassment. Those who were about to become his tenants had nothing to fear.

'The idea is to buy property with people living in it, wait twenty years if necessary until it becomes vacant and then sell it on with vacant possession to a builder for renovation or redevelopment.' It hardly needs to be said that it didn't work out that way for all his new tenants.

Most of those in the buildings he began to snap up wouldn't have known immediately that they had become a Van Hoogstraten tenant. He admitted to the Argus that all the purchases would be through nominees. 'I don't intend to buy anything in my own name.' His reason? He didn't want tenants to become worried because he was their new landlord.

In reality his policy was to use front companies and front people in all his operations, the moneylending and investment companies as well as property. One man whom he used for years as a front, Lebanese-born property millionaire Michaal Abou Hamdan, says: 'Nick always wanted barriers between him and the deal.'

At first Van Hoogstraten concentrated the buying spree in Brighton and Hove. Over a couple of years he and his front men gobbled up almost every house that came on to the market in the quietly respectable avenues just north of the Hove seafront. First, Second, Third and Fourth Avenues and The Drive are parallel with each other, running from the Prom to Western Road, the commercial heart of Hove. The houses are double-fronted, four-storey mansions. They were built in yellow brick with lacy ironwork balconies and high windows. Before the 1980s the Avenues were bathchair country. Retired folk with small pensions made their final homes there. Students and single people rented furnished rooms or flats. These places were Van Hoogstraten's targets. By the middle of the decade he appeared to own almost everything in First and Second Avenues and many of the mansions in the parallel streets as well.

He bought extensively in up-and-coming areas of west London too, like Notting Hill and Maida Vale, and in those that were already upmarket, like Holland Park. As in Brighton and Hove, he tended to go for Victorian and Edwardian buildings. However run down or neglected they were, he knew they would be solidly built and once emptied would command premium prices. 'Quality, I always go for quality,' he explained. 'The Victorians and Edwardians built solidly. I wanted substantial buildings.' Some he 'thieved' for a few thousand pounds. Some cost hundreds of thousands, but he knew that they were potentially worth five or ten times as much.

Rachman's tactics weren't needed most of the time. Some buildings Van Hoogstraten decided to hang on to, and he was happy to keep them tenanted. Of those where this wasn't the case, some emptied naturally as people died or moved on. In the rest, where he wanted tenants out as soon as possible, he tended to pursue a policy of malign neglect. It was purposely designed to wear the residents out. Repairs would not be done. Heating bills would not be paid. When tenants complained, they would be ignored. If they persisted they would be abused or worse. Van Hoogstraten knew that some tenants would respond by withholding their rent. When they did that he immediately went for an eviction order, and he usually secured it. The law insists that you pay your rent whatever hell your landlord visits on you.

When none of that worked – and Van Hoogstraten was determined to get a stubborn tenant out – all kinds of Rachmanite things could happen.

One was the sudden arrival of the neighbours from hell – thunderously noisy and partying all night. Many were drop-outs and drug addicts whom Van Hoogstraten's henchmen had dredged up. He himself specially liked employing Rastafarians. He always got on well with Afro-Caribbeans and made a number of black friends. For a low rent – sometimes a rent-free flat – many were only too happy to move into whatever house he nominated and deliberately turn life there into a nightmare for everyone else.

It was harassment by another name. Occasionally it sparked incidents that reached the courts. In January 1983 an ex-policeman called Stefan Harnisch was arrested after a fight in Hove. He was searched by police and found to be carrying a knife. He claimed that it was for protection against thugs who were harassing tenants in a block of eight flats that Van Hoogstraten had bought in Cromwell Road, Hove, a few months earlier. 'Van Hoogstraten … hired a dozen blacks who moved in with records and amplifiers,' Harnisch claimed in court. The object was to get the tenants out. Harnisch said that he had challenged the leader of the gang and that he was now in fear of being attacked. The knife was confiscated and Harnisch was fined £50.

Mostly what went on behind the front doors of Van Hoogstraten's expanding empire never saw the light of day – like the slow, grubby war of attrition his henchmen waged against Violet Lamont. She had lived at 32b First Avenue, a basement flat, since 1961. A feisty, pretty little lady, she had brought up six sons in India, where her husband was in the colonial service. Her flat was spacious and opened on to its own garden. She was very happy there. Among her friends in the house was a dentist called Paul Lahaise, who had his surgery on the ground floor immediately above Violet.

Life changed for Violet at the beginning of the eighties when a company owned by Van Hoogstraten bought the house. She learned that the new owners wanted her and everyone else out. The flat had been her home for some twenty years, she was a protected tenant and she said no. Most of the other residents were more compliant than she was or they were scared. One by one they disappeared. Soon the entire building was empty except for Violet and Paul Lahaise. He, too, refused to go. So Van Hoogstraten's men got to work on the two of them.

A new set of tenants moved into the first floor. Paul and Violet were soon made to realise that their new neighbours were drug addicts. Used syringes were dropped down into the basement areas. Strange people called. Music thumped endlessly. The colonial servant's widow and the dentist stuck it out. Then the landlord found Paul Lahaise's weak spot – his practice. Heavy wardrobes were moved into the passageway leading to the surgery and they were left there. The wardrobes virtually blocked the entrance. Patients had to squeeze past them or couldn't get in at all. Months went by. The practice suffered. Finally Lahaise told his fellow tenant that he had had enough and he was going.

Left on her own, Mrs Lamont was now to endure nearly a decade of harassment from Van Hoogstraten's men. Nothing violent. Nothing that major. Just the drip, drip, drip of nasty little happenings to make life horrid. Her son Alan recalls: 'To make sure she didn't get any sleep the music was played continually.

They must have used looped tapes or something, because whether they were holding a party or not the music just went on and on. It never stopped. When that didn't shake her, other things started to happen. The cable to her television aerial was cut again and again. Rubbish was thrown into her basement area. The gas flue was blocked. Rubble was dumped all over the garden that she loved. A huge dustbin full of rubbish was set alight outside her door.'

Alan is one of the country's most admired cartoonists. A gentle, softly spoken man, he phoned the managing agents – Van Hoogstraten's office – to complain. 'This rough voice said my fucking mother was the trouble round here. Everybody knew she was a fucking troublemaker. I said that I would report him to the police and he said you can fucking well do that, you fucking fuck.'

'So I did phone the police. They were less than helpful. They said that Van Hoogstraten always knew what he could get away with. If his people were making threats I wouldn't be able to prove it.'

Mrs Lamont went to the council's harassment office. 'He huffed and puffed and did nothing,' says Alan. 'He would come round and noted this and that and said to us do this and do that but nothing would ever happen. He, like everyone, was really too intimidated by the thought of Nicholas van Hoogstraten. Nearly everybody in the town was frightened of him.'

Life became even worse for Violet after her son complained. Every time she went into the garden there was abuse from the floor above. A hole was made in her bathroom ceiling directly above the bath, ostensibly during plumbing work in the room overhead. It was left there so that the bath was open for inspection from the room above. Each time Violet started to run the water she would hear heavy footsteps on the holed ceiling above. The waste pipe outside was broken and her kitchen swamped in sewage. Then one day she found her water turned off. One of her sons came by to turn it on from the mains. Immediately the flat was flooded. A Water Board official was called in. He was astonished to find that someone had twisted the ballcock and diverted the overflow from Violet's water tank so that it flowed back into the flat. Once the water was turned on a flood was inevitable.

Some members of Violet's family wondered if the elderly lady might be paranoid, making it up – until they visited what had been a lovely flat.

By 1984 her beloved home was in such a bad state that an environmental health officer ruled that it was unfit for human habitation. He was going to slap a closure order on the flat. No doubt this was just what the landlord wanted. Now the tenant would have to move out.

Violet Lamont had other ideas. She went to a firm of solicitors. They wrote a timid letter to Van Hoogstraten's office. It was ignored. Alan says that privately they told her they didn't want to upset Van Hoogstraten. It might result in a brick being thrown through their office window. Other local solicitors were approached and they too didn't want to know about taking on Van Hoogstraten. Finally the local Tory MP, Tim Sainsbury, intervened, and a woman solicitor who wouldn't be intimidated took up the case. The unfitness order was never issued and – after a prolonged struggle – a judge instructed the landlord to make the place fit to live in again.

Violet had won. The harassment died down. She kept her home. Van Hoogstraten personally never put in an appearance. But Alan thinks he must have developed a grudging admiration for the old lady. She died of cancer in 1996.

Closure orders, like the one the environmental health officer wanted to issue on Mrs Lamont's home, should be bad news for the bad landlord – in theory. Van Hoogstraten proved that they could be quite the opposite, a handy means to get an awkward tenant out. Just allow the place to deteriorate – or help the process by smashing the house up – and the council will solve your problem by telling your tenants that they can't live there any more because it's unfit for them to do so. This happened time and time again in the Van Hoogstraten empire.

It happened to Madge and Fred Mahood. They were the last tenants remaining in a large, ramshackle corner property, 222 Dyke Road, Brighton. The Mahoods were in their eighties when Van Hoogstraten bought the house. They had lived in the ground-floor flat there since 1962. When they refused to leave, Van Hoogstraten tried to take out an eviction order against them. That failed, so the house was deliberately turned into a slum. The landlord claimed that he had spent £14,000 on the flat in 1983. But lead was stripped from the roof. Windows were broken. Gutters were blocked. Upper-storey windows were boarded up. Water streamed through the roof. The ground-floor walls ran with damp. By 1988 it was a notorious Brighton eyesore.

Fred Mahood was so ill that he was moved into a nursing home. Madge Mahood stayed put. 'It's a terrible place to live and I'm going mad,' she said. 'But I can't leave now. This is my home. Where would I go?… Why should I move just so that a man like Van Hoogstraten can make money.' One night she awoke to find a man climbing through her bedroom window. She shouted and he disappeared. She was certain – though there was no proof – that the intruder was one of Van Hoogstraten's men.

Brighton Council was urged to slap a purchase order on the house. But Van Hoogstraten announced publicly that he would want £500,000 for the property. The council balked at that. They did exactly as he hoped – and imposed a closure order. A council official suggested that it was all for Madge Mahood's own good. 'It was felt that Mrs Mahood's place of residence was unfit for her or anybody else,' he told the press. 'It is unlikely that she would have enjoyed another winter there.' So finally Madge had to leave. Van Hoogstraten had won.

Hove Council was no better than Brighton Council at standing up for Van Hoogstraten's most vulnerable tenants. John Whittington was one of them. A seventy-five-year-old, partially blind and with a bad heart, he and his wife Emily lived in a first-floor flat in Denmark Villas. Van Hoogstraten bought the house in 1979. As at 32 First Avenue and 222 Dyke Road, the other tenants swiftly disappeared and the place rapidly deteriorated. A reporter who visited the Whittingtons' home in August 1980 wrote that the walls of the flat were green with mildew and rain poured through the ceiling.

John Whittington, who was becoming increasingly frail, called in the council's environmental health department. They declared the house to be unfit and took out a court order requiring the landlord to repair it. Van Hoogstraten's company Hamilton Prior ignored the order. A second order was obtained – and that was ignored too. So John Whittington decided to withhold his weekly rent until the repairs were carried out. Hamilton Prior's response was to go for an eviction order.

'We will be taking out a possession order against them,' warned one of Van Hoogstraten's managers, Ron Dedman. 'They would have to pay the rent even if the roof was falling in.'

The council's response? To warn the Whittingtons that because of their unpaid rent they might not only lose their home, but could also lose their place on the council's waiting list for a house. They had been on the list for five years. A housing official explained: 'By withholding rent Mr Whittington may be seen as being made homeless voluntarily.'

At the time John Whittington was so ill that his doctor warned that he would die within six months if he wasn't found somewhere else to live – or the roof was repaired. 'Our life is a nightmare,' his wife said. 'We can't afford to live anywhere else and we can't live here.'

The Whittingtons left. The house was boarded up and left to decline until Van Hoogstraten decided the time was ripe to sell it. He would send in the repair men to deal with any serious structural problem, but no more. The place could rot until he was ready. The same happened with some fifty other of his properties on the coast. He became known for his eyesores and, ever conforming to type, he revelled publicly in the outrage they caused.

Periodically someone on Brighton or Hove Council would suggest that the local authority might take over these wasted assets, but it was never considered worthwhile. Van Hoogstraten laughed when, in 1982, a Brighton councillor suggested a compulsory purchase of one of his boarded-up buildings in Ditchling Road. 'If they think this place is bad they should see some of my other properties in Brighton... It will stay like that until somebody makes me an offer I can't refuse.'

How did Van Hoogstraten see himself at that time, this thirty-seven-year-old tycoon who had been in jail and had come out seemingly intent on making ordinary people hate and fear him?

Here are extracts from a 'My kind of day' newspaper feature on him published on 30 July 1982, when he was still struggling with the Inland Revenue as well as planning his massive spending spree:

'I get up at about 7.30, which I regard as rather late. I don't have anywhere where I really call home. I was living in Paris for a long time and for tax reasons my official home is in Liechtenstein, but you can't live there. It's really plastic.

'I like to be able to smell fish and chips when I walk down the street. I have property in some very seedy areas of London but even there the place has got character and atmosphere.

'I would never eat breakfast in bed. I've got silk sheets and it would really mess it all up... I don't drink alcohol except a bit with meals and I don't smoke. Often I'll have a business lunch which I like because often someone else pays for it. If I don't go out I'll just have a salad sandwich on brown bread and yoghurt. Then it's back to business.

'I don't have a desk to go to. So I just work wherever I am.

'I've got a Cadillac, a Rolls-Royce and a Corvette here, a Rolls in Paris and another one in Geneva... I hate sports cars and I hate the people that drive them. They're all flash Harrys.

'I used to take the train up to London but then they started putting the prices up so I stopped.

'I have a guardian, too, who comes around to protect me. No, they're not former SAS men. We do rather better than that. They're just to protect you from the idiots who try to mug you for £10. I don't really have any enemies. If I did I'd be dead.

'Sometimes photographers try to take pictures of me without my permission. We rip the film out of their cameras, smash the cameras and spit on them.

'I'm very frugal but I do like properly cooked plain English food. The French and Italians seem just to eat chopped-up rubbish covered in sauces.

'I've been in prison twice but I have absolutely no complaint about the food. I thought it was perfectly OK.

'I don't really like restaurants because the food is rarely as good as home cooking. They're full of smoke and there's probably some riff raff at the next table. I'm a terrible snob.

'I don't read much, although when I was in prison I read books on company law and a lot of history books.

'I was brought up a strict Roman Catholic and I believe that there is an ultimate supernatural force. But all organised religions are man-made and were invented by some man who was a bit cleverer and they are just used as a way of keeping the population under control.

'I have my own religion which is power. I control the lives of hundreds and thousands of people just by making decisions about whether to buy or sell a particular business.

'I believe that might is right. The clever and the strong will always survive.

'I believe that all property is theft. If you go back in history all land and property is owned by someone because they nicked it from someone else.

'It doesn't take much to make money, but it takes a lot to keep it. I don't gamble because someone who wins money by gambling or on the pools is just the same as he was when he was poor. I've known bank robbers flying high when they've got £30,000 or £40,000 from a job. Then I've seen them two years later when they're broke and having to think of doing another one.'

Such reflections only hinted at the paranoia and explosive violence of the man. Tony Browne was given a glimpse of the paranoia the first time he encountered Van Hoogstraten. It was 1980 and Browne and a group of fellow students were all looking for a flat, so they made an appointment with Select Management, one of Van Hoogstraten's management companies. They turned up at a house in the Avenues to be greeted by Van Hoogstraten himself.

Browne remembers vividly what happened, and no doubt his mates remember it too. 'We were ushered through a series of steel doors into a dark, dusty room filled with very ornate furniture which was mostly hidden by stacks of files. He sat us all down on this long leather chesterfield. He then went and sat behind this big gilt desk and started ranting and raving. He said he was taping what we said and that if we later came out with anything that contradicted what was recorded there would be some kind of vengeance.

'He then asked each of us in turn what we did, what we were studying. The first one said he was a student of English literature. Nick, as I later came to know him, exploded at that. He called him a parasite who was obviously of no use to society whatsoever. He moved on to the next one. What do you do? He was a drama student. There was even more apoplexy at that. And so it went on. He was verbally assassinating each of us in turn until he came to me. And he said: "What do you do?" I said: "Well, er, architecture." He went: "Ah. Something useful." I was only to discover years later that he meant something useful to him.'

Other students who were looking for accommodation went through the same grilling. One who, like Browne, did become a tenant and then went on to work for Van Hoogstraten as a rent collector, recalls how the tycoon loved to have a go at the students he employed. 'He'd compare himself with us. Here we were with our university degrees. He'd got no qualifications at all at school and here we were working for him.'

Working for Van Hoogstraten was, predictably, a rollercoaster ride. The inner circle called him Nick, the others Mr H. He always paid the wages on time. He was almost always studiously formal and polite. If you made a mistake and admitted it quickly he was understanding. But the slightest hint that you were 'taking the piss' – on the fiddle or lying to him or disobeying him – and all hell would break loose. Browne witnessed it time and again. The last incident was just before he and Van Hoogstraten finally parted company in 2000.

'He found out that some workers in one of his hotels had been using the hotel phone to make overseas calls. There were five workers who might have done it. They were all foreign students working in the hotel as domestics. He lined them up and marched up and down in front of them asking questions until he found out the truth. Two of them had been at it. Nick just started hitting them... Slap, slap, slap around the face, right in front of the others. Everyone was petrified and nobody dared to intervene.'

It was a bully at work.

The climate of fear around Van Hoogstraten on the south coast grew and grew as he expanded during the property boom. By the middle of the eighties he owned an estimated four to five hundred properties in Brighton and Hove and many locals had a friend or a relative who had been one of his tenants or knew someone who had been.

Others only had to read the local newspapers regularly to be taught that a very nasty character indeed was living in their midst apparently unstoppable.

During that period Van Hoogstraten seemed to be Teflon man. Occasionally a tenant might lay charges against him or against one of his lieutenants, but he or she would always think better of it. In April 1981 a student alleged that she had been unlawfully evicted from a Van Hoogstraten flat in First Avenue. Hove Council followed up by trying to serve a summons on Van Hoogstraten. But neither the council's bailiffs nor the detectives it hired could track him down. An order for Van Hoogstraten's arrest was issued. Then, unaccountably, all the witnesses against him abruptly disappeared too. The case was dropped. A year later much the same happened. Again it was a First Avenue tenant, again illegal eviction, again the witnesses vanished, again the case was dropped. 'We are unable to make contact with the witnesses... The council has no alternative but to withdraw the case,' magistrates were told.

The landlord's attitude to his tenants was quixotic. Some he got to know and talked to. At times he bragged that this or that tenant had been with him for years and was as happy as could be. In 1988 he told us that one of his very first tenants, a Mrs Knighton from that terrace of houses in St Magdalene Street that he had bought in 1963, was still his tenant there nearly thirty years later. And he directed the Observer's Duncan Campbell to a woman in Fulham who glowed with praise about him as a landlord. A health service administrator, she had been his tenant for a decade. She told Campbell that she'd always found Van

Hoogstraten 'a very polite and personable young man. There are some tenants who expect their landlords to wet-nurse them.'

However, the hate he exhibited publicly towards tenants – 'scumbags', 'dog's meat', 'filth' – was quite genuine. He tried to justify it many years later by saying he was referring to tenants who tried to blackmail developers by demanding huge sums in return for quitting their controlled tenancies. That did happen, but not to Van Hoogstraten. No, the roots of his animosity lie elsewhere. Tony Browne, who observed his reaction to tenants over a period of twenty years, says there is a simple explanation. Van Hoogstraten's loathing springs from what Browne says every landlord experiences – the careless damage and destruction which tenants tend to leave behind them.

Perhaps Browne is right. Perhaps a broken window back in 1962 or a wall smeared with excrement explain this lifelong detestation. Yet the tenants who most raised Van Hoogstraten's wrath weren't the dirty or the destructive. They were those who had the nerve to take him on.

They took him on as he'd never been taken on before in London. And for once a local council backed them.

Of the two hundred or more properties he bought in London in the eighties, the one that put him in the glare of publicity again was a splendid double-fronted white villa built in Holland Park in the 1860s. Today Sir Richard Branson lives in the same street in exactly the same kind of house. Others there are embassies. They fetch between £6 and £12 million each.

Number 74 Holland Park had been owned by an eccentric old lady. Her tenants were a mixed bunch. They included two actresses, a psychotherapist, a lawyer and a computer analyst, a typical in-crowd mix for this part of west London in the 1980s. The old lady died in 1982, and the house was sold by public auction. A front company owned by Van Hoogstraten bought it. He paid £375,000. Two years later the house would have fetched three or four times that amount with its tenants still in residence, such was the rate of price inflation. Had it been emptied of its tenants it would have fetched ten times as much.

Van Hoogstraten put the house in the name of his mistress, Caroline Williams, the brightest of all his collection of black girlfriends. She informed the tenants in a handwritten note that from now on rent should be paid to Robert Gates and Co in Hove. Nothing at all worrying happened in the house until the following winter. Then the tenants realised that the central heating wasn't functioning. Until then, all that had passed between those living in the house was the odd greeting as they passed on the stairs. Now they got together. The lawyer among them phoned the office of Robert Gates and Co on their behalf and was treated to a tirade from the other end of the line. He was so shaken by it that inside a week he was gone from the building.

It was the start of a six-year battle.

Among the tenants were a psychotherapist Orlee Udwin and her sister Leslee, then an actress and later an award-winning film producer. Leslee had fallen in love with the house when she went to a party there in 1980. A few months later the two sisters managed to get a flat of their own there for a rent of £50 a week. They were the leading lights – and Van Hoogstraten's bêtes noires – in the battle that now began.

When the lawyer neighbour took flight, Leslee phoned around for advice. 'Local agencies ... told us that we were tenants of one of Britain's most notorious landlords... Van Hoogstraten, they said, was dangerous and we should not underestimate his threats. We were advised to fit double locks and chains on our doors.'

In an article for the Sunday Times Leslee described what happened when she took the plunge and phoned Van Hoogstraten direct to tell him that central heating was provided as part of the tenancy agreement. She demanded the heating be put on again. The tenants wouldn't be cowed, she said.

'Van Hoogstraten went ballistic and started screaming at me. He said: "You tenants are fucking scum. You cunt, you're not going to get your car out of second gear.' After that Leslee made a habit of looking under her car before she got in, terrified the brakes would be tampered with or a bomb placed under it.

Next to be threatened was the Irish caretaker, Frank. He was warned of dire consequences to him personally if he put the heating on. Frank quit the job soon after that. All the male tenants in the house quickly took fright as well. Within a few weeks only the women remained.

New men did move into the vacated flats – Van Hoogstraten's men. One was Tony Browne. The others were the architect's friends. Leslee and the other women tenants had no idea the newcomers were friends of Browne and warned them about Van Hoogstraten. Every word went back to the landlord.

Eviction notices were the next move. Two girls sharing a flat were told they were illegal tenants. Others received similar letters.

The two girls made the mistake of going on holiday. At around two o'clock one morning their fellow tenants were awakened by an almighty banging. The girls' furniture was being thrown down the stairs by Van Hoogstraten in person and two other men. After that Leslee began carrying a kitchen knife in her handbag. The spectre of the black-clad Van Hoogstraten able to get in and out of her house at any time of night haunted her.

The landlord's attitude? The girls were 'troublemakers taking the piss'. They had terrific flats in one of the most upmarket addresses in London and were paying peanuts for them. They were indeed living in a desirable place, with large, fourteen-foot-high rooms, huge, balconied windows and a spacious garden. But what really upset Van Hoogstraten was that any tenants should take him on, especially women. He would be just as indignant about an Irishwoman whom he had harassed out of a slum a mile away off Portobello Road as he was about his Holland Park tenants. He told the authors that the woman was 'a prostitute' and the Holland Park women 'a bunch of lezzies'.

No one seemed able to help Leslee and her fellow tenants. The police told them there was nothing they could do unless Van Hoogstraten or his men physically harmed them.

In desperation they hired their own solicitor and spent £2000 pursuing Van Hoogstraten. Two years of injunctions and court orders and summonses followed, all futile. Van Hoogstraten's funds seemed to be unlimited. The tenants' weren't.

The breakthrough came when Leslee and the others linked up with people whom Van Hoogstraten was said to be harassing in other houses in the Royal Borough of Kensington and Chelsea. All were experiencing similar problems – threats, changed locks, disrepair, attempted eviction.

Together they formed a tenants' association and discovered that their own council had quietly taken action against Van Hoogstraten years earlier. In 1979 Kensington and Chelsea Council imposed a control order allowing it to take over a house in Norland Square owned by the tycoon. The building was in such a state that it was deemed to jeopardise the 'health, safety and welfare of the tenants'. Its defects included rising damp, dry rot, a dangerously rotten floor and no fire exit. The order enabled the council to move the tenants out as a temporary measure while it undertook repairs itself and then charged the landlord for them.

Immediately the council had completed repairs, in 1982, Van Hoogstraten's men moved in, changed the locks and prevented the tenants returning. A second control order was issued.

Would Kensington and Chelsea consider taking over four or five of Van Hoogstraten's properties? It didn't look likely. Despite its action over the Norland Square property, the council was a bastion of conservatism. Like all local authorities it had always been timid with control orders. So for months it batted back the tenants' arguments. During this period the harassment went on. Letters came from Robert Gates and Co declaring that they weren't legally tenants at all and were 'squatters'. Possession proceedings were initiated. One tenant, Rod Howard, claimed that Van Hoogstraten personally smashed down the door of his flat and removed furniture while he was in bed.

It was finally too much for Kensington and Chelsea's environmental health officials. An investigation into Van Hoogstraten was ordered. Needless to say, it didn't get much help from the landlord himself. In reply to an enquiry about a tenant in Redcliffe Gardens, his office wrote: 'We are in receipt of your stupid letter of 4 March which should have been returned to you marked "BOLLOCKS WITH TWO LL'S" across it in very heavy black ink.'

Others did co-operate, including other councils where Van Hoogstraten was giving problems. As a result the first-ever dossier on the many sides of Van Hoogstraten was compiled. It listed aliases, convictions, front companies, associates and share-holdings. But the most persuasive fact to emerge was the similarity of what so many tenants in his houses in the borough were experiencing. Kensington and Chelsea, no doubt crossing its fingers, took the plunge.

In October 1985 it issued control orders on five of Van Hoogstraten's properties in the borough: 74 Holland Park, 102 Redcliffe Gardens, 19 Elsham Road, 178 Holland Road and 36 Norland Square. These gave the council day-to-day management rights over the properties. The council followed up with compulsory purchase orders for all five. Worst of all from Van Hoogstraten's point of view, the council then laid charges of harassment against him, against Caroline Williams and against Ronald Dedman, a Van Hoogstraten stalwart in the High Cross siege. Dedman was accused of breaking down a door in the Elsham Road property and threatening a tenant there with 'a nasty accident'.

The harassment trial was set for the following year. If found guilty, Van Hoogstraten could face four years in jail, or even longer.

He was beside himself. A letter signed by Robert Gates and Co attacked the council officers who were acting against him as 'dishonest, incompetent and corrupt'. Inevitably, Van Hoogstraten appealed against the compulsory purchase orders. That meant a public inquiry would have to be held and the harassment trial would have to be postponed.

The inquiry took place in July 1986. As so often, Van Hoogstraten couldn't – or calculated that he shouldn't – keep quiet, and gave vent to a surge of paranoia. 'There is a conspiracy … to thieve these properties from me,' he shouted.

Kensington and Chelsea's QC used the same word. Van Hoogstraten, he said, had organised 'an evil conspiracy' against his tenants. He ensured that they suffered maximum discomfort. 'You do not provide them with hot water. You cut off the central heating... You don't pay the electricity or gas or oil bill... You badger for non-existent rent arrears.' It was all familiar stuff. But persuasive. The appeal against the compulsory purchases was turned down.

The public inquiry went against Van Hoogstraten. Salt was then rubbed in his wounds when the council decided to get back the money it had spent repairing the Norland Square property by selling it. The repairs had cost £126,000. The house was sold to a local housing association for not much more – £148,000. The difference, a mere £22,000, went to the original owner, Van Hoogstraten. The house had been well and truly 'thieved' from him.

Naturally, he didn't take it lying down. Before the harassment trial could be heard, he attempted to jail the mayor of

Kensington and Chelsea and all the councillors. He alleged that in selling the house the council had breached a High Court undertaking, and so sought to have all the elected members jailed for contempt. Inevitably, he failed. The way was now open for the harassment trial.

The case opened in January 1988. Van Hoogstraten faced nine charges of harassing tenants between July 1984 and September 1985. Outwardly, he was his usual confident self. There was no evidence of harassment. The charges would be 'laughed out of court', he forecast.

In Southwark Crown Court tenants reeled off the complaints against Van Hoogstraten, the months of 'hell', the water and power supplies cut off, a door smashed down, the furniture removed in the middle of the night and the landlord's own menacing appearances. Kensington and Chelsea officials backed them and pointed to the same pattern in house after house.

The first week didn't go well for Van Hoogstraten. At the end of it one of his solicitors came up with a suggestion. If he would change his plea to guilty the solicitor could guarantee a non-custodial sentence. Tony Browne, who was there throughout the trial, remembers the nervousness of the man as he made the proposal. 'He was sweating and rubbing his hands.'

Van Hoogstraten, no longer on public display, responded coldly. 'Your opinion is very prejudicial to my position,' he said. That afternoon he sacked his entire legal team, including three barristers and three solicitors.

From then on he defended himself, with Browne acting as his solicitor. They knew they had one advantage. British judges traditionally allow defendants who represent themselves to get away with far more than any barrister could. Van Hoogstraten took full advantage.

'He knew when he was crossing the line and kept doing it,' says Browne. Van Hoogstraten 'deliberately lost his temper during cross-examination', exploding in apparent outrage at what had been said. 'You really must calm down, Mr Van Hoogstraten,' the judge interjected, fooled by his play-acting.

Van Hoogstraten called the case a 'stitch-up'. He claimed that the tenants had manoeuvred for compulsory purchase of the properties so that they could then buy their flats from the council for much less than the marked price. He told the prosecuting council: 'We all know there are villainous landlords around but I'm not one ... None of my tenants, and I've got thousands of them, have lived a life of misery. You don't want to know about the tenants who I send bottles of sherry and hampers from Fortnum and Mason every Christmas.'

A hotel at the nearby Elephant and Castle was Van Hoogstraten's headquarters for the duration of the trial. As everywhere, his office was a table in the restaurant. He had an employee called James Pyeman take notes of everything that happened in court and bring it to the hotel, where he and Browne held a nightly inquest. What had been said? What had been missed? Most crucial of all, how had the jury reacted?

The jury was Van Hoogstraten's top concern. How could he win them over. 'Nick thought the men on the jury would see where he was coming from,' Browne recalls. 'His problem was the women... He needed to sway them.'

Van Hoogstraten's solution was to use the politician's oldest trick – a baby. He arranged for his youngest child to be brought to court almost every day. Outside the court, jurors who had just heard women tenants describe the 'hell' Van Hoogstraten had put them through were greeted with the daily sight of Nicholas van Hoogstraten the gentle father, holding an infant.

If any of the jurors had chanced to venture into the men's lavatory one afternoon they might have seen two other sides of Van Hoogstraten: his paranoia and his violence. Paul Cheston, a rookie reporter on the London Evening Standard, had just entered the WC when he was attacked.

He recalls: 'I had been alone in the press box day after day and Van Hoogstraten kept glaring at me. The day he attacked me I had just gone to the men's room. The door flew open behind me, and I was pushed in the back. I turned around and I saw that it was Van Hoogstraten. He was all dressed in black, his trademark black. He threw me against the wall, both hands round my throat. He's smaller than me but he was very fit, he had the complete advantage. I was terrified. He was semi-throttling me. He was shouting something about me passing press cuttings to the jury about things that he had done in his past. It was a ludicrous idea, but he took it very seriously. He was completely paranoid. It was very, very frightening, and then he stormed out.'

Afterwards Cheston decided that Van Hoogstraten probably feared that the reporter might tip off the jury about his past and that the incident in the men's lavatory was a warning. 'It was a threat, the frighteners,' the reporter says.

He did nothing about it. Neither judge nor jury ever heard about it and the case continued.

Van Hoogstraten's camp believed that a key moment came when he cross-examined Leslee Udwin on the details of the harassment and the fear that she said it engendered.

'What is your profession?' Van Hoogstraten asked her.

She paused, then said: 'Actress.'

Van Hoogstraten left it there.

'"Actress!" That reply said it all,' says Tony Browne. 'The jury knew at that moment that they had been watching a performance.'

The jury returned with its verdict one afternoon in January 1988 during a thunderstorm. The rain was so heavy that it seeped through the roof of Southwark Crown Court and streamed down the walls. The court had to reconvene in a dark old neo-Gothic monstrosity next door. It was an appropriately melodramatic setting for the villain in black. He faced nine charges. With the thunder crashing its accompaniment outside, the foreman of the jury pronounced the verdicts: 'not guilty... not guilty... not guilty...'

Van Hoogstraten had feared the worst. As the first charge was read and the verdict, then the second and the verdict, then the third, tears began to stream down his face. The next time he would cry in public would be at the Old Bailey when he was on trial for murder.

That evening Van Hoogstraten, Browne, James Pyeman and Caroline Williams celebrated over tea and sandwiches. Exultantly, Van Hoogstraten promised the others that he would give them anything they asked for. James asked for an electric guitar. His employer did not approve of such frivolity. He paid for him to have driving lessons instead. Maybe James could be his driver some day.

The next day Van Hoogstraten took Tony Browne off to the Caribbean to continue the celebration at the five-star La Toc hotel on the island of St Lucia. Tony had never seen his tight-fisted boss so generous. 'We stayed for nine days. Everything was lavish. I had a terrific time. On the other hand he never paid me a farthing for all the work I had put in night and day for him on the case for weeks and weeks, so in the end, as usual, he got off very cheaply.'

Although Van Hoogstraten had beaten Kensington and Chelsea in court, the council went ahead with the compulsory purchases. So it ended in a dead heat. The Royal Borough had failed to jail the rogue landlord and the rogue landlord had failed to hang on to his properties.

He wasn't happy. On his return from St Lucia he was the same as ever: 'I will be taking due retribution against the people who brought this case,' he told the Evening Argus in February 1988. As far as is known, he never did.

10

NOTORIOUS

As the Kensington and Chelsea case unfolded, Van Hoogstraten was now under the spotlight not just in the courts but in the Houses of Parliament, too. Yet another new government Housing Bill was going through the House of Commons aimed specifically at boosting the private landlord. Rent controls were to be eased still further. It was a highly contentious measure, and the latest accusations against the tycoon were manna from heaven for its opponents in the Commons. Van Hoogstraten's name dominated debate after debate. So he decided that it was time he changed his image. He sent Tony Browne to consult the public relations people.

Several turned Browne down flat. They didn't explain why. Others, however, were ready to accept the commission. The most impressive was fronted by a former SAS officer. He won Van Hoogstraten over with descriptions of how the dinner parties he'd arrange and charity functions they'd attend would be Van Hoogstraten's entree to new and influential people, the first step in changing the image.

'Then he mentioned the price,' Browne recalls. 'He planned to charge £10,000 a week.' Van Hoogstraten turned him down. It was the same with the other PR men. They were only prepared to take on Van Hoogstraten if he paid top dollar, and as a point of principle he would never do that.

So Van Hoogstraten and Browne conceived a strategy of their own. Van Hoogstraten would present himself as a reformed wrongdoer who was tarred by mistakes that he'd made decades before. The picture he'd present would be of a tough man, yes, but a strictly legal, totally straight one these days. A man to be feared? Yes, but only by those who themselves broke the law in their dealings with him. A bad landlord? No.

The heavyweights of the media and television were now nosing round, and the new PR strategy was tried on them. It did not pan out remotely as planned. Van Hoogstraten and Browne would chat the strategy through first, before the journalist or TV crew turned up, and then Browne, watching from the sidelines, would see it all unravel.

Browne was 'the fixer' for press interviews. Journalists called him on the phone and an evening meeting would be arranged in London. If it was the reporter's first meeting with Van Hoogstraten the venue would probably be an expensive Park Lane hotel. A favourite place of Van Hoogstraten's was the Inn on the Park.

It became a standard routine. The journalist met Browne in the lounge and then, five minutes later, Van Hoogstraten made his grand entrance. At the time he favoured smoked-glass sunglasses, black pinstripe trousers, a starched white shirt, black jacket, black waistcoat, black tie, black pocket handkerchief, black built-up shoes and over all this a full-length white or black mink coat. He had three minks to choose from.

This apparition advanced down the hotel's staircase and up to Browne and the journalist. 'Mr Van Hoogstraten,' Browne announced deferentially. If he hadn't been warned what to expect, the journalist would be transfixed. He'd be treated to the hard Van Hoogstraten stare, and then a diatribe.

Browne told us what usually happened: 'Nick just couldn't contain himself. He had to play the gangster. He couldn't help himself. He'd meet a journalist and every time it was the same. Out he'd come with the half threats and the hints about dark deeds.'

The first of the media heavyweights to come calling when the Kensington and Chelsea case broke was Duncan Campbell, then of the Observer. An incisive and intuitive reporter, Campbell is widely liked among other journalists. He is also hugely envied because his long-time partner is the actress Julie Christie, with whom he now lives in California.

Of all the articles written about Van Hoogstraten, the piece that Campbell wrote for the Observer colour magazine in the winter of 1987 was Van Hoogstraten's favourite.

The six-page article, some five thousand words long, was headed: 'How Nicholas van Hoogstraten played the devil and became a millionaire.' Next to the headline was a full-page photograph of the tycoon posed proudly next to his favourite Louis XV chair.

Campbell began with the quote from Lord Justice Winn when he passed sentence on Van Hoogstraten for the Braunstein grenade attack back in 1968: 'This young man is a sort of self-imagined devil. He thinks he is an emissary of Beelzebub.'

A vivid description followed of 'the landlord with the highest profile since Rachman ... who once sipped tea in the Wormwood Scrubs canteen [and] now has Lapsang Souchong brought to him on a silver tray at the Grosvenor House Hotel in Park Lane'.

The report tracked through much familiar territory – the stamps, the Bahamas, the clubs in the sixties, the Braunstein affair, Wormwood Scrubs, the rupture with his parents, the collections, the palace, Robert Gates, the property empire, the overseas homes and the Kensington and Chelsea case.

It quoted Van Hoogstraten's own view of himself as an innocent man these days who was facing 'what he believes has been a shoddy attempt to deprive him of his properties which, he says, he manages in an exemplary manner'. Campbell left readers to judge as he dug up tenants who were just too frightened to talk and only one with a good word to say about Van Hoogstraten.

Campbell had dug more thoroughly into Van Hoogstraten's background than most other reporters. His knowledge of Van Hoogstraten's life in prison jolted the tycoon. The reporter told him how he'd heard about the relationship with Baron von Benno and how Van Hoogstraten was remembered in the Scrubs for his neatly pressed prison uniform and for never being short of essentials.

'Who told you about that?' asked Van Hoogstraten, who couldn't resist a dive into gangster-speak. 'It wasn't someone who had his legs blown off in the green fields of Surrey?'

The reporter's homework had taken him to Fulham to see Father Gates. The priest told Campbell that he was prohibited by the Official Secrets Act from discussing people with whom he had dealt in a pastoral role. But Campbell had it confirmed that Cardinal Heenan had indeed received a dossier on Father Gates from Van Hoogstraten, but had taken it far less seriously than Van Hoogstraten assumed.

During that evening in the Inn on the Park, Van Hoogstraten opened up more to Campbell than he had to any journalist in the past. He talked for the first time about his love life. 'I am a confirmed bachelor with three or four legitimate mistresses... Although I have more than one "wife", I have a very close relationship with them all. I don't consider anything else other than from an academic point of view. I'm interested in what's out there but I'm not going to pursue it. I've got enough on my plate... My private life is as pure as the driven snow.'

He talked too about his image. One of the PR experts whom he had consulted about that had worked for Aristotle Onassis. 'He was saying the only way from this terrible Mafia-type image is to ingratiate myself by joining "society". Why should these people be interested in me? They're going to be after my money, after my brains and being seen with yesterday's villain. I said: "What's in this for me?"'

The boastful side of the man came bubbling out continually. 'You can take me anywhere, show me anything and within a matter of days or hours I'm an expert. I learnt accountancy in six months. I learnt as much as I needed to know about the diamond business over a couple of years.'

He was keen to impress with his lineage, and talked of his great-uncle Adolph in Sidcup, who, before himself, was the last in the family to be of 'any wealth and consequence'. 'When he died it was in the News of the World because they were looking for heirs to his £8 million estate. If I'd known about him and he'd known about me I'd have got the parcel, wouldn't I? He'd have loved me rebuilding the family fortunes after all these years.'

Campbell ended his report by describing Van Hoogstraten heading off after dinner into one of his properties in Hill Street, Mayfair, one of the most expensive streets in Europe. 'Great Uncle Adolph from Sidcup would have been proud,' he wrote.

Next to come calling was Granada TV's World in Action, the country's top investigative TV programme. Mike Walsh, a reporter on the programme, had been assigned to investigate the growing scandal of winkling in London and homed in on Van Hoogstraten. There were at least half a dozen Rachmanite property developers and speculators operating in the capital at the time. Some were as ruthless as Van Hoogstraten. But none had such a high profile.

Walsh began digging around in Kensington and Chelsea and the neighbouring boroughs where Van Hoogstraten was operating. In Kensington and Chelsea most of the tenants involved in the case brought by the council against Van Hoogstraten were too scared or traumatised to go on camera. It was the same in Notting Hill's All Saints Road, where Walsh discovered another Van Hoogstraten method of getting rid of a woman tenant. She lived in a run-down corner property owned by the tycoon. Her home was the first-floor flat. One day she returned to find the staircase leading up to it was gone. Van Hoogstraten's men had removed it. The tenant lost her home. She was too frightened to go on camera.

Solicitors who had represented tenants were equally scared. One of the most prominent in Kensington and Chelsea said that he'd been thrown down the stairs by one of Hoogstraten's thugs and didn't want a repeat of the experience. He wouldn't even appear with his back to the camera and his voice disguised.

In the neighbouring borough, the City of Westminster, there was a woman with a lot more courage. Jackie Hope was introduced to Walsh by a tenants' rights worker. He knew numbers of other Van Hoogstraten tenants who had been abused but only Jackie Hope was ready to go public.

She wasn't a rent-paying tenant but a leaseholder, an owner-occupier. Her home was in Edgware Road near the Regent's Canal, a raised ground-floor flat with a garden at the back. She bought the lease in the late seventies and understood the garden to be hers.

A delicate woman in her forties with grey eyes and a soft voice, she had been an actress until ill-health prompted her to give up the stage. She spent most of her time during the day in the garden. Then one afternoon she saw two men there. She later learned that one of them was Van Hoogstraten

'I walked out into the garden and walked towards them and said: "Excuse me, are you from the managing agents?" And Nicholas van Hoogstraten spat in my face and pushed me... He said: "I'm the new owner. Get your things out of here." I said: "I'm sorry, this is my garden, you will have to deal with my solicitor." And the man who was with him, who I now know to be Robert Bradshaw, said: "You won't need a solicitor, you'll need a doctor because you're going to end up in a wheelchair, and if you're in a wheelchair you won't be able to get into your garden, will you?" So, again I said: "I'm sorry, you'll have to deal with my solicitor" and I was pushed by Nicholas van Hoogstraten down my garden towards the door, towards my flat and he said: "Get back in there, your property ends there," and he spat in my face again.'

In fact Van Hoogstraten wasn't the landlord. Robert Knapp had bought the freehold using the surname Bradshaw. In a bizarre reversal of roles Van Hoogstraten had chosen to play Knapp's heavy in the confrontation with a tenant. 'Uncle Bob', however, needed no help. Over subsequent months he made Jackie Hope's life hell without anyone's assistance. Nails were hammered into her front door. There were thefts. The garden was damaged.

Mike Walsh approached Van Hoogstraten, and an off-the-record meeting was set up between them. Again it was at the Inn on the Park. The reporter arrived briefed to expect an over-the-top performance full of veiled and not so veiled threats. What he didn't expect was the length of the meeting. It began at 7.30 pm. Van Hoogstraten talked and talked about himself – what he'd done and was alleged to have done, his hatred for tenants, socialists and the Irish, his huge wealth, his collections, his palace, his admiration for Hitler and for Mrs Thatcher. It went on for hours. Walsh finally extricated himself at about 1.30 am.

At Granada it was agreed that if Van Hoogstraten could be induced to say a fraction of what he had said in the hotel, World in Action would have a memorable programme.

At this point Don Jordan was asked to collaborate on the project as producer. He and Walsh had supper with Van Hoogstraten in the Window on the World restaurant at the top of the Hilton Hotel on Park Lane. Van Hoogstraten drank water and ate little.

The two journalists outlined their intention to make a film about the property tycoon and asked if he would participate. The idea was batted about for several hours, during which Van Hoogstraten at one point did his astonishing facial morphing act. One moment he was relaxed and chatty, the next raving mad and threatening. In less than a minute it had blown over, like a summer shower. By the end of the meeting he had agreed that, subject to a letter of intent from Granada Television, he would take part in a film profile of himself and his methods.

Walsh wrote a letter outlining the film they wanted to make and setting out some ground rules. Van Hoogstraten, as he desired, would be informed of who else was appearing and any accusations they made against him – but only immediately before any interview with him. Two weeks later Walsh and Jordan were invited to meet Van Hoogstraten at his offices in The Drive, Hove.

When they arrived, they were admitted by a very languid, good-looking young man and shown into a room furnished with Van Hoogstraten's ubiquitous French pieces. The man himself sat in a dazzlingly bright gilded chair behind a truly beautiful ebonised desk oramented with charming gilded caryatids at each corner.

Van Hoogstraten opened a drawer in the desk and extracted Walsh's letter. He proceeded to criticise it for not being precise and clear. The journalists thought they were about to be thrown out. Then Van Hoogstraten put the letter down and pronounced: 'I couldn't have done better myself.'

This, it transpired, was high praise. Van Hoogstraten was fond of writing letters of ambiguous content to tenants. The qualities he perceived in this letter were to result in his offering Walsh the choice of three things – a job, a 'grace and favour' flat or death. Months later, when the film had been made and transmitted, the three men met over lunch in London, together with another Granada Television colleague. True to form, Van Hoogstraten threatened the other colleague, saying he would give him a 'good spanking'. Walsh brought up the subject of the three possibilities that had been placed before him. Which, if any of these – a job, a flat or death – were still in play? he enquired. Van Hoogstraten pondered for a theatrical moment and then said: 'Well, I think all three are still on the cards, don't you?'

Filming was a stop-and-start affair. Van Hoogstraten was often away in France, so days with him were arranged around his schedule. In between times, the World in Action team researched aspects of his life and business. They interviewed tenants who had experienced a rough time at the hands of their mercurial landlord.

No case history touched the journalists' hearts more than that of a young woman suffering from multiple sclerosis. She was terrified of Van Hoogstraten and only agreed to be interviewed in silhouette and without her name being given. We'll call her Miss A.

Miss A was a sitting tenant in a house owned by Van Hoogstraten in Shepherd's Bush, west London. When she went into hospital because of her illness, Van Hoogstraten telephoned with a fabricated story that her flat had been flooded. She sent him a key. All her belongings were removed, so erasing any trace of a tenant in residence. The house was sold with vacant possession.

When Miss A complained, one of Van Hoogstraten's employees wrote to her suggesting she would be better keeping quiet about the matter if she wanted to see her personal belongings again. The letter said she would be 'well advised to let sleeping dogs lie as we are well used to dealing with the nonsense caused by tenants who one minute are grateful for a place to live and the next minute seek compensation from the owner'.

Miss A tearfully told World in Action that she felt the letter was intended to threaten and frighten her. In an interview at High Cross, Walsh confronted Van Hoogstraten with his behaviour towards Miss A. It was an interesting moment. Van Hoogstraten had not had his behaviour or methods publicly questioned before, except in a court of law. Walsh said he thought his treatment of Miss A was pretty bad.

'You would,' replied Van Hoogstraten. 'It wasn't your property.

You don't think the landlord is entitled to take back his property when he wants to?'

He went on to say that, in his opinion, the small sum Miss A was paying – £12 a week – could hardly be called rent. 'She was taking the piss,' he said. 'And I'm not standing for it.'

'And property is king?' asked Walsh.

Van Hoogstraten thought for a moment and then smiled. 'Isn't that what life's all about?'

The film was full of such moments. On another day Van Hoogstraten sat on the gilded throne behind the gorgeous desk and freely revealed how he saw himself.

'I am probably ruthless and I am probably violent,' he said.

He admitted he knew violent people – 'A few violent associates, yes' – but then 'everybody could be brought to the point of violence, depending on the circumstances'.

He smiled as he said, 'There is always plenty of young blood coming up. Down the line there are people we can call on for things that need doing from time to time.' He was clearly enjoying himself playing the villain. 'One keeps one's insurance policies up to date,' he added. It made for riveting viewing.

There was one moment when he became very agitated. Walsh asked about his connection to specific convicted criminals, mentioning one of them by name. Van Hoogstraten went into a ballistic fury. He fumed that he would not talk about others but was happy to answer questions about himself.

He went on to explain his view of society: 'The most serious lesson I ever learned very early in life, when I first began to have substantial wealth, was that one could not trust those people that ordinary members of the public or business people are told they could trust – their professional advisers, solicitors, accountants, police even – all these people are hypocrites.'

The people one could trust, he proclaimed, were the so-called criminal classes.

At first hearing this sounds deliberately perverse. But when put into the context of the Van Hoogstraten world view, it makes a twisted sort of sense. It starts with the belief that all that matters is oneself. The so-called criminal classes know this. Any notions of society or collective endeavour are only hypocritical bullshit. So the imposition of rules or laws is merely a conspiracy to stop the individual getting what he wants – and the conspirators must therefore be crooked or bent.

So bent means straight and straight means bent.

Other moments were less fraught. Van Hoogstraten and the authors travelled around London in a taxi as he talked about the property world. He described 'winkling' and said how buildings could be worth so much with vacant possession that it could hypothetically be worth bumping someone off – 'if you're that way inclined'.

He said that many of the neighbours did not like it when he bought a house in their street. When asked why this was, he directed the camera crew into the exclusive Holland Park enclave of Norland Square. This pretty garden square is lined with expensive terraces of early-Victorian houses painted a pleasing and uniform pale magnolia. When we asked which house he owned, he replied that we would see for ourselves. We did. At the north-west corner was his house – painted bright purple. It turned out he had other houses around the area in assorted colours – another purple one, a green one and other colours too. A rainbow coalition against the smug conformity of the establishment that hated him and whom he loathed in return.

He hated anyone who stood in the way of making money. Jackie Hope, with a lease of twelve years still to run, finally gave up and left Maida Vale. World in Action helped her to find another flat. After Van Hoogstraten's conviction in September 2002 for manslaughter, she said she finally felt safe. She had spent fourteen years moving from flat to flat, always in fear he would find her.

Another side of this complex man's character came out during filming. He displayed his shrewd knowledge of the property market, and advised the World in Action team that the domestic property market was about to crash. His forecast was proved correct the following year.

He also exhibited the side of his character that is the connoisseur. At the royal jewellers, Cartier of Bond Street, he displayed his astonishing knowledge of big-ticket gemstones. He offered an informed critique of individual stones – 'unusually for an emerald it has fire' – and gave accurate assessments of their value – 'worth about a quarter of a million'.

Back at The Drive, he took pleasure in showing the programme makers some of his fabulous collection of antique French furniture, lovingly describing each piece's provenance – 'from a royal palace' – or the nature of its construction and materials – 'Sèvres plaques, satinwood from the French colonies, mahogany, and the frame is oak.' Unused to such opulent furniture, his guests ventured to suggest it was all a bit over the top.

'Well, I'm a bit over the top, aren't I?' the collector instantly batted back, following this up with a put-down: 'I don't see any onyx tables here.'

He also evidently took great pleasure from cars, although he was not really much of a driver. He drove Walsh down to his High Cross estate in a black Corvette Stingray, a rare collector's machine from the sixties shaped like a shark, with the massive power of a V8 engine. Van Hoogstraten barely drove above 35mph the whole way from London.

Throughout the filming he was touchy but mainly good-humoured. His irascibility would flash through from time to time, but so too would his ready wit. When, in answer to a question, he estimated his worth at about one hundred million, Walsh, seeking clarity, asked if that was in pounds sterling. 'Well, it wouldn't be lire, would it?' came the immediate riposte.

The millionaire was interesting company, with his chippiness, his wit, his hidden empire run from a series of anonymous terraced houses in Hove, his fabulous possessions and his iconoclastic world view. He had a collection of hand-made Italian shoes with what Americans call 'elevator heels' stored in an anteroom off his office, where a hunting rifle with telescopic sights also lingered. He was undoubtedly out of the ordinary.

Of all the days they spent with Van Hoogstraten, the film crew particularly remembered the one when he said he would produce a friend to speak up for him, as World in Action had requested. The man who arrived at The Drive was a small, delicate-looking, middle-aged figure with little hair and a jaunty step. He was David Harris, Van Hoogstraten's former accountant.

What happened next was almost surreal. While Van Hoogstraten looked on, Harris told not of his friendship and regard for him, but about how violent he was. He said Van Hoogstraten was 'dangerous and ruthless', and described the kidnapping incident from the seventies when he was 'lucky to escape' with his life. During this, Van Hoogstraten was having a whale of a time and grinned while Harris told how the millionaire had kidnapped him, held him captive in Paris and fed him on tinned sardines for over a year.

During breaks for the camera to be reloaded, Van Hoogstraten would fill in facts that Harris had omitted. He obviously loved to hear the story and wanted every last detail to be told. The bizarre tableau of the frail-looking accountant relating how he had been in danger of his life, while Van Hoogstraten, attired in his customary black, prowled behind the camera, was to stay with the programme makers for some time.

When the World in Action programme was transmitted, four and a half million people watched the tycoon expound his views and explain his methods of doing business. Thanks to the film, questions were asked in Parliament during a debate on housing. It also received a great deal of attention in the press.

Van Hoogstraten gained instant notoriety and in some circles even a sort of celebrity. He became hooked on television and in the ensuing years was to give countless interviews. But few if any were to reveal quite the degree of menace and comfort with violence that he exhibited in that first appearance.

Soon after, the Daily Star came calling. A tabloid with no time for nuance, the paper found in Van Hoogstraten exactly the sort of black-hearted hate figure that the red-top press loves. It published a two-page investigation by Chris Anderson under the headline 'He sent thugs to strip his family home... Now the family shun tycoon.' Anderson had gone to Rustington to interview Charles and Edna Hoogstraten. He found the tycoon's father to be even more bitter than he had been in the past. Charles repeated his earlier claim that his son had got started in property by ripping off his parents, and then went much further. He claimed that a dozen properties were involved and that in the sixties Van Hoogstraten had also obtained from him and Edna 'antiques, gold, jewellery and a Jaguar' worth around £40,000, a huge sum at the time.

'Britain's most feared landlord,' said Anderson, had gone to his parents' home and stripped it of furniture, carpets and curtains. He then had 'even threatened to have his own parents terrorised by henchmen'. According to the report, Van Hoogstraten admitted that his relationship with his parents got so bad that 'it was getting to the stage of me sending someone round to do something about it. I mean on a personal, physical level.' It was alleged that his plan had been to send in thugs to terrorise his parents in their home and then leave them tied up. Van Hoogstraten admitted to the Star that he was only dissuaded from going further by his younger sister, Betty.

Van Hoogstraten was seldom to be out of the headlines from now on as reporters dug up everything they could. It would be a long time before they realised that he had a parallel – and still more lucrative – business career overseas.

11

BUILDING AN EMPIRE

Harare, capital of Zimbabwe, 1999. It's October – the hottest time of the year. Temperatures average nearly thirty and can easily reach into the sweaty forties. It's the evening now and the daytime heat is finally drifting up into the black sky as Nicholas van Hoogstraten and Tony Browne enter the nightclub.

Browne remembers it well. 'We had a bit of time to kill before we headed up country to the estates. We went into this club which was normally quite a quiet place. It had changed. There were girls and hookers dancing with business types all over the place.'

They sit at a table with a panorama of the dance-floor action. Girls dance with middle-aged whites. One girl is particularly good. She has beautiful features and large breasts. She moves erotically, flicking her backside from side to side while pulsing up and down on her hips in sinuous rhythm. She ripples like an eel, young and sexy.

Van Hoogstraten says: 'What would be good would be to have her naked and shaking her arse over you like that as you lie back in bed.' They laugh. Browne catches the girl's eye. She comes over and Browne does the socials. Her name is Tanaka. She's sixteen at the most. Van Hoogstraten buys her a Coke. Browne diplomatically moves away and one of the girl's friends quickly slides on to the seat next to him.

The following morning the two men drive nearly two hundred kilometres south towards the town of Mvuma to the biggest of Van Hoogstraten's African landholdings, Central Estates. But the millionaire does not forget the girl in the nightclub. Within a year she would be in England, set up as yet another new mistress and living in one of his hotels in Brighton.

Around the corner from that hotel is another of Van Hoogstraten's properties, Africa House. The name conjures up a host of images. There is a grandness about it – Africa House – a sweeping, all-embracing intention. One might think of a government building, a hangover from Britain's colonial age like those grey bulwarks at the corners of Trafalgar Square, Canada House and South Africa House. Whatever it might be, it would hardly be 20 The Drive, Hove.

The Drive is one of the series of grand boulevards sweeping down to the seafront, peppered with houses owned by Van Hoogstraten. Their façades of yellow London brick are stained black with age and their bays jut out grimly over half-basements. Number 20, Africa House, is no exception.

How he came to call it Africa House dates back to the sixties, when Van Hoogstraten was a young man still making his way in the world of international investment. He was in his early twenties and looking for new experiences and new areas of financial speculation. He chose to look in Africa – specifically, in South Africa and Rhodesia – as Zimbabwe then was - – both countries where Europeans could lead a luxurious life at very little expense. And there was, by all accounts, still money to be made. All of this appealed to the penny-pinching, pound-hungry young man from Sussex.

At that time, for a man with an entrepreneurial eye, southern Africa must have seemed a collection of wonderfully free countries, full of opportunity and without the taxation and red tape of England. Van Hoogstraten certainly thought so. Thirty years later he still thought so. In 1997 he told financial journalist James Hipwell: 'South Africa is one of the few places on this planet worth both investing in and living in. The level of honesty and integrity you find down there is much higher than anywhere else in the world.' With prescience worthy of his Irish clairvoyant, he added: 'You don't have all these multiple fraudsters and Stock Exchange scams that you have over here.'

Unfortunately, the young businessman was not so blessed with foresight of the catastrophic political upheavals that were to overtake Zimbabwe, beginning even before the twentieth century ran out. A political tremor was to sweep across the land, putting in question the value of the multi-million-pound investments he had built up in ranching and agricultural holdings.

The Rhodesia Van Hoogstraten found as a young man was a huge, fertile country with a well-run infrastructure built under the British colonial system. Political undercurrents were already rumbling under its placid surface that might have deterred others from long-term investments, but he was made of sterner stuff.

Anyone who travels to Zimbabwe cannot help but be taken by the country. It is part of the great South African plateau, with undulating plains rising up to five thousand feet above sea level. This altitude makes the climate agreeable for Europeans. The first adventurers tended to notice the land but not the people. The things that attracted the young entrepreneur to Rhodesia were the very things that had attracted Europeans since the time of Cecil Rhodes himself – the land, the mineral wealth and the possibility to impose their will on the indigenous population.

The Victorian colonialist Rhodes and the twentieth-century businessman Van Hoogstraten shared a desire for wealth and an ability to take decisive action to gain it. Van Hoogstraten was later to say of his commitment to the country: 'What I do is a bit like what Cecil Rhodes did and nobody could fail to be impressed by what he did.'

Cecil Rhodes founded the De Beer's diamond empire and made political treaties from which nations grew. He had a vision of nothing less than an Africa developed and run for the glory of the British Empire. Van Hoogstraten hated society and craved a world in his own image that would show the rest of them.

But there are real similarities. At the age of seventeen Rhodes was sent for the good of his health to join his brother farming in Natal. That same year diamonds were discovered at Kimberly. Cecil and his brother were among the first successful diggers. By the time he was nineteen Rhodes was rich. Van Hoogstraten was sent abroad in his teens – to cure not physical ill-health but anti-social behaviour – and also seized the opportunity to create the basis of a fortune before he was twenty.

There were other parallels. Here is what one biographer said of Rhodes: 'He so far abused his power as to become intolerant of any sort of control or opposition ... he was lacking in regard for individuals and a great part of his daily life was spent in the company of satellites and instruments, whom he used with cynical unconcern for the furtherance of his ends.'

When Van Hoogstraten first visited in the mid-sixties, the country was in turmoil. The majority of the population supported independence. The minority – the white settlers – did not. In 1964 the Prime Minister, Ian Smith, rejected Britain's plans for votes for all. There would be no votes for blacks. He told one of the authors in the late 1970s how the black population was politically naive, unready for self-government. The twin monsters of racism and self-interest were dressed up in the rags of paternalistic compassion and concern.

In 1965 the opposition parties began a guerrilla war. Despite the thousands of British citizens living in Rhodesia, Britain severed diplomatic links. The United Nations imposed economic sanctions. By the seventies Zanu, largely representing the majority Shona peoples, and Zapu, supported by the Ntebele, amalgamated into the Patriotic Front to form a combined force. They fought a war lasting fourteen years, characterised by guerrilla attacks on Rhodesian security forces and sporadic murderous raids on farms owned by whites. The Smith regime fought back with the help of South African military know-how.

In Rhodesia, Hoogstraten, the perennial outsider and iconoclast, smelled something else he liked: a whiff of the Wild West. Uncertainty and fear are good news for a certain kind of businessman. There was a peculiar swashbuckling atmosphere. From the establishment heart of the Salisbury Club to the hotel lounges and restaurants, and in the easy-going bars and nightclubs, the conversation was the same. The tobacco farmers, the owners of franchises for imported trucks, the cattle ranchers, the mine owners, the drifters and chancers all talked about it. Money. It was why they were here. As Hoogstraten himself would have said, it was what it was all about.

In the roughest bar serving beer from Nairobi, Guinness from Lagos and Scotch smuggled from God knows where, the talk was of money. In the restaurant of the Monopatapa Hotel, where white-gloved waiters served plates of impala steak while the trophy heads of topi, sable and, yes, impala gazed mutely down from the walls, the talk crackled with money or the thought of it. There was gossip of mining concessions that could be had if one knew the right person, and of old mines thought to have been worked out long ago but which some geologist or other had recently seen and declared worthy of further exploitation. Hoogstraten loved it. For a man with a deal in his veins, this was a land running with the drug of money.

Most of this chatter was piffle. But some opportunities

were real enough. While others dreamed over their Shumba beers, Hoogstraten was a man up for action who pursued his opportunities. The result is that today he has interests reputed to range from diamond mines in Congo to coal mines in South Africa.

Back then he was, he says, 'appalled that someone else should own so much of someone's country. It was disgraceful. It was not right.' When he speaks now of the injustice he found, his words carry the tone of conviction. He last spoke of it to the authors in early 2002, when he was facing a charge for murder and, as a condition of his bail, could not leave Britain. He had been in the habit of going to Zimbabwe every few weeks and the restrictions clearly hurt.

Young Hoogstraten quickly reached an opinion of white settlers, or 'Rhodies'. He didn't like them. It was not simply a case of differing views on the black majority, but of style and class. The established ranching class, to which Ian Smith belonged, had old-style manners and courtesies that put them into a time-warped realm of ease which excluded Hoogstraten, the urban self-made man. The white farmers tended to be a rough-and-ready lot who immediately rubbed the essentially urbanite incomer up the wrong way.

For the Rhodies, the young Englishman's cocky, self-assured manner must have rasped against their slower-moving rural skins, snagging like a snake's scales against a cow's hide. The door of social inclusion was shut once more. By now Hoogstraten was turning into the professional outsider, professing contempt for the old order at home and those he found on his travels. He would remain an outsider throughout his life.

Then he discovered Africa. The outsider often pitches up in a new place and sees its opportunities with new eyes. Hoogstraten saw this right away. 'In Third World countries there are no effective laws. Any law there is comes out of a pound note,' he later said.

He also found a kind of freedom. Africa would allow him a status and a space to be himself that he could not find at home in England. He was a European with money. This instantly made him a figure with power and prestige. There was room for a powerful ego to grow here, unencumbered by the class and social barriers at home. The ruthless 'thiever' could create a world of his own and, as a byproduct, he could do good and earn respect in return. In the 1990s all this was to culminate in his becoming a sort of benevolent dictator over nearly a million acres of land.

His commercial interests appear to have begun with straightforward investments made in companies with major African holdings. This move accelerated around the end of the eighties, when the entrepreneur foresaw the crash in the value of domestic housing in Britain. He sold hundreds of houses and began to search for new investments in Africa. As he looked around for suitable investment opportunities, the name of Cecil Rhodes was replaced by a new day-to-day role model. This person was altogether a more modern entrepreneurial spirit – Tiny Rowland.

Rowland was a buccaneering figure who flew around Africa in a private jet, making deals and treating it as if it were all his for the taking. His exploits were to gain him notoriety when Britain's Prime Minister Edward Heath called him 'the unacceptable face of capitalism'. To this, Rowland had replied that he wouldn't want to be the acceptable face. It was a retort Hoogstraten could have made. The two men had a similar disregard for what others might think.

Rowland was born Rowland Walter Fuhrhop in 1917. He had an exotic and controversial upbringing, starting out in the Hitler Youth and then attending private school in England. Despite anglicising his name and taking British citizenship, he was interned during the Second World War. After the war he moved to Southern Rhodesia, attracted by the freedom and high life enjoyed by Europeans.

He made a success of it and quickly came to the attention of the directors of a small company called the London and Rhodesia Mining and Land Company, which in 1961 had profits of £158,000.

Among those who admired Rowland's style was board member Angus Ogilvy, who was later to marry a member of the British royal family, Princess Alexandra. With Ogilvy's blessing, Rowland took over the running of the company. Under a new name, Lonrho, it became a huge corporation. Rowland went on a spree, acquiring companies as avidly as the young Nick Hoogstraten had bought stamps. Among them was the old mining and farming firm Willoughby's Consolidated. It had large assets, but was sluggishly run and ripe for an aggressive takeover. Rowland bought it cheap in one of his many fast and furious dealings as he built up his new empire. In 1989 Lonrho made profits of £272 million. This was almost entirely down to the astonishing abilities of Rowland himself.

When Nelson Mandela became President of South Africa, he awarded Rowland the country's highest honour, saying of him: 'He made an enormous contribution not only to South Africa, but to the whole of Africa.' Rowland had been one of the first European businessmen to criticise colonialism and to support Africa's emerging nationalist leaders, a pattern replicated by Hoogstraten, who was to support the rebel Frelimo cause in Angola and Robert Mugabe's Zanu PF party in Zimbabwe.

Rowland's success in winning contacts across the continent was based on his ability to woo politicians and governments. He used his charm and, if that was not enough, he employed bribery, often on a massive scale. 'Every man has his price,' he said. 'The definition of an honest man is when the price is too high.'

By the seventies Rowland's name had become a byword for daring and corporate flair. He had panache, energy, style and charm. Van Hoogstraten got to know and admire him. An understanding of Rowland helps in understanding something about Van Hoogstraten.

Rowland was a flawed commercial genius. He was a consummate deal maker, flying tirelessly between London and Africa, brokering deals that others found scarcely credible. When he bought a controlling share in the Ashanti Goldmines in Ghana, it seemed nothing was beyond his capabilities.

When he died in 1998, the former president of Zambia, Kenneth Kaunda, said: 'We worked together to empower Africans. He is a great loss to us.' Rowland had gone his own way and did not care a damn what anyone thought of him. It was easy to see how Van Hoogstraten would have been drawn to him.

But as so often in those with restless energy and a will to succeed, there was a destructive self-obsession. In his definitive work Tiny Rowland: A Rebel Tycoon, Tom Bower offers this character assessment: 'Hypersensitive to real or imagined slights to himself, he was not worried about humiliating and manipulating employees ... like a woman, Tiny wanted to be admired and, by the same token, loathed his critics, mistrusted their motives, and would offer no concessions in the countless vendettas he has waged to secure their total destruction. Invariably, Rowland would complain that he was the victim of prejudice, a conspiracy or dishonesty.'

As with that of Cecil Rhodes, the assessment could have been written of Nicholas van Hoogstraten.

It was Rowland who inadvertently gave rise to the younger man's love of aliases. Van Hoogstraten told the authors that during a conversation on a flight, Rowland told him how he never checked in under his own name. He used an alias in case the aircraft was hijacked and the guerrillas sought out wealthy passengers to hold for ransom. Van Hoogstraten took this advice to heart. Soon he had a host of aliases. As we have seen, they were to range from the stolid Nicholas Hamilton to the exotic Adolf von Hessen. They became both a source of amusement and a useful tool for commercial anonymity.

Once, when the authors were filming with Van Hoogstraten at Cartier in London, the tycoon mentioned to the marketing director that he was a good customer of the firm. The Cartier man looked blank. 'Van Hoogstraten?' he mused. 'I don't recall seeing your name, sir.'

'Well, that's because you don't know me as Van Hoogstraten,' came the reply. Van Hoogstraten then opened his briefcase and took out a sheaf of receipts from Cartier in the name of Hamilton. 'That's me,' he announced to the surprise of everyone. This simple subterfuge drew amazement from the Cartier directors, despite the fact that they must have had among their wealthy customers some of the greatest scallywags and villains in the world (as well as several members of the Royal Family). Van Hoogstraten, of course, enjoys the element of shock or surprise. In this case it all began with Tiny Rowland's advice, though Van Hoogstraten was to develop it so much further and make it all his own.

In the late eighties Van Hoogstraten built up a sizeable holding in the Lonrho group. He felt that anything Tiny Rowland thought worth investing in was probably worth a punt. Naturally, he chose to do it by stealth. In the case of Lonrho, this was done through companies based in South Africa. Among his chosen vehicles was a company called Corwil, registered in South Africa with an address in Parktown, Johannesburg. Corwil is an investment holding company. Its sole investment is listed as being in Lonrho-controlled operations.

Van Hoogstraten bought shares in the Lonrho subsidiary Willoughby's Consolidated. This long-established British company, with gold mining and ranching interests in Rhodesia and South Africa, was founded in 1894. Nearly a century later it had become, in Van Hoogstraten's astute eyes, a suitable case for 'thieving'. In other words, he thought the share price undervalued the assets. By 1988 he owned seventy-six thousand shares in Willoughby's. He decided to mount a full bid for control.

According to financial reports at the time, he offered to buy half a million 50p shares at 68p a unit from British shareholders. His attempts to add to his portfolio on the South African market had failed. According to the Brighton Evening Argus, Van Hoogstraten said he was giving shareholders an opportunity to cash in 'an unmarketable investment'.

In the boardroom of Willoughby's the scale of Van Hoogstraten's offer caused alarm. A senior Lonrho director, Paul Spicer, said: 'Mr Van Hoogstraten must be buying shares because he thinks they are undervalued. It's the only reason I can imagine.' He was right.

The predatory move against Willoughby's was reported to the Takeover Panel, a City agency through which both parties could work to ensure fair dealing. It was purely voluntary and so had no teeth. Van Hoogstraten lost no time in exposing the absurdity of the panel. At a hearing, its members were amazed by his brazen lack of regard for the panel's rules. When they asked if he intended to abide by them, Van Hoogstraten simply replied: 'No.' The panel was shown up to be a toothless tiger and the iconoclast did what he always did and went his own way.

Van Hoogstraten's move against Willoughby's highlighted weaknesses at the heart of Lonrho. It was suffering from a lack of hard cash.

By 1993 Lonrho's – and Rowland's – best days were over. Only eight per cent of its turnover was from mining. Rowland had made too many investment errors and had failed to ensure his businesses could generate real profits. His business techniques raised eyebrows in the City and caused anger elsewhere. A deal involving Willoughby's particularly enraged Van Hoogstraten. In 1995 Willoughby's sold its controlling interest in the Zambian amethyst mining company Kariba Minerals to the African Industrial and Finance Corporation. The trouble was that African Industrial was controlled by Lonrho. Van Hoogstraten smelled a rat. He wondered if Kariba was being deliberately undervalued.

Amethysts are one of Van Hoogstraten's favourite gemstones. Their blue-purple colour echoes the colour favoured by Roman emperors, and he adopted it as his own colour.

Willoughby's had a seventeen per cent share in the amethyst company, while Van Hoogstraten's chosen South African financial vehicle, Corwil, had, he says, an even bigger stake. He staged a coup at Willoughby's Annual General Meeting after finding out that the sale of Kariba was not even on the agenda. With his control of a large block of Willoughby's shares, he was able to defeat all the resolutions from the Lonrho-appointed board. The directors were forced to resign.

In 1996 Lonrho begin to demerge most of its African businesses. Perhaps its nadir was reached when it sold a proportion of the Metropole Hotel group to the Libyan leader, Colonel Gaddafi. Lonrho has changed its name to Lonmin and is now primarily a general trading company. Today Van Hoogstraten owns the residue of what was once Willoughby's Consolidated, consisting of ranching and agricultural estates.

According to Tony Browne, who was to go on to manage the Van Hoogststraten estates in Zimbabwe, Van Hoogstraten initially wanted Willoughby's gold mines. Instead he ended up taking over its ranching assets. It was to open a new chapter in his life.

Van Hoogstraten has often said that he hates business. His experience of the Kariba affair no doubt played its part in his reaching that judgement. He told Business Age magazine: 'I don't want my children to go into [business] because they'll become the sort of devious, dishonest person that I've become to protect my assets and I don't want to risk that with my children. To succeed in business, you've got to be an actor, a liar and crook.'

Tiny Rowland boasted he never visited the companies he took over. But Van Hoogstraten is temperamentally different. He takes a direct interest in everything he buys. And so, one day in the late 1990s, he found himself being driven out of Harare, down the long highway from Harare towards Bulawayo, to visit the former Willoughby estates.

When he got to the dusty town of Mvuma he was astounded by what he saw. First, there was the fence. The estate's perimeter was marked by three simple stands of barbed wire. It came up beside the road – and stayed there. For mile after mile. Van Hoogstraten was, he says, amazed as it kept on measuring out the road. The fence described the boundary of the Central Estates ranch and farm, enclosing an area bigger than Greater London.

Van Hoogstraten was no stranger to ownership. He had mines, a country estate back in England, he owned almost entire streets, had homes on the Riviera, hotels, a furniture collection worth millions, a fabulous gem collection, the famed collection of stamps. But this was different. What he had taken over was a vast cattle ranch that saw its beginnings in the nineteenth century in the heyday of the first Europeans to settle on the plateau. The scale impressed even this very wealthy man. He was now not only a property owner, but a landowner on the scale of a prince.

The Central Estates were not all that he had bought. Further south, at Gweru, was the smaller Eastdale Estate, and, near Bulawayo, the Essexvale Estate. In all, over 750 thousand acres.

All this landed Van Hoogstraten with a dilemma. He was now the very thing he hated: a white man in Africa. More than that, he was a white man owning other people's land. The ownership by itself did not trouble him. It was what had always gone with it: the racism, the exploitation, the bigotry. Van Hoogstraten was aware of all this.

He decided to do something about it. He knew he had to be politically astute to ensure his investment would prosper and that he could secure it for the long term in a country whose government was increasingly hostile to white ownership.

He put a two-pronged strategy in place: one part pragmatic, the other more personal and closer to his heart. The pragmatic part was his support for the government of Robert Mugabe, Zimbabwe's mercurial president, while the personal one was to do well by the estate's workers and their families.

He set to work. The company had four directors. As usual, Van Hoogstraten's own name did not appear among them. He was represented by Caroline Williams. Tony Browne was also made a director, as well as general manager of the estates. His brief was to develop the estates along modern and progressive lines. A master plan was drawn up, comprising schools, a hospital, housing for the workers, new roads and other infrastructure. The staff were to be issued with smart new uniforms and their children would be educated on the estate, where the new schools would be equipped and staffed thanks to their beneficent owner.

Browne looked after the Zimbabwe enterprises from 1998 to 2000. During that period several million pounds were spent on developing the infrastructure and on restocking the land. The local development manager told BBC reporter Jenny Craddock in 2000 that £200,000 a month was being spent at Central Estates. It was coming directly from Van Hoogstraten.

Investing hard currency in a developing country is a risky business. Buying power has to be measured against the possible loss of value of the assets due to inflation and other hazards, such as political instability. To make the equation even more complicated, there is the consideration of lower production costs to be set against possible export earnings.

Central Estates became a mixed development, with ranching, a safari business and ostrich farming. Ostriches may seem a whimsical venture but they are far from being so. Their meat is high is protein and low in cholesterol, while their hides are sought after for making shoes and handbags, especially in Japan, where they can earn welcome hard currency.

As the programme of building and social reform began to take shape, the regime on the estates resembled a form of benign paternalism. Van Hoogstraten's standing with his workers and their families grew. Browne found his employer's change in style remarkable. 'He was able to do a lot of good. Maybe it was him searching for redemption or some type of salvation in investing in the ordinary working person down there.'

Browne had reason to be surprised and to think of his friend and boss as searching for redemption. He had seen how Van Hoogstraten had dealt with employees in England who he felt had cheated him. He had witnessed the summary beating meted out to employees in Brighton.

With Van Hoogstraten's temper appearing to be worsening and his fuse shortening with the advance of middle age, his African ventures seemed all the more remarkable. In Britain, he was a notorious figure whom one crossed at one's peril, but in Zimbabwe he was a benefactor and was thought of on his estates as an elder of the tribe. His Zimbabwean girlfriend Tanaka Sali – the girl he picked up in the Harare nightclub – was a visitor to the estates. She vouches for the extent of his kindness to his staff, exemplified by issues of free milk and the provision of free education.

'Nick is very kind,' she says, adding the rider: 'Whether that is coming from the bottom of his heart or not, that's not for me or anyone to judge. He is a nice person as well, but he is a selfish person, too.' And there, simply put, is the paradox of the man. But it is also the dilemma facing the rich: what one should do with one's money and how one should ensure one holds on to it?

The answer to the latter question, in Van Hoogstraten's case, was to use all necessary force. In Africa, he employed armed guards to protect his grazing lands against cattle rustlers. The guards had the right to shoot if they came under threat from armed gangs. According to Browne, this has happened and several poachers have been shot and killed. He says the shootings took place according to standing orders and that such action is viewed as normal by local police. Van Hoogstraten has said that he regrets that in Britain a landowner cannot shoot trespassers with impunity.

In his defence of his Zimbabwean assets, he has another strategy: make political allies. Taking a leaf out of Tiny Rowland's book, he has long been a supporter of President Mugabe's Zanu PF party. He has backed this up by providing funds and by attending rallies. He has a portrait of Mugabe on the wall of his office but he has yet to meet the man.

In 2002 Van Hoogstraten was reported to be backing the purchase of fighter aircraft by the Zimbabwean government. The deal, reputed to be for $250 million worth of Russian MiG aircraft, could be in breach of international arms embargoes against Zimbabwe. If the story is accurate, it is little wonder that Van Hoogstraten should want to broker arms deals. They are so very lucrative, with large commissions payable to many of those who participate. In some instances, the commissions – which include anything from genuine payments for middlemen to bribes for government officials – can account for twenty per cent or more of the total contract.

Van Hoogstraten's good relationship with Zanu PF has enabled him to conduct business very effectively in Zimbabwe. It is unlikely he would have been able to purchase pyrites mines without government agreement. But his special relationship as a white supporter of the government has not prevented the sequestration of some of his assets. At the time of writing, two of his estates, Essexvale and Eastdale, had been taken over by the government as part of the land reallocation programme. Families are already settling on the Central Estates and there are tales of looting

In its accounts for the year ending 30 September 2000, Willoughby's Consolidated's tangible fixed assets of land, buildings and machinery were listed at £9 million and its total assets at £18,588,636. After depreciation and other costs, a loss was made of £550,000.

Only in the long term will one know how successful Van Hoogstraten's diversification into African investments has been. He has played his hand astutely on many occasions. Like Tiny Rowland, he has supported nationalist politics and, in a nod towards Cecil Rhodes, he has tried to do something for the ordinary people.

This sad and ravished continent has given the entrepreneur a wider canvas for his investments and for his personal dreams. While Rhodes left his vast fortune in trust to provide scholarships so that students from Africa and other colonies could study in England, Tiny Rowland's empire turned to sand. What will happen to Van Hoogstraten's African wealth is anyone's guess, but the future in Zimbabwe currently looks bleak.

12

AT THE COURT
OF KING NICK

Van Hoogstraten promised that when his great palace was finished, he would hold a party. It would be 'the first and only party' that would ever be held there. All the great and the good would be invited to see his treasures and his park. Then Hamilton Palace would be closed up for good. There'd be no more parties, no more guests. No outsider would ever clap eyes on his priceless collections again. No one would even get into the grounds. Other self-made men can't wait to get into the county set, entertain lavishly and see themselves accepted. Much of the history of the English countryside is of the corrupt and the ruthless, parvenus and villains, buying their way into society by building a mansion which everyone who matters comes to time and again. Needless to say, Nicholas van Hoogstraten, the perennial outsider, had no such plans.

High Cross House had originally been the home of the Thornton family, who had built it in the 1840s. Half a century later, in a typical expression of Victorian benevolence, Major Robert Thornton spent a fortune restoring the local church in nearby Framfield. When the estate passed out of the Thorntons' hands that kind of paternalism went too. But even Cyril Newton Green, the publican who acquired High Cross before Van Hoogstraten, happily let locals wander and pick holly and bluebells and the local angling club fish for trout in the lake.

Not the new owner. After he took over High Cross, the message went out that no one was welcome on the estate. The notices that were pinned up at the time of the siege warning that trespassers would be shot were left there. The angling club was kicked out. Van Hoogstraten's men could be seen in the grounds with shotguns. As he outlined his plans for the palace to the press he emphasised the malevolent treatment any interloper could expect: 'Trespassers will be dealt with really viciously,' he told the Daily Star. To the Observer he said: 'People think they can come on and start cutting holly at Christmas time, come sightseeing... We deal really viciously with people when we catch them especially when they know they are not supposed to be there.'

His nearest neighbours were the two hundred or so souls living in and around Palehouse Common, mostly in groups of cottages along the road from nearby Uckfield to Lewes, some isolated in smallholdings. They were understandably terrified by what they heard about the new lord of the manor. One local did try a courtesy call on the estate. He was told by a man he took to be a caretaker that he wasn't welcome. Others living in the group of cottages just outside the estate were approached by the press about their new neighbour. The only one who chose to speak would only do so off the record, explaining that he was frightened of 'a brick through the window.'

The fear spread to the little town of Uckfield, just a over a mile away. Mike Skinner, a Liberal Democrat councillor all through the nineties, says that Van Hoogstraten didn't have to do anything to intimidate people in the town. 'His reputation was enough. Almost everyone seemed afraid. I remember sitting with a police inspector over something Van Hoogstraten was up to, and being told: "Don't do anything, he's dangerous." He wouldn't go into any details. He said he couldn't tell me why and just repeated: "He's dangerous."'

It needed only the subtlest moves from Van Hoogstraten to reinforce that intimidating picture. When he applied for planning permission to resite his palace a little to the south of the skeleton of the gutted old mansion, local councillors visited the site to see for themselves. As they got out of their vehicles and filed down the lane leading to the estate, they saw people with video cameras. Van Hoogstraten's men filmed each councillor entering the grounds, and made what they were doing very obvious. The planning application went through quickly, almost on the nod.

Quietly Van Hoogstraten began buying up parts of Uckfield. It was rumoured that he owned whole parades of shops there.

Like the police, council officials were loath to take him on. There was one case that infuriated councillor Skinner. An eighteenth-century Methodist chapel in Palehouse Common was being rebuilt as an expensive residence. It was sited in the middle of a terrace of modest houses along a country road called The Street. Complaints came in from the houses either side – both the homes of women living on their own – that they were being harassed by Van Hoogstraten's men. The two women said that hedges had been ripped up and their boundaries pushed back by the builders. When a council official eventually called round it was claimed that he joked about their complaints with the developer.

Skinner wrote to the chief executive of Wealden District Council, and was told that there was no evidence of Van Hoogstraten's involvement. The tycoon had been seen driving by the chapel one day in a black American car and stopped to have a laugh with the builders. That was the only link. Skinner wasn't satisfied and began to dig.

He found that the man named as developer of the chapel, a Ukranian called Roman Antoniuk, had an address on the High Cross estate and a registered office at another building owned by Van Hoogstraten. Skinner demanded action from the council. 'The chief executive told me: "Leave it, leave it ... we're all frightened of him,"' he recalls. He wouldn't leave it, insisting that the council should act to force the developer to give his two neighbours their land back. A council committee was convened to discuss issuing an enforcement order. It met, but to Skinner's frustration was adjourned sine die. Nothing was ever done. The two women had to put up with it. A disgusted Skinner was helpless.

The dark persona which Van Hoogstraten had cultivated so thoroughly didn't put off everyone. The reverse in some cases. A coterie of admirers gathered around him. The common denominator among them seems to have been that, like Van Hoogstraten himself, they were all outsiders. They ranged from career criminals like Robert Knapp to smaller fish in the property field – usually foreign-born – who tried to ape Van Hoogstraten or to live off his leavings, or who tried both.

Knapp was only at the 'funny farm' intermittently because he was in jail most of the time. When he first met Van Hoogstraten in prison he was a comparatively minor criminal who had served a few years for burglary and forgery. Later he became his alter ego and happily played the role of his enforcer, but he had other strings to his bow as well. Sometimes they involved Van Hoogstraten, but not always. Like many of Van Hoogstraten's associates he dabbled in property on his own account. He was also the registered owner of a wine bar in Hove. Police suspected that he was merely the front man and that Van Hoogstraten was the real owner, but they may have been wrong.

'Uncle Bob' had a taste for the glitzy life and always seemed to be driving a new – usually American – car. To fund his lifestyle he developed into a major-league hold-up man. One acquaintance who witnessed Knapp talk about his 'jobs' thinks that he loved the adrenalin rush of being a robber. Like some character out of a Humphrey Bogart movie, he seemed to get a buzz out of being behind a gun. But though he impressed everyone who knew him as being an intelligent man, he nevertheless kept getting arrested. In 1986 he led a raid on a Post Office van and stole £100,000. Police caught up with him just as he transferring the money from the getaway car into another vehicle.

While Knapp was away in jail for the hijack his parents Sylvia and Arthur were given one of the 'grace and favour' cottages at High Cross by Van Hoogstraten. Later, in court, Van Hoogstraten would break down and describe his fondness for old Mrs Knapp. 'She was like my mother,' he said.

Knapp was released from jail on licence in 1993, but he wasn't out for long. Just six months later he got twelve years after a botched raid on a jeweller's in which his fellow robber killed himself rather than be caught.

Another violent friend – also another outsider – was the tough Greek-Cypriot restaurateur Andrew Emmanuel. Van Hoogstraten and he had always enjoyed a fiery relationship ever since they met in the sixties. Emmanuel was the one man who consistently stood up to him and was treated by him like an equal. They were a disparate pair, the carefully brushed, neat Van Hoogstraten and the muscular Emmanuel with his yellow teeth and excited gestures. They did business together and rowed continually, cursing each other, hurling every kind of threat. 'At one time or another each one was going to murder the other or break his legs ... we were always on the brink of calling the police when they were at it,' says a regular witness of their fights.

However serious their rows appeared to others, Emmanuel stuck by Van Hoogstraten through thick and thin, and vice versa. Asked once by the authors if he had any friends who would be willing to talk honestly about him, Van Hoogstraten could think only of Emmanuel. We duly approached Emmanuel. 'Yes, I will give you an interview,' he said. 'I want the world to know about the man I love and the man I hate.' In the event, on Van Hoogstraten's instructions, he had second thoughts and told the world nothing.

The most dramatic role of all in the Van Hoogstraten story would be played by a third outsider who couldn't be more different from Emmanuel. This was a polite, obsequious, even fawning Pakistani, Mohammed Sabir Raja.

A burly, genial-looking figure, with big black eyebrows and a carefully clipped moustache, his appearance belied his behaviour. In his white shirt, silk tie and striped blue business suit and with his purposeful, military stance, Raja could have been mistaken for an ambassador or an international banker. In fact he was a slum landlord.

Born in 1937, Raja grew up in the tiny village of Tatral near Rawalpindi in Pakistan. He married in 1951 and had three sons. At the age of thirty-five he set out for England, leaving his family behind until he had made enough money to send for them. So began a classic climb from rags to riches. The young immigrant took a room in Brighton and began a course in business administration at the local college. While studying in the evenings he worked in the day for the Post Office, then as a guard on the railways.

It took him five years to save and borrow enough money to buy his first property. That was in 1967, the year that his friend-to-be Nicholas van Hoogstraten was first starting to appear in the headlines. Raja bought a house in Lorna Road, Hove. A controversial career as a landlord had begun. Three years later he was doing well enough to bring his wife Starbie and their three sons over from Pakistan, but it was to be another six years before he had enough capital to become a full-time property dealer.

Later Mohammed Raja would credit Van Hoogstraten with teaching him the tricks of the trade. But from the early days he was no angel. He specialised in crowded bedsits, squashing in as many tenants into the smallest space he could. A fellow property dealer says of his bedsits: 'You smelled stale human sweat from the moment you walked in until the moment you walked out. They were the pits.' In 1976 Raja was criticised for housing up to sixteen tenants in a property in Goldstone Road, Brighton, which had just two WCs and one bath. A few years after that he was fined £750 with £600 costs for trying to bribe a council official. Raja said that it was 'a clear misunderstanding'. He was not used to dealing in 'the English way'. Eventually he would notch up more than a hundred convictions all over the country, mostly for health and safety violations. In 1989 the Evening Argus investigated his activities and dubbed him 'Brighton's worst landlord'.

Raja was unrepentant. He told the paper: 'Tenants, including the young people and those who are on the dole, they have nothing to do except fight each other and damage the property... If people want to live in a doss house or a palace it is their choice.'

He ultimately did so well in the bedsit business that at the time of his death he had amassed a portfolio of more than a hundred properties. Most of them were in the Brighton area, but he also had houses in London and as far afield as Manchester, Liverpool and Newcastle.

Oddly for a man judged to have broken the law so many times, Raja clearly brought up his family to respect it. He and Sarbie had three more children, all girls, and each one became a lawyer.

Van Hoogstraten says that he first clapped eyes on Raja in the early eighties. Raja needed a top-up loan to complete the purchase of a 'modest' property which he had bid for at a London auction. He put down a deposit of ten per cent, but he didn't have the funds to complete the deal. So he came cap in hand to borrow the money from Van Hoogstraten. However, Raja couldn't have offered enough security for the loan because the tycoon turned him down. As a result, Raja lost his deposit. Van Hoogstraten's story – told with typical relish – is that he himself then 'thieved' the property, which was now going dirt cheap.

Raja, a proud man, never mentioned the episode. He claimed not to have met Van Hoogstraten until some years later. He said that it happened in 1987. He was at a property auction when he was 'persuaded' to borrow from Van Hoogstraten in order to buy a property from him. Raja outlined the deal in a statement to a lawyer some years later. The arrangement was slick and it dodged taxes. Van Hoogstraten lent him the money at twelve per cent, a cheaper rate than the banks charged. Raja paid off the loan, bit by bit every month, usually in cash. When they were square he got the deeds from Van Hoogstraten. There was nothing on paper. As extra security, Van Hoogstraten had Raja sign blank property transfer documents. These could be used to transfer other Raja properties into Van Hoogstraten's name if Raja reneged on repayments. Raja held his breath and agreed to everything. It was all cemented with a handshake. It was a gentleman's agreement.

The deal worked perfectly. Within a few months Raja had paid back the loan and Van Hoogstraten handed over the deeds. It was the first of a number of similar loans that would eventually total well over £500,000.

As in so many of his business dealings, Van Hoogstraten got to know this new associate. They were soon on first-name terms: Mohammed and Nick. Raja's son Amjad says: 'It was nice to know the man. He seemed genuine enough at the time. He was

OK to do business with because he had clout. He had money as well, so that seemed OK.' They became friends. Such good friends that a few years later Van Hoogstraten was invited to be the guest of honour at Amjad's wedding.

Van Hoogstraten began letting Mohammed Raja in on some of his money-making secrets. Raja later described one of them – a breathtakingly simple way of reneging on debts. Van Hoogstraten would deliberately run debts up on company A and meanwhile transfer all assets out of that company to companies B and C. Then he would dissolve the company with all the debts, company A, and its creditors could go hang. Raja called it 'wiping the slate clean' and appears to have approved. 'I learned quite a few tricks of the trade from him for which I am still grateful,' he said.

According to Raja, one of the tricks involved buying freehold properties and then getting hold of the leasehold tenancies dirt cheap. From Raja's description it appears to have worked like this. Van Hoogstraten bought a freehold. He then squeezed the leaseholders unmercifully by imposing high management charges. Some couldn't keep up payments and defaulted on their mortgages. Their flats were then repossessed by their building societies with a view to putting them on the market to get their money back. At this point Van Hoogstraten's men vandalised the repossessed flats, usually making it impossible to sell them on the open market. As freeholder, Van Hoogstraten then made an offer for the flats and usually got them 'at a knock-down price'. He went on to give Raja's son and business partner Amjad lessons in how to do this.

The tycoon boasted to the Rajas of his tough approach to associates who owed him money. He described the kidnapping of his accountant David Harris and invited the Rajas to witness a violent repossession he was planning. 'He told us that he was "sequestrating" a shop and all the contents in it,' Amjad recalls.

'He said he was going to surround the place with thirty men to make sure the job was done properly.'

In the late eighties and early nineties Raja borrowed more and more from Van Hoogstraten as he tried to build up his empire. Each time Raja borrowed to buy another property, Van Hoogstraten kept the deeds of the property plus a blank transfer document with Raja's signature. It was a procedure that years later would prove a recipe for disaster.

Shortly before Van Hoogstraten started doing business with Raja, another foreign-born property dealer struck up an acquaintance with him. Michaal Hamdan set out to become a friend of the tycoon. He was to become closer to him than almost anyone, and then, like Raja, become a bitter opponent.

Today Hamdan is living the life of a millionaire playboy in Beirut. An overweight forty-something with a liking for silk shirts, low-slung sports cars and gold jewellery, he whiles away his time between villas, yachts, the beach and the casino. He seems a dedicated hedonist with a penchant for young girls. Hamdan lived in Britain for twenty years, then fled back home to the Lebanon in April 2002. He is afraid for his safety because he thinks that his old friend Van Hoogstraten may have put out a contract on him.

Hamdan is from a rich Christian family in Beirut. He came to Britain in 1978 to study business and settled in Brighton. In the mid-eighties he started dabbling in property and attending auctions. You couldn't do that in Brighton – or London for that matter – without becoming aware of Van Hoogstraten. When the tycoon wasn't at the last auction in person, his doings or suspected doings were usually part of the gossip afterwards in the bar.

Watching Van Hoogstraten's struggle with Kensington and Chelsea Council in the late eighties, Hamdan became a fan. He studied Van Hoogstraten at auctions but didn't make himself known. He liked the chutzpah of the man, and the two fingers he waved at authority. From everything Hamdan said subsequently it is clear that he decided to model himself on the tycoon. 'I think I idolised him,' he says.

'He was stalking me,' Van Hoogstraten said later. 'He kept trying to bump into me.' Hamdan finally succeeded. He buttonholed the tycoon as he emerged from a branch of Lloyds Bank in Bayswater in 1987. Hamdan remembers introducing himself as a property dealer who would like to do business with Van Hoogstraten, hastening to add that he was only a small fish. He remembers Van Hoogstraten's reply: 'Big fish eat little fish.' Van Hoogstraten's recollection of the meeting was: 'He came up to me and I effectively told him to go away.'

In fact Van Hoogstraten was quite taken with this eager little fish. He said he'd check him out with contacts in the Lebanon. A few months later he called in at Hamdan's flat and soon the two became friends. The young Lebanese wanted to be big in property and Van Hoogstraten told him how. Hamdan became an avid pupil at the feet of the master. Mean in so many things, Van Hoogstraten has always been generous with advice – where to live, who to trust (or more usually who not to trust), when to buy, when to sell. He looked at Hamdan's modest portfolio and at his debts and told him that he was insolvent. To dodge his creditors Hamdan should 'warehouse' some of his properties – transfer them out of his name – and sell some of the others, then declare himself bankrupt.

Hamdan took Van Hoogstraten's advice and survived the crash. He later bought properties from the tycoon for himself and also acted as his front man. Like Van Hoogstraten, he painted himself as a man it would be very unwise to cross because he had dangerous connections he could always call on.

The two men were so often together that some people assumed the Lebanese was a new bodyguard. Van Hoogstraten was in

London sometimes twice or three times a week. Hamdan invariably found that he had business in the capital at the same time. He'd give Van Hoogstraten a lift from Hove in his Porsche in the morning and meet him for a Park Lane dinner at dusk. The highly sexed Hamdan might have preferred to go clubbing in Soho, but instead he usually listened as Van Hoogstraten talked and talked and then he dutifully drove the tycoon all the way back to the coast.

In 1990 the relationship was further cemented – or so it seemed – when Van Hoogstraten offered this pupil the management of some of his holdings on the Riviera. At the time he was expanding fast in France. He later told the Daily Telegraph's David Millward that because of the authorities' attitude he found it easier to deal with tenants on the other side of the Channel. The French police just stood by and watched 'while you do the villainy', he explained.

The deal with Hamdan involved the Lebanese managing Van Hoogstraten properties and renovating them at his own expense in return for half the rents and half the profits once the properties were sold. But they weren't sold. Hamdan later complained that he spent £80,000 of his own money renovating them and then got fifty per cent of nothing.

Hamdan played a key role in another new venture for Van Hoogstraten – hotels. In the 1990s the tycoon was set on building up a hotel chain. By the end of the decade he owned, directly and indirectly, at least seven hotels in the Brighton and Hove area alone. As usual he tended to use front men in acquiring them. Hamdan was one of them. When the seventy-bedroom Imperial Hotel in Hove came up for sale, Van Hoogstraten put in different offers using different front men, including Hamdan. He orchestrated it so that at least one of his highest bids was withdrawn at a key moment, so that a lower bid, notionally from Hamdan, got the hotel.

The torched white transit van in which Croke and Knapp made their escape from the scene of Raja's murder.

Cottage 4, High Cross Estate.

Montana   Garages

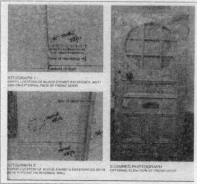

Location of blood
Exhibit ref: SB/11
Location of blood
Exhibit ref: SB/18
SB/19

Top: A police photograph of
Hoogstraten's estate.

Bottom left: The door frame removed
from the scene with the location of the
blood spatters marked.

Bottom right: A computer generated
image of the scene of the crime.

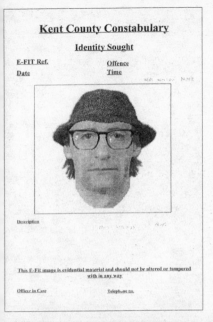

Top: The e-fit images created by the Metropolitan Police, which assisted the apprehension of Knapp and Croke.

Bottom: Van Hoogstraten on his way to court.

Top: Van Hoogstraten outside court.

Bottom left: Police mugshot of Croke.

Bottom right: Police mugshot of Knapp.

Top left: The Metropolitan police posters appealing for help in solving the crime.

Top right: The victim Mohammed Raja, who was brutally murdered outside his family home in front of his grandsons.

Bottom: The court artist's impression of Van Hoogstraten and his co-defendants.

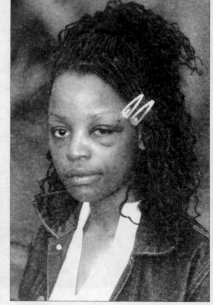

Top: Van Hoogstraten leaving court with girlfriend Tanaka.

Bottom left: Tanaka leaving the Old Bailey during the murder trial.

Bottom right: Tanaka sporting a black eye.

Van Hoogstraten enjoyed a life of immense wealth and luxury.

Nicholas Van Hoogstraten in the foyer of one of his hotels.

The purchase money was put up by Van Hoogstraten, and ownership of the Imperial was quickly transferred from Hamdan to one of the tycoon's companies. Meanwhile Hamdan managed it. He says that Van Hoogstraten promised to make him part-owner of the hotel but reneged on the deal. When he pointed out that he'd been managing it unpaid for seven months, Van Hoogstraten told him it was good experience.

All this didn't stop Hamdan continuing to front for Van Hoogstraten in some property deals and partner him in others. He became so close to the tycoon that he was made a director of some of Hoogstraten's key enterprises, including the Zimbabwean holding company Willoughby's Consolidated. But the Lebanese was increasingly unhappy. Secretly he decided that Van Hoogstraten wasn't giving him his due. He said later: 'I expected Nick to take the lion's share but I did expect crumbs, and I didn't even get them.' The admirer was turning into an enemy.

13

FIRE!

At the beginning of the nineties the Van Hoogstraten empire had taken on a radically different look, which should have kept controversy at bay. Foreseeing the property crash, the tycoon sold the bulk of his residential properties in the UK. He concentrated instead on the commercial stuff – hotels, shops, office blocks, warehouses. Fewer residential properties meant fewer 'difficult' tenants to deal with and that should have meant fewer 'devil's landlord' headlines. But it did not turn out that way. In 1990 the gravest landlord-tenant crisis yet was about to break over him. And this would involve deaths.

This time the crisis involved not rent-paying tenants like the Mahoods or the Udwin sisters but a trio of leaseholders. They were owner-occupiers of three flats in a house in Hove and were trying to use the new Leasehold Reform Act to buy the freehold.

The Act had been introduced by Van Hoogstraten's heroine, Mrs Thatcher, as part of her crusade to boost home ownership. It gave leaseholders the right to club together and buy their freehold as long as a majority among them agreed. Van Hoogstraten regarded the measure as a personal affront.

Like other ruthless freeholders, he had always made big money through exorbitant service charges and management fees. He reacted to the new law with a typical burst of paranoia. He complained that it was unjust and told Michaal Hamdan that he knew that it was directed specifically at him. 'They're trying to stop me,' he told Tony Browne.

The house the three leaseholders lived in was 11 Palmeira Avenue, a gracious, magnolia-painted Victorian terrace. As well as the leasehold flats, it contained two rented flats. In 1989 the leaseholders, led by a man called Andrew Crumpton, decided that they wanted to buy the freehold on the house. A bizarre game of pass the parcel now began.

In 1990 Crumpton and his neighbours approached the company they assumed to be the freeholder with an offer. Sorry, they were told, the freehold has just been sold. They tracked down the new owner. Same story. Sorry, it's just been sold. The same with the next buyer and the next and the next. The title was passing around like a red-hot brick. In two years it changed hands six times.

While the leaseholders chased after the title, hurried conversion work was under way in the two tenanted flats. It seemed innocuous enough – refurbishing for new tenants, no doubt. However, when the work was finished the three leaseholders found that these two flats had become three flats. They were being 'sold' on short leases to three different companies. At a stroke, Crumpton and the others had lost their majority and their legal right to acquire the leasehold.

It was a brilliant, if unscrupulous, dodge.

But the three owner-occupiers included a trainee solicitor, and they challenged it. A protracted legal dispute developed. It ended two years later in victory for the leaseholders. They must get their freehold, the courts ordered. The night that the decision came through, Crumpton received a threatening phone call. He immediately told the police. He was so frightened that he and his wife moved out.

A few weeks later, on Easter Saturday, there was a party on the third floor of number 11. It was to celebrate the twenty-eighth birthday of the flat's tenant, Tim Sharp. The day before the party Tim felt a bout of flu coming on and tried to postpone the celebration, but it was too late. He was homosexual and word about the party had gone round the large gay community in Brighton and Hove. As the pubs closed people began to congregate in Palmeira Avenue and mount the stairs to Tim's flat. One was an unemployed airline steward called Trevor Carrington, who arrived with his partner. He wasn't a friend and hadn't been invited. Apparently he'd just heard about the party and had scribbled the address on a piece of paper. In the free-and-easy camaraderie of such gatherings nobody objected. But Carrington was drunk when he arrived and got drunker. Nobody complained when he decided to go, and followed his partner down three flights of stairs, past an old sofa outside the ground floor flat. They left behind maybe sixteen or seventeen people.

Shortly after 2 am, fire broke out. The blaze took hold so quickly that Tim Sharp and his remaining guests were trapped on the third floor. There was no fire escape. One partygoer got out by shinning down a drainpipe. Others stumbled across to the parapet next door. Tim tried to climb down the drainpipe too. He lost his footing and fell fifty feet.

Firemen arrived just after 2.30. In the basement area they found Tim Sharp's body. He was dead. A forty-eight-year-old nurse from Wales, Mabel Roberts, and twenty-nine-year-old Andrew Manners both lay nearby. Both had jumped from the third floor. Both died. Another badly injured man was trying to crawl up the basement steps.

As one crew tried to battle its way through the flames on the ground floor stairwell, another was told to get a platform up to roof level to tackle the blaze from there. Just before the fire engines arrived a passer-by had seen two faces at the front window immediately below the roof. Flames and smoke now obscured the window. Speed was essential. But there was no room on the roadway to put down the stabilising jacks needed for the hydraulic platform. There was an unbroken line of parked cars next to the pavement and a double line of cars down the centre of Palmeira Avenue. Firemen and policemen desperately bumped parked cars out of the way. They estimated that this lost them between five and ten minutes. It took three hours to douse the flames completely. Two hours later the remains of thirty-three-year-old Paul Jones and thirty-one-year-old Adrian Johns were found under the roof on the third floor.

Five were dead. All might well have escaped but for one thing. The freeholder who had struggled so determinedly to hang on to the freehold had struggled just as determinedly to avoid paying for fire doors – let alone a fire escape. Four years earlier Hove Council officials had judged the place a firetrap and demanded action by the owners. They'd got nowhere.

The day after the fire, Easter Sunday, Trevor Carrington took a stiff drink, swallowed some tablets and slashed his throat and wrists. He was rushed to a hospital in Haywards Heath. The following morning his brother visited him there, and a terrible story stumbled out. On the way out of the party Trevor, in his drunkenness, had used his cigarette lighter to set alight the settee on the ground floor. He'd wanted to 'cause a panic' and 'liven up' the party. It was 'a prank that had gone terribly wrong'. Carrington pleaded with his brother to help him flee abroad. Go to the police, or I will go to them, his brother told him. Three days later Carrington walked out in front of a lorry. Death was instantaneous.

To Hove police it was an open-and-shut case. A malicious prank by the drunk Carrington had caused the fire. But was it so simple? A fire brigade report on the fire suggested that fires might have been set in other parts of the house as well as the ground floor. It pinpointed two areas of severe charring on upper landings which it said were 'not consistent with a fire that had originated at ground level'. Had more than one person been involved in the arson?

Then the Daily Telegraph had a tip-off from a fire-brigade source that Van Hoogstraten might be involved and sent reporter David Millward to dig into the freehold dispute. The reporter talked to the leaseholders and heard that while they were trying to buy the title it had whizzed between five companies and a woman called Lucia Tavarini. He discovered that each of the companies was run by a close associate of Van Hoogstraten or had an address associated with the tycoon. Millward couldn't at that time find any link to Ms Tavarini. But there was one. In preparing this book, we discovered that she had been a girlfriend of Van Hoogstraten's front man and sometime partner Michaal Hamdan.

Before the inquest into the deaths was held, David Millward unearthed the dismal history of Hove Council's attempts to have fire precautions installed. Rumours circulated about who was really responsible for the five deaths. Hoogstraten's name was to the fore. Trevor Carrington was rumoured to have had £30,000 in an Isle of Man bank. Journalists speculated wildly that he might have been paid by Van Hoogstraten to fire the house and that he might then have been murdered to keep him quiet. To some people, nothing was beyond Nicholas Van Hoogstraten. The Evening Argus decided to put Van Hoogstraten on the spot over his links to the house. It demanded that he appear at the inquest into the deaths. 'He should come forward and clear the air,' an editorial declared.

Van Hoogstraten didn't oblige. But although he wasn't there in person, his was the dominating presence at the inquest when it opened in Brighton in August 1992. Colm Davis-Lyons, counsel representing two of the bereaved families at the inquest, wrote to the coroner, Dr Donald Gooding, asking that Van Hoogstraten be called as a witness. Dr Gooding turned him down, saying that the millionaire wouldn't be able to shed any light on the deaths, so he wouldn't call him. In protest Davis-Lyons and two of the families walked out of the inquest and demanded a judicial review of the decision.

The inquest proceeded. Over two days jurors heard senior officials try to explain Hove Council's futile attempts to force the landlords of 11 Palmeira Avenue to take fire-safety measures. They listened as witnesses took them through the awful events of the previous Easter – the party, the fire, the five deaths, Carrington's confession to his brother, his death.

They also heard something indicating that maybe there was more to this act of arson than a drunkard's moment of madness. Andrew Crumpton was in the witness box, describing the disputes over the freehold. When he had finished, the coroner asked if there were any further questions. In the press box David Millward stood up. 'Can the press ask questions?'

'Yes,' said Dr Gooding.

'Well, Mr Crumpton,' said Millward. 'Can you tell us what happened the night that you won the case?'

'Yes,' said Crumpton. 'Someone phoned me and threatened to burn the place down.'

The jury brought in a verdict of unlawful killing and, in Carrington's case, suicide. The jurors added an afterthought. They called for changes in the law to bring absentee landlords to heel.

For five bereaved families it was nothing like enough. They wanted to see Van Hoogstraten in the witness box. They also wanted to know much more about the four years in which the council had tried and so abysmally failed to make the landlord install a fire escape. 'You can't sweep five deaths under the carpet,' said Dennis Johns, whose son died in the fire, overcome by fumes.

There was an outside chance that Mr Johns and the other grieving relatives would get their wish. The day the inquest ended a judge accepted Davis-Lyons's plea for a judicial review. This meant that two appeal court judges would put the coroner's actions under the microscope and maybe order a new inquest. The world might yet see the tycoon called to account.

At the time Van Hoogstraten was far away, living on the French Riviera with his latest black mistress, a twenty-seven-year-old Sudanese called Fatou. Reporters and press photographers flew down to Cannes to interview him. They found the multi-millionaire enjoying his riches. Snappers photographed him in outsize Hollywood shades with Fatou's arm around his neck. He radiated confidence, and as ever he provided terrific copy.

He told the Daily Telegraph's David Millward that it was 'outrageous' to link him to the deaths: 'If I had been involved, number one, there would not have been anyone in the building. Number two, it would have been done in the basement. If you are going to do it you do it properly.'

Millward asked him about Davis-Lyons. Van Hoogstraten replied, in his typically threatening style. The lawyer 'was liable to get a whack ... entitled to get a spanking... He knows what the position is. If anybody causes me any kind of personal hardship they don't get away with it. They may get away with it for six months or a year or two years or whatever until sufficient time has passed and it is nothing to do with me. I deal with people in cold blood not hot blood.'

The Evening Argus sent its Van Hoogstraten expert, Adam Trimmingham, to Cannes. He fixed on the tycoon's sybaritic lifestyle. 'On his right hand he wore a ring worth anything up to £250,000. On his left he sported a watch given him years ago by an Arab sheikh.' His latest girlfriend was 'stunning', the reporter added. He described how the millionaire 'conducted a public, teasing, affectionate hands-on relationship' with her throughout ten hours the Tringingham spent with them.

'I asked him,' Trimmingham said, 'if he was more mellow now. He replied: "Not more mellow but less hot tempered. I may have done something immediately ten years ago but now I stop and think about it."'

The quest for the truth went on for nearly two years. It culminated in December 1993 when the judicial review opened at the High Court in London. The families vented their feelings to the court. The coroner had appeared 'to be more interested in getting the inquest over as quickly as possible than addressing any of the issues relating to the means of escape,' declared Lee Homberg, who lost his brother in the fire. The inquest jury were 'repeatedly misled' about what Hove Council could have done, claimed Edward Fitzgerald QC, acting for the families.

It didn't impress the High Court. Lord Justice Simon Brown savaged the coroner's handling of the inquest but was even more critical of the families' lawyer and of the press. Barrister Colm Davis-Lyons had been 'high-handed' and 'tactless', which had riled the coroner. Dr Gooding had erred but he was right not to call Van Hoogstraten. 'There was no useful evidence which Mr Van Hoogstraten could have given, even assuming, contrary to all likelihood, that he would have been a willing and co-operative witness.' As for the media: 'Much of the pressure to call Van Hoogstraten came from the media who were undoubtedly intent on exploiting the tragedy to the full, not least by capitalising on Van Hoogstraten's suggested link with the property.' There would not be a new inquest, the judge concluded.

The ruling didn't allay the rumours and suspicions, let alone satisfy the bereaved families. Years later an even wilder story circulated. It was claimed that the house had been fired by members of a notorious paedophile ring who were being blackmailed by people attending the party.

The Argus kept an eye on Van Hoogstraten over the next few years but with less and less reward. There was a running scandal about a decrepit eyesore on the seafront that he was rumoured to own and there was the odd landlord-tenant dispute to report. But the only headline story about him in the mid-nineties was an account of how he bought a hotel and promptly cancelled a club booking because the terms offered by the previous owners were too cheap. The Argus gave front-page prominence to the predicament of forty bewildered trippers who had been turned away by Van Hoogstraten.

He was much quieter all round. Maybe he had decided to enjoy his wealth and his mistresses and concentrate on the palace and his kids. Maybe middle age was catching up. Whatever was going on in his mind, something seemed to be changing in Nicholas van Hoogstraten. Readers of the Argus even began seeing good things about him. The paper reported that he made the News of the World pay £2000 to a Sussex charity as the price of giving an interview. It revealed that when sponsorship for the giant Christmas tree in Palmeira Square was suddenly withdrawn, Van Hoogstraten had stepped in and paid for the tree. There was a report that he was regularly giving thousands to charities. The Argus columnist Adam Trimmingham wrote that Van Hoogstraten was a complex man with his own set of moral standards.

But Van Hoogstraten was not to settle into a tranquil middle age. His past was going to catch up with him and bring him to his knees. And two of those fellow outsiders who had been so drawn to him would be the agents of destruction – the eager front man Michaal Hamdan and the obsequious Mohammed Raja.

14

A THORN IN
THE SIDE

As he reached his fifties, Nicholas van Hoogstraten had begun to wonder about his own mortality. 'For the first time in my life in the last few years I've been involved personally with people who have died, dealing with funerals and that sort of thing. And I don't like the feeling,' he told one of the authors in 1997.

The first death to affect him was that of Bill Bagot, the burly old millionaire from west London whom he'd met thirty years before and who had been so important to him ever since. Bagot died in Charing Cross Hospital on 3 September 1993.

Doctors had expected the old man to survive. He had a heart condition and had lost the use of his legs. But the view was that he could safely be discharged as long as there was constant medical care on hand. Van Hoogstraten set about providing it. Bagot's home in Acton was converted to provide a flat for a nurse next to his bedroom. Van Hoogstraten paid for the work and was planning to pay for the nurse.

Others had flinched at the eccentric old man, who got shabbier and filthier as the years went by. But Van Hoogstraten, so meticulously clean himself, didn't seem to notice. He was genuinely fond of Bagot. 'My father figure and my mentor,' he called him.

News of Bagot's unexpected death affected Van Hoogstraten deeply. Tony Browne was amazed to see tears coming down his employer's face. 'Nick is an actor but this was no act,' he says. 'He really was upset... He began some soul-searching, why-are-we-here? soul-searching, that sort of thing.' But then sensibilities gave way to practicalities.

'We were straight round to Bagot's house in Acton to search it,' recalls Browne. 'The old man was a miser. He hid things, like Nick hid things. Nick wanted the place taken apart... What was he looking for? Valuables, bank notes, bearer bonds, gold, anything with high value. He was sure Bagot had lots of things hidden away.'

The house and the house next door, also owned by Bagot, were both ransacked. Over a period of weeks the garden was completely dug over, the cellar was searched, the walls examined for hollow sounding bricks, floorboards taken up, and lavatory cisterns searched, always with Van Hoogstraten looking on.

The search was suspended for a few hours for Bagot's funeral. Then the digging and stripping at the two houses in Cumberland Road resumed. Van Hoogstraten insisted on being on hand throughout. He didn't trust any of his lieutenants to let on if they found something. He watched as every bed knob was unscrewed and every picture on the wall taken down so the paper backing could be ripped off in case something was underneath.

Something was found. Gold coins! Browne didn't see them and never knew how many had been unearthed or what the value was. But he saw Van Hoogstraten's delight after the discovery.

A will was produced. Drawn up almost exactly twenty years earlier, it was a sparse document for a man known to be immensely wealthy. Of the four hundred properties Bagot had owned in and around Paddington only one was mentioned, along with just one other property – a house in Surrey. They were left for the lifetime use of two friends.

The residue of the estate was willed to Van Hoogstraten. He was named as Bagot's sole executor and trustee. What the residue consisted of wasn't specified. Apart from a rough sketch of a cemetery monument and the words 'Red Granite Obelisk as here', that was the only information which the old eccentric had put in his last will and testament.

'Putting the estate in order' can mean a lot of things. We can only guess what it entailed for Van Hoogstraten as he went through Bagot's effects. The two adjoining houses in Acton were full to the ceiling with junk. But they also yielded up antiques, a collection of forty or fifty carriage clocks worth thousands of pounds and, of course, the gold. That, however, couldn't be a fraction of what Bagot had really owned. His fingers had been in many pies. He had been variously described as 'an accountant', a 'merchant banker', a 'businessman' and 'the owner of a property empire'. There had to be a fortune somewhere.

Van Hoogstraten spent a long time looking for it. He put Bagot's estate in for probate in June 1994, nine months after his old friend died. The probate document made no mention of the hundreds of properties the old man had owned. Maybe he'd passed them on to Van Hoogstraten in his lifetime. But the documents made no mention either of gold coins, shares, antiques or carriage clocks. Indeed Van Hoogstraten claimed that the net value of Bagot's estate in Britain was less than £10,000 – about the value of a lock-up garage next to one of the old man's houses in Paddington. Probate appears to have gone through without problems. There were no death duties.

Two more deaths occurred in the 1990s – those of Van Hoogstraten's parents, Charles and Edna. For three decades he had hated both of them and they, it seemed, had hated him in return. But towards the end of their lives there was a reconciliation between them. Again Van Hoogstraten shed genuine tears.

The passing of those people who had been so important to him left a more introspective figure who sometimes surprised visitors who had come expecting the same old posturings. In the spring of 1997 one of the authors, who had not seen him for years, was treated to what was almost a display of humility when Van Hoogstraten showed him around the shell of the projected palace in the spring of 1997.

Predictably, Van Hoogstraten began by enthusing over the half-built edifice. He still appeared to be the megalomaniac intent on leaving a monument of mind-blowing extravagance behind him. 'There'll be frescos on the ceilings, the columns will have to be painted in gold, there will be tapestries on the walls,' he boasted.

But in the next breath this vainest of men was mocking himself for being so mean about everything else: 'We do things and we don't exactly know why. Most of the things that I do, from when I get up to when I go to sleep, I don't know why I am doing them. I wonder to myself sometimes why I am wasting my time using second-class stamps to save sixpence. Even if I do it a million times it adds up to a hill of beans.'

In this confessional mood Van Hoogstraten then admitted why the monument he was building, and the kids he had fathered, wouldn't bear his family name. 'The name is Hamilton Palace... Hamilton after Hamilton, capital of Bermuda. It was one of the few places in my youth that I fell in love with... My children are called Hamilton. It's a fine colonial name ... and I couldn't foist my own terrible name on them, innocent children.'

Those close to Van Hoogstraten have no doubt that whatever mellowing there was in him was down to the effect of fatherhood. In the eighties it was impossible to see him even developing into a fond parent. By then Caroline Williams had borne him two children, but he was never pictured publicly with them, and he made clear to those who asked that the kids would have to make their own way in the world, unaided by him or his wealth. He wasn't leaving his children anything. If they expected to benefit from his death he would never be able to trust them. The only time he was seen to be the loving father was when he cuddled his youngest child in an attempt to influence women jury members during the Kensington and Chelsea trial.

Ten years on, paternity had transformed him. He now had five children, four sons and one daughter. Company searches suggest that far from letting them fend for themselves, he had settled a fortune in shares on each of them. He demonstrated a tactile affection for them which was obviously genuine. It was reciprocated. He also began to talk about them, coupling their interests with his. In interviews with newspapers and on television he now talked enthusiastically about the 'importance' of his children in his life.

But despite the children and the moments of introspection, fundamentally Van Hoogstraten hadn't changed. At the slightest challenge the temper could still go way over the top. He'd been out of the headlines for four or five years when, in December 1998, the Ramblers' Association announced that he had closed a public footpath at High Cross and must open it again. His reaction turned a trivial dispute into a major event and made him a national hate figure once again.

Van Hoogstraten was just what militant ramblers were looking for – an arrogant large landowner who had barred a public right of way. Parliament was debating the decades-old issue of public access to the countryside and Van Hoogstraten was God's gift to those urging the government to take on unreasonable landowners. The footpath that now became a cause célèbre was on his High Cross estate. Known as Framfield Nine, it ran to a disused church and had once been a lovely walk with glorious views of the South Downs. When Van Hoogstraten had closed it years before, no one had noticed, but suddenly ramblers discovered its existence and found that it had been a public right of way for 140 years.

The landowner responded to the Ramblers' Association's call to open the footpath with all his old villainous extravagance. He had his men dump old fridges, car batteries and all kinds of other rubbish on the path and string razor wire everywhere. A ten-foot fence was erected. Men with shotguns were reported to be patrolling. No one was going to walk on his land.

Once more the media made for East Sussex. Van Hoogstraten was ready for them all with a different epithet for every interview. The ramblers were 'just a bunch of the dirty mac brigade', 'the great unwashed', 'disgusting creatures', 'a lot of herberts', 'anarchists', 'perverts'.

The 'Enemy of the People' column in the Sunday Times described Van Hoogstraten as 'one of the least likeable people this column has ever attacked'. The Daily Mirror called him 'Britain's vilest millionaire'.

He enjoyed himself hugely. In one live TV interview he libelled an MP by saying he was surprised the man hadn't yet been arrested because of his activities on Clapham Common, 'if you get my meaning'. When the cameras turned off he said to the studio manager: 'Did you like that bit about Clapham Common? I thought it was rather good' and laughed unproariously.

Van Hoogstraten would need all the light relief he could get. At the beginning of 1999, when so much seemed to be going so well – with his kids, his palace and his plans in Zimbabwe – he was in reality heading for a fall. It wouldn't come through his property dealing but that still murkier side of his business – the moneylending. The catalyst would be the slum landlord, his one-time friend and admirer Mohammed Raja.

Until the early nineties everything had gone smoothly between the two of them. More than a dozen properties acquired by Raja had been bought with loans from Van Hoogstraten. Each month Van Hoogstraten phoned to tell Raja what he owed in interest and capital repayment. Each month Raja or his son Amjad turned up at Van Hoogstraten's Hove office with a cheque or a bundle of £50 notes. The cheques were never made out to Van Hoogstraten but to one of his finance companies, Unifox.

Outwardly, relations were amicable. Raja was polite and always full of compliments for Van Hoogstraten. In turn Van Hoogstraten drew both Mohammed and Amjad Raja more and more into the fold. Amjad began managing some of Van Hoogstraten's properties in west London.

But it was a mutually suspicious partnership. Van Hoogstraten always insisted that he was fond of Mohammed Raja, yet he told a friend that Raja had 'dirty fingers' and sneered about 'this slum landlord' to journalists. As for the Rajas, privately they appear to have resented the arrogance of the man they were in hock to. Amjad said later that Van Hoogstraten 'acted like a king', treating other people as if they were nothing.

Relations went downhill after the house-price bubble burst in 1989, sending the property business into recession. Between 1991 and 1992 the number of house sales fell by half. A lot of property men got caught as prices slumped too. Van Hoogstraten, seeing what was coming, sold much of his residential property, but Mohammed Raja wasn't as far-sighted and went on buying.

He was soon in trouble financially. In desperation, he raised a building society mortgage on a property for which he already owed money to Van Hoogstraten. Technically that was fraud. Van Hoogstraten found out about it and demanded extra security for his loans. Raja agreed to give him deeds to other properties he owned. In his desperation he also signed blank property transfer forms. This extraordinary step left Van

Hoogstraten in a position where – if Raja did default – he could fill in the name of a Raja property and transfer ownership to himself.

Michaal Hamdan recalls Van Hoogstraten telling him that he was giving Raja 'enough rope to hang himself'. Sure enough, Raja couldn't keep up repayments and Van Hoogstraten promptly repossessed several of his properties. He also sued Amjad Raja over unpaid rents.

Open war broke out in 1993 over how much Raja still owed Van Hoogstraten. In May that year he asked for a breakdown of borrowings and repayments and meanwhile stopped all further payments to Van Hoogstraten. The tycoon refused to detail everything on paper. All he'd do was tell Raja the total figure owing – £300,000. Raja refuted it. In October he went to the High Court alleging breach of trust and demanding the return of the deeds he had lodged with Van Hoogstraten. He claimed that Van Hoogstraten had used the blank transfer forms to fraudulently take properties from him.

There followed a series of heated phone calls from Van Hoogstraten. 'He was very abusive,' says Amjad Raja. 'He phoned me... He called my father a maggot... He said my father "doesn't know who I am".' Hamdan witnessed one confrontation between the two men at the Grosvenor House Hotel in London. 'Nick suddenly raised his voice and began saying he would not trust Raja to go to the toilet in his house without expecting to lose his girlfriend's jewellery...'

Van Hoogstraten, meanwhile, moved in on Raja's properties. Locks were changed and letters sent to tenants telling them their old landlord was bankrupt, and the new one was Robert Gates and Co. Raja in turn sought an injunction preventing Van Hoogstraten from 'interfering' with his property or making threatening phone calls and of conspiring to cause him injury. The injunction wasn't granted.

Later, in court, Van Hoogstraten would insist that despite all this he and Raja remained on good terms personally. It is difficult to believe. In 1996 the tycoon fingered Raja as a 'fraudster' in a letter to the Bradford and Bingley Building Society which had given Raja that mortgage. Van Hoogstraten suggested to the building society that it launch bankruptcy proceedings against Raja and he offered to pay the costs himself.

The fight with Van Hoogstraten became Raja's obsession. He talked about it continually. He went to the Sussex police with information which, he said, proved Van Hoogstraten a fraud. The police sent him away. He went to 'every solicitor in Sussex', as one of them put it, asking them to take on the case.

Some turned him down because of the fear the name Van Hoogstraten induced. A standard reply to anyone asking in Brighton and Hove to be represented against Mr H or one of his companies was – and still is – 'but we could get a brick through the window'.

Raja's case seemed moribund. He was largely to blame himself because he appears to have been almost as slippery as Van Hoogstraten. He was loath to give the full facts. It eventually emerged, for example, that he knew Van Hoogstraten had used the blank transfer forms to assume title to some properties, and had accepted it. But he said that he didn't know the extent of the transfers or expect that he wouldn't get the deeds back.

Van Hoogstraten didn't seem to have much to worry about. It was minor stuff to him, just an irritant. But Raja wouldn't leave it. In the summer of 1998 he found a new lawyer in London and took the decision to up the ante. In July he gave notice that he planned to ask the High Court to let him amend his charges against Van Hoogstraten to fraud. The minor irritant was now serious.

Raja was not the only litigant brave enough to take on Van Hoogstraten. As Van Hoogstraten himself saw it, a more serious threat came from a barrister who had once represented him. Michael Kennedy was a specialist in company law. He had represented Van Hoogstraten against the Palmeira Avenue leaseholders in 1992. He lost the case but – unlike other lawyers who unsuccessfully represented Van Hoogstraten – had remained on good terms with him. So good that when Kennedy needed £350,000 to invest in a high-tech company he went to the tycoon. A complex deal was struck. It involved Kennedy borrowing the £350,000 from a Van Hoogstraten company and providing security for the same amount.

In October 1996 Kennedy paid off the £350,000 and asked for the security to be released. He told a friend that when he went down to see him in Hove, Van Hoogstraten just looked at him and said: 'Michael, I'm not giving you a penny back.' The barrister was stunned and left.

Ripping off Kennedy so blatantly was a grave miscalculation by Van Hoogstraten. This was a top barrister who knew the workings of the law and was a member of one of the leading chambers in the Inns of Court. He was neither a confused tenant nor a terrified provincial solicitor. Kennedy sued for return of the security. An acrimonious legal battle began. By 1998 it looked as if Kennedy was winning it.

Both the Raja and Kennedy cases continued to go badly for Van Hoogstraten. In October 1998 the High Court rejected his move to strike out the Raja action. In January he was ordered to pay Raja's costs. Meanwhile Kennedy was granted an injunction which froze £350,000 of Van Hoogstraten's assets. Then in April Raja finally got the go-ahead from the High Court to sue Van Hoogstraten and his companies for conspiracy and fraud.

Of the two antagonists, Van Hoogstraten seemed to take Kennedy much more seriously. He would refer to the Raja case as the 'Raja nonsense' while cursing Kennedy and telling his associates he would 'do' him.

The Kennedy case came to court on 15 April. It was bitterly contested. Accusations about front companies, disreputable business practices and fraud flew around for five days.

Then, out of the blue, Van Hoogstraten waved an olive branch. With the court case still due to run a week, he phoned Kennedy personally and suggested the two have supper that night. They met in London, in the discreet elegance of a French restaurant off Sloane Square. Neither party will tell the details of what transpired. But an out-of-court settlement was reached. Kennedy got his security back and – it was rumoured – Van Hoogstraten also promised him one of his farms in Zimbabwe. If that was the icing on the cake, Kennedy never got to taste it. Before the summer was out war veterans from Zanu PF had taken over the farm. A friend of both men suggested that Van Hoogstraten himself might have tipped his Zimbabwean friends the wink.

Kennedy was off Van Hoogstraten's back, and it might briefly have seemed to the tycoon that Raja would soon be off his back too. As the Kennedy case was coming to its climax, Raja appeared to be making his own peace overtures. On 9 March and again on 23 March he wrote fawning letters to the tycoon suggesting they 'clear this mess up'. Addressing him as 'Dear Nick', he was full of compliments – about Van Hoogstraten's integrity, his wisdom, and even about how well he came over on TV. Van Hoogstraten replied that he agreed 'entirely' that they should settle.

Raja's letters, however, contained no concessions. He still wanted a breakdown of what was owed and what had been paid, and Van Hoogstraten still wouldn't provide it. On 22 April the High Court gave Raja permission to amend his claim against Van Hoogstraten to that of conspiracy to defraud.

Van Hoogstraten would later treat the Raja claim as trivial, small beer to a man of his wealth. If he had lost the case, he said, he would have just written it off against tax.

But, according to the Rajas, the money now involved certainly wasn't small beer. Amjad Raja says his father was talking in terms of Van Hoogstraten owing him millions – maybe three million or more.

The 'maggot', whom he so derided, was standing up to Van Hoogstraten in a way he wasn't used to. What's more, the media were starting to take notice. His desk diary records his irritation. The entry for 5 May says 'BBC Raja nonsense'.

At a property auction attended by Amjad Raja and Michaal Hamdan the tycoon couldn't stop himself giving vent to his feelings. Amjad and Hamdan were talking about the basement flat which Hamdan and Raja senior were fighting over. Amjad asked if his father was a thorn in his side. 'Van Hoogstraten was standing maybe a yard away from me. He stepped forward and said: "You know what we do with those thorns. We pick them and one by one we break them." That hit me. It was a threat. I knew he was talking about my father.'

15

VOICE FROM THE GRAVE

A summer morning on 2 July 1999. A Ford Transit turns into Mulgrave Road in Sutton, south London. What could be more normal, more English? A white van in a suburban street. Tradesmen tending the needs of the middle classes. Plumbers. Builders. Kitchen fitters. Loft converters. No one pays them much attention.

The van stops across the road from number 63. Two men get out. They are wearing blue overalls and matching floppy hats. From the van they take a canvas tool bag and a long-handled fork. Gardeners.

But these white-van men have a secret. The man with the fork has a knife hidden in his overalls. And inside the bag carried by his mate is a sawn-off, single-barrelled shotgun. They ring the doorbell of number 63. Mohammed Raja rises from his desk and goes to answer it. The surprising thing is that he, too, is carrying a knife.

What happens next is seen by people across the street. A scuffle breaks out in the doorway between Raja and the two men. Then a shot is heard. It wakens Raja's two grandsons, Rizvan and Waheed, both students and still in bed though it has gone half-past nine.

'I was sleeping and I was wakened by a really loud noise,' recalls Waheed.

The scene that met them could not have been more horrifying. Their grandfather was bleeding and in obvious pain. A man was standing over him with a knife. Another man was kneeling and reloading a single-barrelled, sawn-off shotgun.

'I saw my granddad and he was in lots of pain. He was bleeding and he was looking at me in my eyes,' says Waheed. 'And I saw these two other men standing there and then I saw one of them was holding a gun. And that's when I realised that it was actually a gunshot.'

The shot they heard had hit the ceiling by the stairs. Mohammed Raja was bleeding because of knife wounds. He had been stabbed five times, and the injuries were sufficient to kill him. But Raja was not going to go quietly. He shouted to his grandsons to call the police – and he screamed something else that stuck in their memory.

'And my grandfather shouts out to us in our native language, Punjabi, that these are Van Hoogstraten's men that have come and hit me,' says Rizvan.

Waheed ran upstairs to dial 999. His brother tried to pull his grandfather away from his assailants, before shielding himself behind the kitchen door. Though grievously injured, Mohammed Raja stumbled out of the hall and into a lounge at the rear of the house.

While this was going on, Waheed was having trouble getting through to the police – he was put on hold by an automatic queuing device. When he finally did get through, he heard another loud bang.

Although he had lost a great deal of blood, Mohammed Raja

was still defiantly holding his knife when the gunman followed him into the lounge. This time the intruder made no mistake, and fired at point-blank range into the dying man's left eye.

As the attackers ran out of the house, they were watched by a couple taking their pet to the vet's surgery across the road. The woman said she thought they were in their twenties or thirties. But they were odd-looking. They had moustaches and wore heavy-framed glasses. Both had long hair that could have been wigs.

The murderers drove off. They turned into Manor Road and after only half a mile pulled into a driveway behind a block of flats. They doused the van with petrol and set it alight. An elderly resident, Margaret Perry, heard the noise. She looked out of her window and saw the white van and the two men, one of whom she later described as being about eighteen years old. When the men spotted her, they ran off.

The driveway was right beside the A217, a major route running south through Sutton towards the M25. If the murderers had accomplices waiting with another vehicle, they could quickly have driven anywhere in the country.

When Waheed Raja's call was received in the 999 call centre, it put in motion a series of rapid events. An operator routed the call to a Metropolitan Police operations room which dispatched local police officers to Mulgrave Road. The ambulance service was also alerted.

Shortly afterwards a call was made to a run-down Victorian pile in Eltham, south-east London. The building sits on Shooters Hill, at the junction with Well Hall Road – the road on which Stephen Lawrence, a black teenager, was killed by a racist gang in 1993, a notorious attack for which no one was brought to justice. Just around the corner, two of the suspects in the Lawrence case hurled racist abuse at an off-duty black police officer in 2001. For this, they were imprisoned for eighteen months the following year. It is not a place for the fainthearted.

At first glance, the building on the corner appears derelict. Leaves and rubbish collected around the main entrance indicate it is never used. Only the cars parked in the sloping yard at the back give any sign that people work here.

This is the unlikely headquarters of AMIT – the Area Major Investigation Team – the branch of the Metropolitan Police that investigates all serious crime in south London.

To enter their shabby HQ, the detectives climb an iron fire escape from the yard and go through a steel door on the first floor. This takes them directly into a long, shabby kitchen that doubles as a canteen. At the far end, a dismal corridor leads away to the offices.

When the news of the Raja murder came through to AMIT, a call was made to Detective Chief Inspector Chris Horne, the unit's senior investigating officer. He was at the Old Bailey, attending a murder trial.

Chris Horne was a career detective who had made it into the CID after three years in uniform. He was a no-nonsense type whose twenty-five years' experience as a detective gave him a low-key but decisive manner.

After taking the call DCI Horne immediately ordered a forensics unit to Mulgrave Road. Their first task would be to cordon off the scene and make sure that no clues could be disturbed. In any murder case the best thing any investigating officer has going for him is the scene of the crime itself. The murder scene is the physical link to the perpetrator.

Horne got in his car and drove to Sutton. When he arrived he found to his dismay that local police and ambulance men had trampled through the scene of the crime. They had gone through the front door – just as the murderers had done. They had followed their route to the lounge at the back of the house, where the body of Mohammed Raja was found. Furniture had been moved to give paramedics more room to examine the victim.

As an old hand, Horne knew what to do. He stood at the doorway and looked down the hall, noting the many bloodstains. Then, instead of going through the house, he went around to the garden and peered in through the French windows. On the other side of the glass he could see the body of Mohammed Raja lying on the floor. His first impression was that Raja had been trying to escape through the French windows when he was shot. Near the body, by a doorway from the lounge into the kitchen, lay a bloodstained knife.

Horne called a meeting of his forensics team. They discussed what evidence should be collected. There was an enormous amount of blood around the house, smears, blobs and pools of it, on floors, walls, furniture and on the dead man himself – forty or fifty separate bloodstains in all.

One of the forensics team asked: 'How many swabs do we take, boss?'

Horne did not hesitate. 'Every single one,' he replied. It was important to know if all the blood at the scene of the crime was solely that of the victim. If it wasn't, then some could have come from one of his attackers, injured during a struggle. It was a painstaking approach that was to pay off handsomely later in the inquiry.

The team went to work. Among the bloodstains they noticed some small blobs on the front door. What made them interesting was that they were on the leading edge, where the door fits against the frame when closed. The blood could only have been deposited there while the door was open. The door was carefully unscrewed from its hinges, wrapped in polythene and taken to the Home Office forensic laboratory in Lambeth for testing.

The investigation was helped by Mohammed Raja's grandsons

having seen a great deal. So the fact that their grandfather had been attacked by two men was immediately established. Then there were the dying man's last words – that he had been attacked by Van Hoogstraten's men. It seemed that Mohammed Raja was reaching out from the grave and giving the police a steer as to where to go.

Chris Horne was too seasoned a campaigner to fall for the first theory that presented itself. 'One of the worst things for an investigating officer is to have tunnel vision,' he says. 'You have to look at everything.' However, he knew that if there was a link between Raja and Van Hoogstraten, his job was to find it, analyse it and either discount it or act on it.

The burned-out van was examined minutely for clues. In the back were the burned remains of blue overalls, a charred knife and several burned fertiliser bags. The van was towed away to be minutely examined at the forensic laboratory for fingerprints and DNA traces.

That evening at Sutton police station Horne had an unexpected visitor – Commissioner Hugh Orde. It was unheard of for such a senior officer to attend the scene of what was, after all, just one more murder. But the killing at Mulgrave Road had rung alarm bells for top brass at New Scotland Yard.

The McPherson Report on the way police had handled the Stephen Lawrence murder had just been published. It made several damning criticisms of the Metropolitan Police, including incompetence and endemic racism within the force.

Now two white men had murdered an Asian man in south London. The Met could not afford this one to go wrong. Hugh Orde left Chris Horne in no doubt that a quick and efficient investigation was required.

Horne reflected that this was no more than what he intended. He knew that time was both an ally and an enemy of detective work. It was important to gather intelligence about all suspects as quickly as possible. Speed would provide suspects with less opportunity to cover their tracks.

The first people Horne questioned were the murdered man's family. Had they any idea of who could have done it? Mohammed's son Amjad was asked for the names of people who might have had a reason to want his father out of the way.

Amjad said his father had a number of continuing disputes, mostly over property or money. Among them was one with a businessman from the north-west of England, and another with two brothers in Essex.

Two disputes stood out from the rest – the squabble with Michaal Hamdan over the flat in Brunswick Square, and the litigation against Nicholas van Hoogstraten over the loans.

Hamdan was a close associate of Van Hoogstraten and might conceivably have shared a taste for violence. But given the dead man's last words and Van Hoogstraten's reputation, Van Hoogstraten looked much the stronger suspect.

Rizvan said that a few months before the attack, Mohammed Raja had told him he was about to win his case against Van Hoogstraten. Then his grandfather had advised him that if anyone rang the doorbell, he should always look through the window to check who it was. Whether or not he took his own advice, we shall never know. But if he did, it was not enough to save him.

If Van Hoogstraten was behind the murder, could one of the attackers have been the tycoon himself? The team ruled out this possibility because of his age. Van Hoogstraten was fifty-four, while eye-witnesses put the attackers in their twenties or thirties. But Raja's words were enough to put Van Hoogstraten at the top of their list of suspects.

The police had to keep an open mind. Even members of the immediate family had to be eliminated as suspects. A list was drawn up of just about everyone who knew the dead man. Having thrown their net as widely as possible, the detectives set about their next task: going through their catch to gradually eliminate people from their inquiry.

Detective Constable Hugh Ellis was given the task of gathering intelligence on Van Hoogstraten. A few hours after the murder he was in Uckfield to talk to the local police about their best-known resident. He remembers that the Uckfield police had little information beyond the millionaire's well-known reputation as a forceful person not to be trifled with, who had a hobby of feuding with the Ramblers' Association. Why should they have more?

DC Ellis travelled on to Brighton, hoping for better luck with the police there. The local CID were helpful and Ellis was soon looking through their intelligence file on Van Hoogstraten. The millionaire's past was about to come back to haunt him.

The file listed Van Hoogstraten's various brushes with the law, including his prison sentence for the grenade attack on the Braunsteins. It also contained a list of people he knew. This was much more like it. Among the names Ellis wrote down was that of a career armed robber called Robert Knapp.

It was late at night when Ellis returned to London, but the information he carried with him was to prove central to the investigation.

Robert Knapp had a record stretching back twenty-five years or more. It included sentences for attempted robbery, for possession of a sawn-off shotgun and a revolver without a licence, another for theft, another for burglary and two very long stints for armed robbery.

Knapp and Van Hoogstraten had remained in contact ever since they had first met in prison around thirty years before. Knapp had continued with his career as a heavy-duty gangster. His 'previous' was impressive. One of the investigating team later said of him: 'Here was somebody who had some association with Van Hoogstraten and had a long history of criminality himself.

He was clearly an individual who perhaps had the right frame of mind to carry out this type of offence.'

The spectacular nature of one particular robbery told a great deal about Knapp's character. This was the Putney jewellery shop raid in 1994. Knapp went armed with a handgun and his accomplice carried a shotgun. When they entered the shop, they fired into the ceiling, leaving staff under no illusions as to their intent.

They fled with a large quantity of jewellery and ran slap into a reception party of armed police. There had been a tip-off and the Flying Squad was waiting. Faced by superior forces who had the drop on them, most robbers would have given themselves up. But not Knapp and his accomplice. They exchanged shots with the police and held them off long enough to form an escape plan. They made a dash under a hail of bullets to a police car and leapt in. They drove off, pursued by the outwitted and furious Flying Squad officers.

After a short chase a police car managed to ram them. Knapp's accomplice ran off, firing repeatedly at the pursuing police before being wounded. At that point he turned his gun on himself and committed suicide. Knapp, more wisely, realised the game was up and surrendered. He was given twelve years. Ellis noted that Knapp had been released from Long Lartin prison on 21 April – only ten weeks before the murder of Mohammed Raja.

Ellis did some more digging. He came across a Home Office record listing all those who had applied to visit Knapp in prison. Permission had to be granted because Knapp had been a high-security Category A prisoner. Among his visitors was Nicholas van Hoogstraten.

At a meeting of the murder team on 27 July, Knapp and Van Hoogstraten were discussed in detail. Neither was looked upon as a suspect for the actual hit. Van Hoogstraten was too old. Knapp, too, was getting on a bit and, like many an old con before him, had a serious liking for Class A drugs, especially heroin. There were also the eye-witness reports of the hit men being much younger.

It was felt that if Knapp was involved it would have been to organise the hit, hiring the assailants and so on. Horne asked his team for more information on Knapp, his connection with Van Hoogstraten and with any other likely villains who could have been involved.

The team reviewed the case so far. It could have been an attempt to frighten or threaten Mohammed Raja. Or the intention might have been to injure him, either as revenge or a warning. It was thought unlikely that it was a robbery gone wrong. If it had been, why did the gunman feel it necessary to run after the dying man and finish him off with a shot to the head? If this was so, could it have been a contract killing?

The main puzzle facing the police was why was the hit so badly done? It did not appear to be a properly planned murder at all. Two men had gone to Raja's house armed with a single-barrelled shotgun and a knife. If they had merely intended to threaten or scare him, surely they could have found more subtle methods. If their intention was simply to rough him up, why the knife, why the gun? So much seemed so odd.

And that took them to Van Hoogstraten. If he had hired them, why these amateurs? This puzzled Chris Horne.

'Van Hoogstraten was rich. He could have afforded to hire the best,' he says. 'I thought if he had wanted Raja killed, he would have been more organised, done it in a better way. For £1000 you can hire a professional hit man.'

The murder did not fit the usual pattern of contract killings. They typically involve a hit man approaching his victim in an accessible place such as the street. They would shoot with an automatic pistol at point-blank range before making a swift getaway, perhaps on the back of a motorcycle driven by an accomplice.

In the case of Mohammed Raja, the attackers turned up in elaborate disguises involving false moustaches, glasses and wigs. They were primitively armed with a single-barrelled shotgun and a knife. They grappled with their victim by the front door in view of people on the street, before having to run through the house to deliver the coup de grâce. As one of the investigation team, Detective Inspector Andy Sladen, observed: 'It's not a fantastically professional contract killing – certainly not the sort of thing that Frederick Forsyth would write about.'

He had a point. In the film of Forsyth's novel The Day of the Jackal, the dashing assasin played by Edward Fox drives an Alfa-Romeo sports car. Mohammed Raja's attackers made their getaway in an old Ford Transit van. It had been bought by a man giving a false name and address, who paid £200 cash. The van had been customised, making it stand out from all the thousands of other white vans on Britain's roads. Two green stripes had been painted along its sides and on a large sign above the driver's cab was written 'THUNDERBIRDS TWO'. It was more Del Boy than Carlos the Jackal.

Horne needed to find a motive. The place to look for it was in the dead man's office, among his business papers.

DC Ellis began the task. Every scrap of paper had to be gone through. 'The papers were put into three large piles. Between them, they measured six feet high,' he remembers. Some of the papers made no sense by themselves. Ellis would seek clarification with Amjad Raja, who would help to put them into context. Among a lifetime's correspondence, contracts and legal documents, three documents stood out. They were copies of letters exchanged between Mohammed Raja and Van Hoogstraten three months before Raja's death.

The first one, dated 9 March 1999, was from Raja to Van Hoogstraten. In the Asian style, it was rather flowery and flattering, and spoke of Raja's respect for Van Hoogstraten's integrity and sincerity. It went on to describe him as 'unusually unique' and added, 'By the way, you looked nice on BBC on Monday night.'

But the letter's real intent was not flattery. Raja asked Van Hoogstraten to provide 'further explanations and clarifications' to help clear up what he referred to as 'this mess between us'. Ellis realised the letter's importance. It provided written confirmation of a dispute between the two men.

Van Hoogstraten replied on 17 March, saying that he agreed entirely that they should try to settle their differences – and do so 'without legal proceedings which only enriches the lawyers'. He had always been willing to meet to arrange a settlement and he would telephone to fix up a meeting. He signed off, 'Kind regards, Nicholas.' An amicable letter, thought Ellis.

He found a reply from Raja, dated 23 March, saying: 'I wish I was brought up in such a wise atmosphere as yours which makes you a winner.' Raja went on to say that 'as you expressed your honourable intention' they should think what he would get for several properties. The letter listed eight addresses in Brighton and London and added, 'and other properties in your possession'. To Ellis, the implication was clear: Van Hoogstraten may have had possession of the properties but Raja believed they belonged to him.

Raja's letter continued: 'Please Nick! You know I am honest and truthful and sincere and genuine. Thus I expect you to respond accordingly, probably we can sort out our differences in daring way and keep these money grabbers and greedy solicitors out of the way.' He ended with a reference to the legal action he was pursuing against Van Hoogstraten: 'Please Nick! Send me replies to my further and better particulars so that I don't have to make further applications and avoid embarrassment.'

Ellis thought that, despite the polite tone, the letter was that of a man making a last effort to settle a dispute and threatening stronger legal measures. It could not have had the desired effect, for a few weeks later Raja successfully applied to the High Court to bring an action against Van Hoogstraten for fraud.

For the next few weeks the murder team sifted through evidence, interviewed friends, relations and business contacts and whittled away at their initial long list of suspects. They began to look at Knapp's associates and soon discovered he knew another seasoned robber with a taste for violence and guns. His name was David Croke. He and Knapp had done time together for similar offences.

Croke's criminal career had an all-too-common trajectory. He began with shoplifting, quickly moving up to armed robbery and then sliding into long stretches at Her Majesty's pleasure. His career effectively ended in 1986 when he and two accomplices hijacked a security van containing £283,000 in cash. There had been a tip-off and they were under police surveillance. The rest was the usual downward spiral of arrest, charge, trial and sentence.

That was only the beginning of the bad times for Croke. A long-time accomplice turned Queen's Evidence. Croke was found guilty of several other serious crimes. Among them were taking £250,000 from another security van, stealing £90,000 from a security depot after strapping a mock bomb to a guard and robbing £480,000 cash from a bank after holding a security guard and his wife and daughter hostage.

Croke got twenty-three years, reduced to twenty on appeal. His many victims got a lifetime of trauma after being held captive, bound and gagged, threatened with guns and – ultimate horror – having what they thought were real bombs strapped to their bodies.

David Croke had been released from prison on 6 May, two months before the Raja murder. Here was a man who would do anything for money, thought the detectives.

The results of the DNA blood tests came through in early September. Almost all the samples from the house matched those taken from Mohammed Raja. But a tiny amount – taken from the blood on the edge of the door – did not.

This was important news. The unidentified blood could be from one of the attackers. Police had to eliminate all other possibilities. The DNA from the anonymous sample had to be compared with DNA from the Raja family and everyone else who had a legitimate reason to have entered the house.

The DNA samples were collected by taking swabs of saliva from inside the mouth of each person, and were sent for analysis to the Home Office forensic laboratory. Swabs were taken from the immediate family, their relations and in-laws, their friends, the postman, taxi drivers and even the milkman. More than a hundred people voluntarily had their DNA tested.

The painstaking sifting of all the connections to the murdered man – their possible motives and their whereabouts on the day – continued throughout the summer. The team kept an open mind, looking into every possibility, while keeping their main theory and suspect uppermost.

Contract killings are notoriously difficult to investigate. Even if police quickly identify someone as a strong suspect with a clear motive for ordering the hit, it is difficult to pin the crime on them. The simple fact is that there is usually little or no evidence linking the person who pays for the hit with those who carry it out. Nothing is ever in writing and there are no witnesses to the contract.

By the autumn, the investigation was going slowly. There was no evidence linking Van Hoogstraten with the murder and no motive for Knapp or Croke. Usually, murder cases are solved quite quickly. If a result is not obtained after about six months has passed, the inquiry may be scaled down or put on the back burner so that manpower can be diverted to the wave of new cases rolling in.

Chris Horne and his team felt the pressure. The Metropolitan Police were still receiving criticism over the botched investigation into the Stephen Lawrence murder. If they failed to find sufficient evidence even to charge anyone for the murder of an Asian businessman on their patch, the bad smell could become overpowering.

By now it was business as usual for their number-one suspect. In a case similar to that in Palmeira Avenue, Van Hoogstraten was involved in a struggle over ownership of a building divided into flats. Once more the leaseholders were moving to buy the freehold. In order to prevent them reaching a majority to force the sale of the freehold, Van Hoogstraten created a new leasehold flat for one of his companies – out of a broom cupboard.

He also had some pressures on his cash flow. In 1999 he was spending large sums from his own resources on improving his hotels, building his palace and developing his African estates.

At Shooters Hill, detectives still had insufficient evidence to arrest or interrogate Van Hoogstraten. There was nothing connecting him with the murder that they could put to him. In fact, Horne was still far from sure that he had anything to do with it.

If all the uncertainty was not enough, Horne had something else weighing on his mind. He had been asked to take up another job. His newly appointed boss, a superintendent, wanted Horne to review other murder inquiries. The idea was that weekly check-ups would help ensure that officers on all inquiries were always making progress.

Horne was unhappy about the idea. He was an investigating officer at heart and did not want what he saw as merely an administrative job. He told his boss he wished to continue with the Raja case and see it through. The superintendent pressed Horne to take up the new position. Horne refused. A sort of stand-off developed, with neither one giving way.

Meanwhile it was obvious the Raja murder team needed more leads. Horne decided they should seek publicity on BBC's Crimewatch programme. Every week the programme appeals to the public for information to help solve crimes. These appeals are often very successful and the programme has contributed to many a villain being convicted.

On 10 October 1999 the show carried a report on the murder. It was carefully prepared so as not to tell the whole story. Key facts were changed or kept back.

'I made a deliberate decision, as in all murder investigations, to withhold information,' says Horne. 'This is something we do as a routine.'

The reason for this is to help police discount false confessions. People often come forward and claim to have committed murder. They may be deluded, attention-seekers or time-wasters who love a twisted thrill. Whatever their reason, some facts are always kept from the press to catch them out.

If a person walks into a police station and says they have committed a particular murder, the first thing they are asked is how they did it. If their description of the murder tallies with the deliberately erroneous one given out by the press, police know they are not the real murderer.

There is, of course, another good reason for keeping some details back. In a rare case, the real murderer might be interviewed and let slip a detail unknown to the general public. This is the kind of thing that often happens in television detective series but in reality almost never does.

The Crimewatch report included a reconstruction of the murder with actors playing the parts of Mohammed Raja, his grandsons and the two hit men. The Raja family bravely allowed it to be filmed at the house. The reconstruction was to play a major part in the investigation, so it is worth describing how it went.

At the beginning Mohammed Raja is seen in his office on the

first floor. Then two men dressed as gardeners and aged in their twenties or thirties get out of a white Transit van and walk up to the front door. Raja opens the door and the men burst in.

The film then cuts to Raja's two grandsons asleep in their beds. A bang is heard and they wake up and come downstairs. They see their grandfather in the hall. We see no blood, but he shouts: 'I've been hit.'

Next one of the intruders is seen reloading a single-barrelled shotgun. Mohammed Raja and one of his grandsons run into a room and shut the door. The gunman bursts in and points the gun at Raja. The two assailants flee.

At no time does the film show Mohammed Raja being stabbed, nor do we see the first shot missing. We only hear a shot being fired.

Next we see the gunman reloading the shotgun, and then pointing it at the doomed man. We do not see or hear him shoot, but it looks as if Raja is about to be killed.

There was a good response to the programme. People phoned in, reporting that they had seen the van in various locations in the days before the murder. Horne set his team to follow up all the new leads.

Then he went on holiday. He had been working solidly all year, going from one case directly to the next without a break. He felt this was as good a time as any to get a rest. But he was not to get the relaxation he had hoped for. Within a day or two one of his team telephoned him to say that a new Chief Inspector had moved into his office.

Horne was devastated. He knew the person who had been moved in to replace him. Dick Heselden was a much younger man who had been promoted into the CID after coming first in his sergeants' exam. He had been fast-streamed for promotion to high rank and had been parachuted into Horne's job at Shooters Hill.

The older man was crushed. His friends and colleagues on the case were shocked. A change in leadership can unsettle any team – but this one had happened without warning and behind the current leader's back. The trouble was that the tenacity that makes a good detective can, in different circumstances, manifest itself as stubbornness. For Horne's superiors, it had, sadly, seemed the only way.

If all of this was not unsettling enough, the Raja investigation team received another bolt from the blue. They had been working every hour they could, running up large amounts of overtime. Now overtime was cut. It was a double blow.

The Raja family heard the news of the changes with dismay. They had got to know and trust Horne. So why was he being moved? The investigation into the murder of Stephen Lawrence had suffered from several destabilising changes at the top. Because of that, one of the recommendations made in the McPherson Report was that there should be continuity of leadership in all murder cases.

There was a sense of unease, especially among the members of the Raja family. Perhaps the Raja inquiry was about to go the way of the Stephen Lawrence affair.

16

THE CHICKENS COME
HOME TO ROOST

The murder team was anxious to see how the new Chief Inspector would shape up. Dick Heselden was a stocky young Londoner, still in his thirties, and very ambitious. His manner was restless, that of a man keen to move on. His speech was rapid and fluid. There was a feeling of energy.

He would need it. He had vigour and intelligence on his side, but not the experience of his predecessor. Chris Horne had largely built the team Heselden was taking over. Not only had the new boss to handle all the new murder cases coming in, he had to read himself into those already up and running. But his first crucial task was to show leadership and win over the team.

Heselden's arrival coincided with the investigation's six-month review. This is standard practice for every murder inquiry. It was carried out by Chief Inspector Brian Bowden-Brown. His main recommendation was simple: that Nicholas van Hoogstraten should be investigated urgently.

To mount a case against the tycoon it would require perseverance – and the co-operation of the Raja family. And here was a problem. The Rajas had written to the local paper in Sutton and to their MP, Paul Burstow, asking for Chris Horne to be kept on the case.

Heselden met the Rajas and reassured them that the case was not being sidelined. He told them he would do all in his power to ensure the murderers were brought to justice. The Raja family promised their support.

However, the Rajas were far from passive by nature. From then on, they bombarded Heselden with calls, asking what was happening and when an arrest would be made. They were a tenacious family. The traits that had enabled Mohammed to claw his way up to create a business had rubbed off on his children. All three of his daughters were lawyers and they were determined to see their father's killers brought to justice.

Heselden decided on a change of strategy. Van Hoogstraten would be invited in for questioning. The Chief Inspector reasoned that the tycoon would expect to be questioned anyway, so an interview should not ring any extra alarm bells for him. They had nothing on him so the move was a gamble. It was merely a fishing expedition.

On 18 November Van Hoogstraten voluntarily walked into Hove police station for questioning. As usual he was punctual and politely greeted the detectives who were to interview him. Hugh Ellis and Chris Moore had expected him to come with his solicitor and were surprised that he turned up alone.

The detectives showed Van Hoogstraten through to a small room. They switched on the tape recorder and the interview began at eleven minutes past four. For the benefit of the tape, Ellis and Moore read Van Hoogstraten his rights and asked if everything was all right. He answered that everything was fine except that they had been given the broom cupboard. The three men laughed.

The detectives asked Van Hoogstraten about his business dealings with Raja. He told them he had first met Raja in the early eighties at property auctions. Their first business dealings had taken place around 1987 or 1988 when he sold Raja a terraced house in Chippenham Road, Maida Vale.

To help Raja complete the sale, Van Hoogstraten loaned him £30,000. He wanted to get rid of the property, otherwise he would not have done business with Raja at all. Van Hoogstraten said it was well known that Raja did not pay his debts and was hard up. After the property crash at the end of the 1980s Raja was 'in a sinking ship'.

Disarmingly, Van Hoogstraten appeared happy to tell the detectives all about his commercial property dealings. He disliked doing business with Mohammed Raja, but got on better with his son Amjad, whom he helped out by asking him to manage some of his property lettings. He told how he gave Amjad houses that had what he called problem tenants. In return, he would split the profits when there were any.

All of this poured out almost unprompted. The tape kept running and the detectives listened.

Unbidden, Van Hoogstraten brought up what he saw as the crunch moment between himself and Raja. At auctions, Raja got carried away and bought properties for which he didn't have the ready cash.

'He would come running to whoever he could run to, and sometimes it was me,' said Van Hoogstraten.

Sometimes things were so bad for Raja that his cheque for the deposit bounced. Van Hoogstraten helped him out. Either he himself or one of his companies bought the property for Raja. This gave Raja breathing space. He would then have anything from one to three months to come up with the balance. If he failed, Van Hoogstraten ended up with a property he usually didn't want and that was that.

The picture Van Hoogstraten painted was of a rich, clever man helping out a poorer, not very clever one. 'You know,' he told

Ellis and Moore, 'he just didn't have a clue, honestly. He used to buy unbelievable shit.'

Eventually Raja stopped paying money back. According to Van Hoogstraten, Raja owed money to several companies connected to him – Rarebargain, Robert Gates and Co, Unifox, Barnhill. And he owed money to Van Hoogstraten personally. The time came to repossess some Raja properties on which he had lent money.

This was Van Hoogstraten in full flood. For the two detectives seeing it for the first time, it was an experience. The millionaire liked nothing so much as a captive audience. The detectives were paid to listen. Even better, they were being paid by someone else.

With a dismissive wave of the hand, Van Hoogstraten said he viewed Raja's allegations of fraud as 'a source of amusement'. He said all he was doing was buying buildings from the receivers after they had been repossessed from Raja. It was 'a joke'. Raja had already ceased to own the properties.

He laughed again. He was having a good time – the millionaire instructing a couple of mere detective constables on the ways of the rich.

Finally the bemused Ellis and Moore got their act together and asked about the disputed properties. On the first one, Van Hoogstraten said he had bought it for cash from Raja – so what was the problem? As for the next one, Raja had defrauded him in a double scam, raising a loan with him while also taking out a mortgage with someone else.

The air in the small room was getting murkier. The detectives moved to the alleged fraud. Raja had claimed Van Hoogstraten had fraudulently transferred ownership of the building to himself.

Van Hoogstraten batted this aside. He claimed that Raja's answer to anything he didn't like was to claim someone had forged his signature on a contract. The atmosphere was thicker now. Van Hoogstraten told how he sold another house to the

Rajas and bought it back – or maybe it was the other way round, he couldn't remember. The detectives were seeing less and less clearly now.

The conversation entered a truly surreal realm when Van Hoogstraten declared that when the money from Raja dried up it was funny.

Anyone who knew Van Hoogstraten knew there was one thing he never ever joked about – money. And now here he was, in a cramped little room in a police station, chewing the fat with two men who earned less between them in a year than he had been spending in a week. Van Hoogstraten had amassed his wealth because money was what mattered. After all, money was what had moved him to make many of his most memorable public utterances: Isn't that what it's all about? She was taking the piss. He deserved to have his bollocks chopped off. I'm not standing for it.

When the first tape began to spool out after forty minutes, the detectives asked Van Hoogstraten if he wanted a break. 'No,' he said, 'put a new one on.' Their guest was clearly staying.

When the new tape was running, Ellis enquired if Raja had ever asked him for a breakdown of whatever he thought Van Hoogstraten owed him. Van Hoogstraten said Raja had never asked him but he might have asked his solicitors. Ellis then asked if he had threatened Raja – had he said he was going to slap him? Van Hoogstraten laughed, saying that it was a joke. Had he called Raja a maggot? No, he hadn't. 'But it could be a very apt description of him … a maggot in our society.'

Ellis moved on to the next subject, the house in Brunswick Square. Was Hamdan fronting for Van Hoogstraten – did he have some control over the building? Absolutely none, which was a shame because 'it must be worth half a million pounds'.

By now Ellis and Moore had learned a great deal more about the twists and turns of the property business than they had bargained for. As so many had found before, Van Hoogstraten is happy to chat away for hours. And he is never happier than when delivering a master class in investment to the uninitiated.

Ellis decided to wind things up.

By the way, he said, the murder had been on Crimewatch. Van Hoogstraten said he had seen it. He wanted to know if what was shown was what had actually happened.

Moore carefully gave a noncommittal answer. 'They achieved what they wanted.'

Somehow the subject changed and Van Hoogstraten said that he had something to tell them he had never told anyone before.

One day Raja had arrived at his office with a bag full of grubby US banknotes, about $120,000 worth, that he wanted to pay him with. 'Well,' said Van Hoogstraten, 'you know what's going through your heads – the same as went through mine. I'm being set up here.

'The next thing that's going to happen is the door's going to crash in and we're going to get nicked for money laundering, drugs, all that.'

He got hold of the bag and thrust it back to Raja. Took him by the scruff of the neck and booted him out.

Raja later explained to Van Hoogstraten that the money had been obtained from traditional Muslim bankers, who ran a system parallel to the Western banking system and known as Halawi banking.

The interviewee was playing with the minds of the listening detectives, fingering the dead man for serious crimes. If any of it were true, Raja could have been hit by all sorts of people.

Van Hoogstraten brought up the subject of Crimewatch once more. He was tickled by it. The way it was put in the papers, he said, it was obviously 'a professional hit. Somebody's gone and done him. But when you see it on the television, well, it's a joke. That's not a professional hit.'

DC Moore once again deflected the question. 'They achieved

their objective, didn't they?' The detectives next discussed the letters between Van Hoogstraten and Raja that had been found at the house in Sutton. Yes, Van Hoogstraten vaguely remembered them. Ellis suggested that the letters related to a recent allegation of fraud. Oh no, said Van Hoogstraten, the fraud allegation came much earlier.

It was a classic Van Hoogstraten moment. The disarming honesty. The unexpected swerve. Ellis decided to get to the heart of the matter. He told Van Hoogstraten that the fraud allegation could be a motive for the murder.

Van Hoogstraten replied that it would be 'scraping the barrel'. 'I mean, it's ludicrous.' With a derisory laugh, he asked: 'Is that the high point of the case?'

Ellis asked bluntly: 'Do you know where you were on 2 July 2002?'

'Oh, just listen, just a minute – seeing that blinking Crimewatch, was I the one? Come off it!' exclaimed Van Hoogstraten. He'd never had a gun in his life. One of his people would have a record of where he was. He'd get David Englehart or Andrew Emmanuel to tell them. Tie up the loose ends.

It was a blooming joke. 'I shouldn't be laughing, really, should I? Because at the end of the day, the poor guy's dead.'

So did he have any ideas? It could only be drugs. 'Drugs or someone he owes a lot of money to.'

By now Ellis wanted to end the interview. As a fishing expedition, it was getting nowhere.

But Van Hoogstraten had a question. 'A couple of my girlfriends and other people that know about all this asked me about this Crimewatch thing. Is that what really happened?'

'Yeah,' said Ellis. This single word opened the first real dialogue of the interview. Until now, it had been a one-way street, with the millionaire giving tuition in property investment and moneylending.

'Is that what goes on?' he asked.

'That was an accurate account of the incident.' DC Moore was playing his straight bat.

'But when they went there, how did they miss him the first time, then?' asked Van Hoogstraten.

This was the moment that much much later rang bells for the two detectives. But it was the end of a long interview. Van Hoogstraten had said something that would eventually seem revealing about his knowledge of the murder. How did he know the first shot had missed? The Crimewatch reconstruction did not show a shot missing. For an hour and twenty minutes they'd been round the houses in the whirligig world of moneylending, freeholds, leaseholds. They failed to pick up on the question.

'By this time we'd been trying to shut him up,' says Ellis.

They wrapped up the interview at 5.32 pm. Van Hoogstraten walked back to the Courtlands Hotel.

As Ellis and Moore returned to London, it seemed their boss's gamble had not paid off. But Van Hoogstraten's curiosity about the Crimewatch report was like a little clock. Unseen, unheard, but ticking.

It was back to work as usual for the investigation team. They held a meeting to discuss the relative merits of all suspects. Using a system to award points for motive, opportunity and so on, suspects were put in order of preference. Those with the fewest points were dropped. Among them were women and any men outside an age band of twenty to fifty.

Several suspects remained. Detectives travelled to Liverpool to see a businessman that Raja had been in dispute with. He was ruled out. They went to Dagenham to see the two brothers he had had a spat with there. They, too, were dropped from the list.

It was decided to have a closer look at Michaal Hamdan. Amjad Raja told the police that after the murder, Hamdan had suggested to him that two people were likely suspects for killing his father: 'Me and Van Hoogstraten, and I didn't do it.'

The row over the flat at 6 Brunswick Square came under the spotlight. Michaal Hamdan was a perplexing figure. Was he his own man or was he a protective shield for Van Hoogstraten? The murder team found him difficult to work out. Amjad Raja thought that Hamdan was acting as a front for Van Hoogstraten, the real owner of the freehold. The team invited Hamdan in for questioning.

On 19 January 2000 Hamdan went to Chelsea police station, where he was met by Hugh Ellis. The conversation quickly got on to the subject of Brunswick Square. Was he fronting for Van Hoogstraten? He said he was not. It was his own property. He had been trying to buy the flat from Raja for ages to gain vacant possession. Around the time of the murder, he and Raja were close to a deal. The Lebanese claimed that the death of Raja scuppered that deal and left him back at square one.

The conversation moved on to Van Hoogstraten. To Ellis's surprise, Hamdan began to bad-mouth his friend and then made a surprising offer. He could keep in touch and inform them about what Van Hoogstraten was doing and thinking.

It seemed that the police might now have an inside track on the tycoon ... if Hamdan meant what he said.

In the meantime, the man who sold the Transit van used in the hit was helping police. He remembered that the man who bought it said he supported Leyton Orient. Police asked him to watch hours of video footage recorded by CCTV cameras at the team's Brisbane Road ground to see if he could spot the buyer. They even took him to a match to scour the crowd. It was a long shot and produced nothing except eye strain.

In the spring of 2000 a £20,000 reward was offered for information leading to the arrest of the killer or killers. The Raja family put up £17,500 of it. Usually the offer of good reward money brings out whispers from the underworld. On this occasion there was nothing. Dick Heselden found the lack of new leads dispiriting.

'Never had an award that size produced less information,' he says. The team began to think the killers must have been brought in from abroad.

Hamdan's offer of help was put into play on 10 April 2000. Hugh Ellis walked into Harrods department store in Knightsbridge to meet him for lunch. The detective was wearing a concealed microphone and a tape recorder was running in his inside pocket. As soon as they sat down to eat, Hamdan began to describe conversations he'd had with Van Hoogstraten about Raja. What he alleged seemed compelling to the detective. And Hamdan was willing to go further. He offered to have himself miked up by the police and then attempt to get his supposed friend to incriminate himself on tape.

Ellis was non-commital. Later, after he reported in at Shooter's Hill, the murder team discussed Hamdan's offer and his motives. Much hung on his story that he and Raja had been near to a deal over Palmeira Square. If that were true then it certainly wouldn't have made sense for him to have Raja killed – Raja's death would leave him as far away as ever from gaining vacant possession of the building. On the other hand, if he was lying about the deal, maybe he was lying about everything. Maybe he was himself behind the murder. What better cover than to frame Van Hoogstraten?

Raja's papers didn't provide an answer, but his son Amjad did. He confirmed that, in the weeks before his father was killed, he and Hamdan had been on the point of agreement. Hamdan, it seemed, was in the clear

But using him in an attempt, even if there was no basis for the thought that he might, to get Van Hoogstraten to incriminate himself might be self-defeating. If the police did mike him up it might well be seen as entrapment. Instead, they decided to try to keep meeting Hamdan, get everything they could out of him and persuade him to put it all down in a signed statement.

Meanwhile, at the murder HQ in Eltham, all energy was directed towards the search for accomplices who could have carried out the murder.

Knapp's mobile phone records were checked. They were a revelation. During the weeks before the murder, Knapp and Croke spoke daily, sometimes even several times a day. On 2 July, the day of the murder, the calls stopped. The inquiry team deduced that Knapp was calling Croke to arrange for him and someone else, as yet unidentified, to do the hit.

For DCI Heselden, this was a much-needed breakthrough. 'It seemed unusual to us that people would be in touch with each other two, three, four times a day, early in the morning, late at night, and then on the day of the murder the contact would stop.'

The investigation had a new momentum. Now the full weight of the investigation was on Croke. Detectives trawled for known villains connected to him in an attempt to find the other hit man. They found none. But they did come up with a link between Croke and the getaway van. This came about because the van had been spotted in Clacton.

Clacton-on-Sea, a down-at-heel Victorian resort in Essex. A great deal of time and manpower revealed that Croke's ex-wife lived there. Surveillance revealed Croke was staying with her.

This was a breakthrough. And then calamity. Croke vanished.

He had been tipped off that the police were on to him. The tip-off came from the police themselves. Letters had been sent out to everyone wanted for the voluntary mass screening for DNA samples – the milkman, the postman and so on – and David Croke. Because of his association with Robert Knapp, his name was on the list.

The investigation team had no option but to write to all the known criminals on their list of suspects. Collecting DNA samples covertly by putting those with criminal form under surveillance and then picking up discarded cigarette ends or paper coffee cups for testing would be no good. Any such evidence would not be admissable in court. A direct approach was substituted. Old lags are often asked to account for themselves in serious crime investigations so that they might be eliminated from inquiries.

Dick Heselden now had a choice. He could go looking for Croke, arrest him and get a sample. Or he could wait for him to turn up. He chose the latter course. Croke's name was put out on the Police National Computer as a suspect. All forces around the country were alerted that if they came across him to contact the Met.

Then Knapp disappeared. He had been staying at his mother's cottage on the High Cross estate. There had been a robbery from her garage. Some furniture belonging to Van Hoogstraten had been stolen. Van Hoogstraten blamed Knapp's girlfriend.

When Croke discovered he was a suspect, he could have called Robert Knapp, he called his old mate Robert Knapp. Cash from some tasty Van Hoogstraten furniture could have smoothed his way into hiding. The investigation team learned that Knapp had fled to Ireland.

Knapp's absence meant police could not take a sample of his DNA either. But his mother Sylvia still lived at High Cross. She agreed to be tested. While the police were at her cottage, Sylvia showed them the garage where the robbery had taken place. In the corner they spotted fertiliser bags of the same unusual make as the ones in the burned-out getaway van.

A fingerprint check revealed Robert Knapp's dabs on the bags. There were none on those in the van, but it was another little piece of the jigsaw.

In October Croke was arrested in Lowestoft on a drugs charge.

His car was stopped and police found heroin and amphetamines. Suffolk police immediately contacted the Met. A swab for DNA was taken and sent off to the Home Office forensic laboratory. Croke was released on bail.

Four months went by, and the investigation was flagging. There were no new breakthroughs, no new connections being made, no new witnesses coming forward. On 23 February 2001 the post arrived mid-morning at Shooters Hill, as usual. It lay for a while before someone went through it. Among the letters was one from the forensic laboratory. And there it was – Croke's DNA result. It matched the blood on the Rajas' front door.

The team were jubilant. It was their first big success.

Andy Sladen explained how important it was: 'If someone has stabbed you they've had to come very close to you to do it. That's how we think the assailant was injured and then came to leave his blood on the leading edge of the front door in such a position that it could only have got there with the door open.'

More than a year and a half had gone by since the murder of Mohammed Raja, and here at last was real evidence linking one of the suspects to the scene of the crime. 'Whilst we'd never given up hope,' says Heselden, 'and whilst we were always confident, that was the breakthrough we had been waiting for.'

Four days later detectives called at Croke's new home in Bolney Road, Moulscombe, Brighton. They arrested him for the murder of Mohammed Raja. He was taken to Bexleyheath police station, where he denied ever having been in Sutton. When the DNA evidence linking him to the scene of the crime was put to him, Croke replied: 'No comment.'

It was now vital to discover Croke's movements on the day of the murder. If Knapp had organised the hit, it was also important to discover his whereabouts. While they puzzled over that, Hugh Ellis sat down one day to check the accuracy of a transcript of his interview with Van Hoogstraten the previous November.

Near the end, he read Van Hoogstraten asking: 'How did they miss him the first time?'

'Something just clicked,' recalled Ellis. 'I suddenly thought – how the hell did he know that, how did he know they'd missed with the first shot?'

He could hardly wait to get the video tape of the Crimewatch programme and push it into a video player. To Ellis, the reconstruction suggested that the first shot had definitely hit Mohammed Raja. It showed the grandsons upstairs where they hear a bang like a gunshot. Raja is shown in the next set-up holding his side, shouting, 'They've hit me.'

The reconstruction is ambiguous. As the shot is only heard, the viewer can't be certain that it has hit its mark. There is a degree of vagueness over just what has taken place. However, the more likely conclusion would be that the first shot had hit home.

To the police, then, the man who always boasted that he was too smart to get caught had incriminated himself. In the interview he gave to World in Action in 1988 he had boasted about being so clever that he didn't get caught any more.

'One is clever enough to organise things to ensure that the chickens don't come home to roost,' he said.

At last the chickens looked as if they might be coming home.

Meanwhile Michaal Hamdan was making increasingly interesting accusations about Van Hoogstraten's behaviour in the months before the murder. He still wouldn't put them in a signed statement. Nevertheless Heseldon reckoned he now had enough to charge Van Hoogstraten with the murder of Mohammed Raja. But would a charge stick? The team at AMIT sought the views of lawyers at the Crown Prosecution Service. Their opinion was not heartening.

The CPS saw three problems. Firstly, there was no specific link between Van Hoogstraten and Croke. Secondly, Van Hoogstraten might be able explain his knowledge about the second shot. For example, he might have been told about how the murder really happened by a member of the Raja family or someone who knew them. Thirdly, Hamdan's accusations were unsubstantiated and he was afraid to make a statement.

It was a setback.

Heselden decided to take the fight to Van Hoogstraten. They would arrest him and see what they might get out of him. If he had made one error, who knows, he might make others.

On 16 July 2001 Hugh Ellis and two colleagues walked into the Courtlands Hotel in Brighton and asked for Van Hoogstraten. When he appeared, they arrested him in connection with the murder of Mohammed Raja. This time he did ask to call his solicitor. The police officers had a warrant to search Van Hoogstraten's cottage at High Cross and they asked him to accompany them there.

Van Hoogstraten watched while they searched. The main item of interest they found was his diary. After the search, the police drove him to Bexleyheath police station, where he spent the night in a cell.

That evening the officers read the diary. They noticed several interesting entries. One was a meeting in 1998 with someone called Jim Croke. Could this have been David Croke? More importantly, there were several entries in 1999 listing loans to 'Uncle Bob'. They added up to £7000.

'He was saying he had almost nothing to do with him, hadn't seen him hardly at all since he had come out of prison and wanted nothing to do with him,' says Heselden. 'Yet here he was making a number of substantial loans to Mr Knapp, and we also knew that Mr Knapp was living in a premises owned by Mr Van Hoogstraten rent free.'

The next day Ellis and Detective Sergeant Chris Crowley questioned Van Hoogstraten in the presence of his solicitor, Danny Solomon.

Van Hoogstraten said he had genuinely liked Raja. He was a

'nuisance', that was all. 'There's no big money involved in any of this. We're talking about relative peanuts,' he said. The litigation was worth only around 'twenty or thirty grand ... it's not even a week's pocket money'.

But the police knew that, according to the Raja family, the disputed properties were now worth several million pounds. Ellis suggested that Raja's allegations were the catalyst for Van Hoogstraten to arrange the murder.

'Absolutely not,' Van Hoogstraten replied.

He went on to say that Raja had been less than honest in his dealings with him.

Ellis replied that he was not there to defend Raja. However, Raja's actions had brought out what he called Van Hoogstraten's 'second character'.

'Do you know Robert Knapp?' Ellis asked.

Van Hoogstraten replied that he did. He'd known him since about 1969. In 1979 Knapp's parents had come to live on the High Cross estate and Knapp himself became the estate manager. He had a flat near the estate but in later years Van Hoogstraten really had nothing much to do with him because of a serious drug problem. He made some quite large loans to Knapp, but only out of friendship for his parents.

Ellis asked if he knew David Croke. Van Hoogstraten said no. Did he know anyone with the surname Croke? Again, he said he did not. Ellis suggested that he was involved in the murder, together with Knapp and Croke.

Van Hoogstraten replied: 'The idea horrifies me.'

They took a short break. When they resumed, Ellis asked Van Hoogstraten about his first interview. How did he know that the murderers missed the first time?

Van Hoogstraten answered that he knew that from watching the BBC Crimewatch programme: ''Cause we heard the bullet, heard the gun going off.'

Ellis pressed him further. How did Van Hoogstraten know there had been two shots? Why did he suggest the first one had missed?

Van Hoogstraten answered: 'Because they shot him again. I couldn't understand how if somebody's opening a door and presumably the gunman's standing there, how he couldn't have hit him.'

Ellis wanted to make certain that Van Hoogstraten's knowledge could not have come from some other source than Crimewatch. He asked: 'Which of your friends told you that they'd missed the first time, then?'

'Nobody. I didn't know anything about it,' Van Hoogstraten replied.

From this simple answer, the two detectives believed they had been told all they needed to know.

Ellis asked Van Hoogstraten about Rizvan Raja's evidence that his grandfather said he had been hit by Van Hoogstraten's men: 'Do you have any comment about that?'

Van Hoogstraten remained silent.

For the benefit of the tape recorder, Ellis said: 'No comment.'

Van Hoogstraten then said: 'Well, I can't possibly comment on it.'

At the end of the interview the detectives told Van Hoogstraten he was going to be given bail. Then something happened that amazed them.

'At that point when he knew he was being bailed from the police station,' remembers Ellis, 'he turned away and cried. I had to look at him twice to see if it was the same man that I had seen in these programmes, how he was portrayed on television.'

Police continued to pursue the links between Robert Knapp and David Croke. Finally they had a success. Croke had used his credit card at a service station on the M25 near Crayford in Essex at 1.25 pm, four hours after the murder. Within minutes, Knapp made a call on his mobile telephone in the same area. So, on the day of the murder, both men were in or around Crayford.

At first, detectives could not work out why the two men might have been there. Then they discovered that Knapp knew someone in Crayford. Her name was Doreen Tong and she was his heroin dealer. Doreen told police that she remembered Croke and Knapp visiting some time in the summer of 1999. They smelled of burning or smoke and Knapp had superficial burns. They said something about a job 'gone wrong'.

On 24 September 2001 Van Hoogstraten was called again to the police station in Hove. He gave the taxi driver a £50 note and told him to wait. He never came back. He had become the wealthiest man in Britain ever to be charged with murder.

Unusually for a murder suspect, Van Hoogstraten was remanded on bail. It was set at £23 million. He provided £1 million in cash and the rest in various investments. Dick Heselden reckoned that Van Hoogstraten would never flee the country because of the potential harm to his business interests. Besides, if he did a runner, the state could always sequester all his assets.

Three days after Van Hoogstraten was charged, word reached AMIT that Robert Knapp had returned from Ireland. He was arrested and charged with murder.

The police had now charged Croke, Van Hoogstraten and Knapp. All three denied the charges. The case against Van Hoogstraten was thin, almost wholly circumstantial.

Heselden still counted on Michaal Hamdan agreeing to testify. Hamdan remained reluctant until he discovered that Van Hoogstraten was about to find out what he had been saying about him.

It was due to a legal process known as discovery. The prosecution lawyers had to provide the defence team with all relevant information. Hamdan's claims had suddenly jumped into that category. Van Hoogstraten was going to claim in court that Hamdan had organised Raja's murder. This meant that his defence team had the right to see everything the prosecution had on Hamdan.

The Lebanese was horrified and scared. Hamdan agreed to make a statement. In return, he wanted protection. Heselden offered to put him on the witness protection scheme. When Hamdan learned that this would involve a false identity and a fictitious new life, he refused. He had too many business interests to look after.

Then an unexpected witness appeared. A few weeks before the trial, the Brighton police called AMIT to say that they had a visitor with a black eye. It was Tanaka Sali. She explained that Van Hoogstraten had beaten her up because she had been seeing a younger man, a bouncer at a nightclub. Later she was to describe their fight in vivid terms: '...he just came to the bed shouting like, "You fucking bitch!" He grabbed me by the hair and he pulled me out of bed. He took off his slipper and he was whacking me in the face with it, and the slipper split. And he said: "You're not to go anywhere, you bitch." Then he left the room. Later on I went to my friend and she took me to the police station. And it just started from there, really, at the police station.'

The investigation team wasted no time. They went to Brighton to question the teenager. She told them about life with the hugely jealous tycoon and about several potentially significant things he'd allegedly let drop in the months before the murder. She agreed to repeat them in court. The police were ecstatic. Here was a star witness.

There was more good news too – Hamdan. He had at last given his crucial statement. It ran to 32 pages and covered everything he knew about Van Hoogstraten, from their first meeting to the tycoon's attitude to Mohammed Raja. All that remained was for him to sign it ... and agree to go into the witness box.

However, the nearer the trial, the colder Hamdan's feet. A week before the trial was about to start, a contact invited Mike Walsh to a mystery meeting at a hotel in Gloucester Road, South Kensington. When he arrived, the mystery turned out to be a very nervous Hamdan.

For three hours Hamdan agonised about his statement and his safety. He wanted the police to give him twenty-four-hour protection – armed bodyguards, the lot. They had refused. It was too expensive. What should he do, he asked? What would happen if he did give evidence? What if his statement to the police disappeared?

Over many bottles of Grolsch, Hamdan fretted away. He had not wanted to finger Van Hoogstraten. He expected what he had told the police to remain confidential. When he learned that the defence had a right to see his statement, he was horrified. The police had not treated him fairly, he complained.

Two days later Hamdan agreed to meet Walsh again. At his flat in Mayfair, he produced a copy of his statement. They chatted about it. Then Hamdan said he was exhausted because of sex with a girl he had picked up a few days earlier. He went on to talk about Van Hoogstraten's taste for teenage girls. Hamdan, paunchy and middle-aged, grimaced and shook his head with disapproval. The meeting was brought to a halt by the arrival of the girl he had been enthusing about. She looked about fifteen.

The trial was set to start on 16 April 2002. That morning, Andy Sladen got another telephone call. It was Hamdan. His father had died and he had to go to Beirut immediately. The scene was set for the trial of Nicholas Van Hoogstraten to be played out at the Old Bailey ... without the prosecution's star witness.

17

THE RECKONING

The trial of Nicholas van Hoogstraten and his two alleged hit men for the murder of Mohammed Raja was always going to be a major drama. Everyone knew that Van Hoogstraten would provide fireworks. But no one could anticipate the devastating impact the tycoon's personality would have on the trial.

The venue was Court Number One at the Central Criminal Court, where some of the most infamous criminals in history have faced justice. Normally the senior judge at the Old Bailey, Michael Hyams, would have presided. But a decade earlier, Judge Hyams had been threatened by an angry litigant, who called him a 'bastard' and promised to 'get him ... sooner or later'. The litigant making the threat – none other than Nicholas van Hoogstraten. That incident ruled him out. He could not try a man who had threatened him.

Mr Justice Newman, next in seniority, took over. A tall, eagle-eyed man with a touch of Alastair Sim about him, Judge Newman would find his patience tested almost to breaking point by the accused. But only at the end would he reveal anything of his feelings.

The Crown chose David Waters QC to prosecute. He was known for building cases meticulously, surrounding the accused with a slowly mounting wall of evidence until all avenues of escape were closed. A Pickwickian figure, Waters effected a gentle, enquiring smile, and prodded and prodded, then struck: 'Er, Mr Van Hoogstraten, could you, therefore, help me with…?'

Van Hoogstraten's counsel was Richard Ferguson QC, an Irishman who was said to be one of the sharpest defence barristers at the bar. Physically he was the opposite to the well-fed Waters. A handsome, ruddy-faced six-footer, Ferguson gave his hobbies in Who's Who as watching Arsenal and drinking Guinness. He had represented the Birmingham Six, Rosemary West and the Brighton bombers. 'Dick Ferguson always has tricks up his sleeve,' said a fellow barrister before the case.

The trial opened on 16 April 2002. In some Old Bailey cases the accused are judged to be so dangerous that paramilitary police watch outside. Van Hoogstraten was not in that category. Even so, the authorities were taking no chances. The jury was to be bussed in and out from a secret rendezvous somewhere in London. Prosecution witnesses were given panic buttons. And, to his reported irritation, Mr Justice Newman was given armed protection.

Every eye focused on Van Hoogstraten as he followed Robert Knapp and David Croke up from the cells and into the dock. In the press box journalists who knew him saw how much he had aged. The beautifully cut hair was still thick but turning grey. He looked as if he had shrunk a little. His skin was a greyish colour. But he was still the same Nicholas van Hoogstraten: expensive pinstripe suit, silk tie and matching handkerchief, gold wrist watch and menacing, slightly tinted glasses. As he stared at the judge, then glanced up at the public gallery, his look was as piercing as ever.

In the gallery Caroline Williams blew down a kiss. Van Hoogstraten grinned.

His two co-defendants showed no emotion. The contrast between them and the elegant Van Hoogstraten was marked. The bespectacled Croke, deeply lined and weary, was wearing a sweater and looked like a harmless old man. Robert Knapp, tall, close-cropped and watchful, looked formidable. Dressed in a T-shirt, he stared unblinkingly at every journalist in the press box in turn. Some joked uneasily about it afterwards.

Over the first two days Waters outlined the case against the accused. Van Hoogstraten, he said, had ordered 'a contract murder' because of 'the problems and difficulties' he had encountered with Raja. Waters related the alleged threats to Raja, the 'maggot' remark and the fears that Raja had expressed in the weeks before his death. He went though the links between Van Hoogstraten and Knapp, and between Knapp and Croke. Then the jury heard what happened on the day of the killing, the events in Mulgrave Road, the blood spot linking Croke to the crime, the burning of the van and the alleged visit by Croke and Knapp to the Tongs in Crayford.

On the surface it all fitted together. In reality it was entirely circumstantial except for the blood spot, and even that was open to challenge. It emerged that the sample taken from the doorway at Mulgrave Road had been used up by prosecution scientists before defence experts were able to test it. In such circumstances the defence hoped that the DNA evidence might be ruled out as inadmissible later in the trial.

The defence had a major fear too. Counsel dared not do anything that might lose what is known as their 'shield'. This is the rule which prevents previous convictions being revealed to the jury except in special circumstances.

This fear constrained defence lawyers at every step. They dared not question the truthfulness of any prosecution witness, knowing that Waters would immediately leap in and argue that as his witness's character was under scrutiny, the past character of the defendants should be scrutinised too.

The last thing the defence wanted was the jury to get an inkling that they were trying two professional armed robbers and a man who had had a friend's home bombed. 'Myself and Croke were advised by counsel from day one by all costs our "form" must not come in,' Knapp explained in a letter after the trial.

Knapp told us: 'That is why all witnesses were stroked instead of bashed!'

Waters's first witness was the victim's eighteen-year-old grandson, Rizvan Raja. He came into the witness box to relive that terrible morning: the bang that brought him and his brother down the stairs to find their grandfather bleeding and struggling with his assailants... Rizvan's futile attempt to ring 999... and the moment when he saw his grandfather's attempt to defend himself, vainly holding a knife as the gunman fired at him from point-blank range. 'I just heard a loud bang and it hit my grandfather. He fell down and the gunman ran away.'

The full brutality of the murder was brought home by pathologist Dr Richard Shephard. He told the court that Mohammed Raja had been shot in the eye and stabbed five times. Dr Shephard couldn't say whether one of the stab wounds or the gunshot had killed him. Either would have done so.

Up in the public gallery, sitting eight or nine feet away from Caroline Williams, Mohammed Raja's three daughters and his elder brother listened. They would be there every day for three months, hearing every word.

A procession of witnesses followed as Waters built up a picture of what had happened on the day of the murder. Defence counsel picked away at them and began to score.

First the identification evidence began to wobble. One witness had picked Croke out of an identity parade. But all the others who had seen the hit men in Sutton that morning described them as being between eighteen and forty. Yet Croke and Knapp were in their fifties and Croke looked more like seventy.

An E-fit poster compiled by police just after the murder was shown to the jury. It looked nothing like either of them.

Then Doreen Tong came into the witness box and admitted that she couldn't be sure that Croke and Knapp had visited her on the day of the murder. Her father's work records seemed to show he couldn't have been there to see them that day.

It wasn't going too well for the prosecution. Much depended on their four star witnesses. What Waters could not know was that three of them would not deliver.

First came Amjad Raja, the murdered man's youngest son. He had been part spectator, part participator in the legal battles with Van Hoogstraten. Over two days Amjad answered questions on his father's relationship with Van Hoogstraten – the loans, the friendship, the souring of the relationship, the 'fraud', his father's pursuit of Van Hoogstraten through the courts and the 'we take thorns and we break them' remark.

Like his dead father, Amjad is a polite man who keeps his feelings to himself. But his bitterness towards Van Hoogstraten was clear to see. The tycoon, he said, was a loan shark who had demanded a down payment of £10,000 before he would even see Amjad. He was an arrogant man who behaved as if others were nothing. And he was, Amjad made clear, very dangerous. Once, when Amjad was having problems with a tenant, Van Hoogstraten had suggested Amjad 'do him' with a knife, then offered to do it himself when he said no.

Amjad was pressed about his father's other antagonists – notably Michaal Hamdan. He insisted that the row with Hamdan over the basement flat in Brunswick Square was near to a solution when his father was murdered. Amjad left no doubt that in his mind Van Hoogstraten alone could have ordered the killing. In the days just prior to the murder his father was on his guard. 'He felt that Van Hoogstraten was going to take some sort of action against him, some sort of revenge... I was there the weekend before he died. He seemed quite upset, but he didn't tell me why.'

Amjad's testimony was damaging to the defence but there was nothing concrete in it, no smoking gun. That was to be provided by the prosecution's second star witness – the girl who only three weeks earlier had been sharing Van Hoogstraten's bed, Tanaka Sali.

Tanaka looked sensational as she arrived at the Old Bailey. A plain, dark-blue robe with a cowl enveloped her from head to toe. Only her wide-eyed face could be seen. No one could take their eyes off the tall, voluptuous young woman as she slipped past the dock containing her lover and into the witness box.

She had come to give what's called evidence voir dire. This is an ancient peculiarity of the judicial process which allows evidence to be tested in the absence of the jury. It helps the judge decide what can and can't be admitted as evidence in the trial proper. It also shows the press what to expect later in open court – a taste of dramas yet to come.

The witness box in Court Number One is an ordeal for anyone, let alone an eighteen-year-old. But not for Tanaka.

This was no brainless bimbo. She thought a moment about every question and answered so lucidly the judge almost glowed.

She told of her tempestuous relationship with Van Hoogstraten, how she'd come to England with him and of what she'd learned about him. She discovered that he was a man with no friends, just people who worked for him. She was at pains to make clear that she didn't think him guilty of murder. But she related incidents that the prosecution claimed suggested otherwise.

Mr Justice Newman was visibly impressed with Tanaka. She was told to come back in a week's time to tell her story to the jury. Police and prosecution were elated. Hoogstraten's ex mistress could be his downfall. Meanwhile someone else who'd once been close to the tycoon was called to give evidence against him: Tony Browne. The architect had fallen out with Van Hoogstraten.

He told friends that he wasn't going to kick his former client in the teeth, but he would tell what he knew. The police had high expectations. They thought he would lay bare Van Hoogstraten's violence and his use of Knapp as an enforcer. Once he took the stand, however, they decided he was pulling his punches.

The architect vividly described his experiences of the volatile Van Hoogstraten and recalled violent actions involving tenants. But when it came to Knapp and the murder his answers were qualified. Yes, Bob Knapp was a menacing character who had acted as Van Hoogstraten's 'persuader', but that was years ago. Latterly Knapp had become a junkie and Van Hoogstraten wanted nothing to do with him. Yes, Van Hoogstraten had 'a spectacular falling out' with another business associate and said 'he was going to have him done, whatever done meant', but then 'he was going to have lots of people done'. And yes, Van Hoogstraten had talked about the murder of Mohammed Raja, but only after the event and then only to ask Browne what happened when police interviewed him about the killing.

Waters, who had been expected to keep Browne on the stand for hours, abruptly stopped the questioning, and the witness was discharged. The architect, puzzled, said afterwards that he had always wondered whether what he knew would be more beneficial to the defence or to the prosecution.

Worse was to come for the prosecution. It was now Tanaka's turn to lay bare what she knew, but it didn't happen. The day she was due to appear the court learned that she wanted to retract her statement. The judge had Tanaka brought up from Brighton so he could question her. Tanaka was transformed. Gone was the articulate, co-operative young woman in her long, sweeping robe. This Tanaka was a bolshie, monosyllabic teenager in jeans who didn't want to say anything. She refused to take the oath but insisted that what she'd told the court a week before was untrue. The judge was openly furious. But Tanaka was immovable. The jury never even got to hear of her existence.

A day after Tanaka's retraction there was more bad news for the crown. Hamdan wasn't budging from Beirut. Every day, Detective Inspector Andy Sladen phoned him, but Hamdan wouldn't even agree to give evidence by video link, let alone fly back to give it in person. A desperate Waters pleaded with the judge to allow Hamdan's statement to be read to the jury. The judge said 'no'.

It was the lowest moment in the trial for police and prosecution. Privately, one of the team admitted that the case might not even last beyond half time. In other words, it might be dismissed before the defence had even begun to present its case.

As the prosecution limped on there were some consolations. One was the court's decision to admit the results of the DNA tests. If it had been ruled out the entire case might have collapsed.

Another boost for Waters was that the court looked likely to allow the jury to see some of the damaging admissions about the use of violence which the property magnate had made over the years, especially on the World in Action programme in 1988.

The jury heard little of this. Instead of watching a drama unfold with advantage swinging this way then that, they kept being sent home. Days elapsed between one witness being cross-examined and the next. They didn't know that Ferguson was continually having to ask for time to 'take instructions' from his client.

So much time was lost the judge made the jury part-timers. He told them he would generally only expect them in the mornings. The afternoons he gave over to 'consultations' with clients, voir dire evidence and challenges in chambers. At one point when he once more had to send the jury home, he told them they could watch Italy in the World Cup on TV that afternoon.

Among the press few believed the prosecution would now succeed. But the defence had a huge problem of its own – the ego of Nicholas van Hoogstraten. He was said to have overruled Ferguson time and again. In closed sessions, when his QC wanted him to wrap up, he would not. The cavernous corridors of the Old Bailey buzzed with rumours about the Ferguson – Van Hoogstraten relationship. It was said they were on screaming terms, and that both used the same four-letter word to describe each other. It was even rumoured that at one point Van Hoogstraten's cheque had bounced and the QC had nearly quit.

Ferguson opened the case for the defence on 10 June. The police, he said, had found no evidence against his client. It was guilt by association. As a motive for murder the Raja lawsuit was 'scraping the barrel'. The consequences for Van Hoogstraten if he lost were trifling.

As for Van Hoogstraten paying Knapp to do it: 'Can you get your head round paying for a killing by instalments? Not only by instalments but paying by cheque.' Another business contact of Raja's had more reason to want him dead than Van Hoogstraten had.

The jury now heard about Michaal Hamdan and how Raja had thwarted his plans to acquire the whole of the Palmeira Square property. Before he was killed a number of threats had been made to Raja, and Hamdan was behind them, said Ferguson.

The nature of the killing alone showed that it couldn't have been his client, said Ferguson. Van Hoogstraten was a man of means. 'Do you not think that if he had wanted Mr Raja killed he would have had a vastly more sophisticated plan? This was a bungled farce, more like an attempted robbery than a contract killing.'

It was going well for Van Hoogstraten. The consensus around the court was that at the end of the trial he and Knapp would probably be acquitted, although the blood spot would do for Croke.

Then Van Hoogstraten made the most stupid move of his life. He couldn't resist the temptation to give evidence in open court. Every one of his legal team urged him not to. Waters would get to him, needle him, make him lose control. He could lose everything. But the vanity and the mistrustfulness of the man prevailed. Only he could do justice to his own cause.

He began well enough in the witness box, speaking quietly and switching on that charm that had worked so well on so many occasions. He referred to an episode in the past. As if in an afterthought, he added softly that, of course, the jury were all too young to remember. At that all six women on the jury looked at the handsome man on the stand and kept looking.

He rubbished the idea that Raja's fraud action was a motive for murder. Raja's case against him was 'laughable'. His diary entries showed that he called it the 'Raja nonsense'. The money involved was peanuts.

He bore no ill feelings towards the murdered man. 'I don't believe Mohammed and me ever had a cross word with each other. Hard as this may seem or sound like, my relationship with Mohammed basically stayed the same from the day I first clapped eyes on him.'

What, Ferguson asked, had he to say to the allegations that he'd ordered the murder? Van Hoogstraten seemed almost overcome. He'd never been asked the question direct, he said.

'Do you deny the allegations?' his QC asked.

'Absolutely, I have five children…' His voice broke off. There were tears in his eyes.

He told the court that if anyone did have a motive for the killing it was Michaal Hamdan, whose hopes of acquiring the Brunswick Square property in Hove had been thwarted by the murdered man. That building had been a 'battleground', he added. In his campaign to get possession of it the Lebanese had been involved in arson, vandalism, flooding and intimidation.

As for himself, the picture Van Hoogstraten conveyed was of a much misunder-stood, misrepresented man.

'You would agree that you are an astute businessman?' said Waters.

'No, because I'm standing here... I was quite a successful businessman, yes... It hasn't been easy. I wasn't born with a silver spoon. I haven't had an easy life. Far from it.'

He talked about his money.

'Would you agree that money means a great deal to you?' Waters asked.

'It doesn't mean much to me now... It used to when I was young and didn't have any... It's all relative really. Even if one has five hundred million it does not go very far.'

He talked about his palace. So far it had cost between £25 and £28 million. It was his 'pride and joy'. He pressed the judge to let him show the jury an aerial photograph of it.

He talked about his generosity. In another emotional moment he said that Robert Knapp had only been allowed back to live on the High Cross estate through consideration for his infirm old mother.

This led to the nitty-gritty. No, he hadn't paid Knapp for a killing. The £7000 mentioned in his diary was loans.

The Waters technique was to allow the man in the dock to talk his head off and then switch abruptly to a more dangerous subject. The sign that he was getting down to business was a bend in his knees as, almost imperceptibly, he started to bounce in polite anticipation of blood.

He drew some blood on Van Hoogstraten's third day in the box. The tycoon was asked about his own remarks that Raja was 'a maggot' and that he'd give him 'a slap'. Van Hoogstraten insisted that no threat was implied. He bore the Pakistani no ill will.

'You're lying, aren't you?' Waters said.

The tycoon denied it. He was visibly irritated. No one talked to him like that.

Waters continued, pressing Van Hoogstraten on his real feelings towards Raja. Bouncing perceptibly, he accused the man in the dock of being 'desperately keen to pull the wool over the jury's eyes'.

Van Hoogstraten, goaded by the earlier digs from the prosecutor, exploded. Waters was trying to trick him.

The judge intervened. He told the property magnate: 'Mr Waters ... has a job to do.'

That night Van Hoogstraten realised the mistake he had made in insisting on taking the stand. In one more move that astonished everyone in court he wrote a long letter to the judge. It said that for the past twenty years he had led 'a blameless life'. But he had been called a liar and dared not call witnesses in rebuttal for fear that his past record would be revealed. Waters was trying to trip and trap him. He demanded fair treatment and protection from Waters or he wouldn't continue to answer questions.

It was too late for second thoughts. The judge made that clear. Van Hoogstraten had to continue or the jury would be allowed to draw its own conclusions. The tycoon and Ferguson consulted. Van Hoogstraten would continue to face the music.

He should have been at his most aware immediately after the letter episode. Instead he made the gaffe of the trial.

He was talking about his tenants and a drug problem in Hove in the mid-eighties: 'The police complained to me about a number of drug-related incidents. They were effectively trying to say a lot of these people were living in my properties. Eventually I had a meeting with someone high up in the police and I said: "I can deal with this."'

He did so by sending 'hefty builders' round to kick the drug addicts out. Sometimes that didn't work. 'On those occasions we sent in a couple of dogs.' Obviously amused, he went on to describe how hippies had been forced to jump from second-floor windows to escape his Alsatians.

Paul Cheston, the Evening Standard reporter whom Van Hoogstraten had assaulted in another courthouse fifteen years earlier, reckoned that this was the turning point in the trial. 'It was a chilling moment. There was silence. It was as if at that moment the jury's minds were changed, I think for ever. At the time I thought that if it wasn't the beginning of the end for him it would take some very clever talk to take the image away of this man in black glorying in sending in the dogs.'

There was more to come as Waters told the jury about Van Hoogstraten's admissions on World in Action. The most damaging of those admissions amounted to just seven words: 'I'm probably ruthless and I'm probably violent.'

'You're scraping the barrel,' Van Hoogstraten sneered. 'I was the subject of a programme put together by left-wing journalists who were trying to scupper the government's intention of opening up the housing market. It was politically motivated.'

Waters: 'It was a programme made ... with your co-operation?'

Van Hoogstraten: 'I was conned ... these people are all bent. The media across the board is bent.'

On the programme Van Hoogstraten had admitted kidnapping accountant David Harris and beating him up, spitting at Jackie Hope and having violent associates he could call on for work he would not talk about on television.

If women jurors had been charmed in the early stages, they looked stony-faced now as he tried to explain and inadvertently revealed more and more about the workings of his mind.

Yes, he had beaten Harris up after getting 'very irate' because the accountant had stolen from him. But that was fifteen years before the TV people came along. It was 'a disgrace' that they'd brought the Harris business up.

Yes, he had spat in Jackie Hope's face. But 'she was a druggy.

She was dressed in a long kaftan-type thing. She was a weirdo.'
And she wasn't his tenant anyway.

Yes, he had talked about violent associates he could call on.
But he was a nightclub owner and, of course, he had to
employ bouncers.

Van Hoogstraten was blind to the effect his admissions were
having. In his eyes most people would surely understand the
victim of a theft beating the thief half to death. Most people
would agree that the weirdo in the kaftan had been dealt with
astutely. Most would accept that, of course, a nightclub owner
must employ violent young men.

Only one other person in Court Number One that day
probably saw it his way: the adoring Caroline Williams, still an
anxious daily spectator in the public gallery.

After Van Hoogstraten finished giving evidence, a reporter who
had quoted odds of 7 – 3 for acquittal reduced them to 6 – 4.

Robert Knapp did not follow his old friend into the witness
box. The evidence against him was minimal. If he'd been charged
on his own, his case wouldn't even have come to court. He said
on being arrested that he had a complete answer but would keep
it until later. In the end, however, he stayed silent.

David Croke did take the stand. It was on 28 June, his sixtieth
birthday. Bent, tired and beaten, he was a miserable figure. No
one could have guessed that once he had been one of the
deadliest bank robbers in the country or that his speciality had
been tying mock bombs to bank managers' wives. If Van
Hoogstraten really did pay him to kill Mohammed Raja he
couldn't have known the state of the man.

Croke said he had an alibi. He was at home. In the face of the
DNA evidence it was anything but convincing.

On 9 July the case for the defence concluded.

Then the judge, summing up, produced a final surprise. Only
two verdicts were possible for Knapp and Croke. Guilty or not

guilty of murder. But there was another option in Van Hoogstraten's case. If the jury decided that he had sent the two men to Mulgrave Road to frighten Mohammed Raja but not to do him serious injury, they could find him not guilty of murder but guilty of manslaughter. No one had mentioned this possibility during the previous thirteen weeks of the trial.

The jury were out for five days. On Friday 19 July the usher announced that they were ready to come back. Had they reached a unanimous verdict on Van Hoogstraten? No. Had they reached verdicts on Croke and Knapp? Yes. Guilty. Both of them.

The judge sent the jurors home. They would return on Monday to try to reach a majority verdict on Van Hoogstraten. Over the weekend each of the twelve must have been thinking very hard. On Monday they were secretly bussed in for the last time to reconvene in the jury room at 10 am. They were out again, with their verdict, within forty-five minutes.

It was the one morning in the whole trial that the Raja family were late in court. They more than anyone were convinced of Van Hoogstraten's guilt and prayed for a guilty verdict. But they weren't there to hear it. The foreman announced that they'd found Nicholas van Hoogstraten not guilty of murder but guilty of the manslaughter of Mohammed Raja. It was a majority verdict – eleven to one.

The judge gave Robert Knapp and David Croke life. It was a formality. Croke wasn't in court to hear the sentence. Knapp was. As he was taken down he turned to the jury and for the first time addressed them: 'You have convicted an innocent man.'

Van Hoogstraten was not sentenced that day. The judge announced that, having observed him for three months, he felt that a psychiatric report might serve the interests of justice. Pending that, he delayed sentencing until 2 October. But he warned that a life sentence was in his mind.

The prisoners were taken down, and journalists streamed upstairs to the cafeteria, where the Raja family and the police staged a press conference. They were delighted to have some result but disappointed it wasn't murder. In the cafeteria doorway Caroline Williams watched. She said nothing.

Later, outside the Old Bailey, Caroline was on the outskirts of the crowd again, this time watching the TV cameras crowding round the Rajas. With her was another of the tycoon's old lovers, Jennifer Prouse. When the cameras had had their fill of the Rajas, Caroline and Jennifer linked arms with Van Hoogstraten's solicitor, one on each side of him, and walked away very slowly. Every film crew captured the moment. Every press photographer snapped it: two women, parading their defiance and their belief in Nicholas van Hoogstraten. And not one frame, not one shot was ever used. On the night of his conviction the world didn't want to know about anyone who cared for the 'devil's landlord'.

The next morning all that the press was interested in was the life of villainy of the man. Van Hoogstraten was accorded the kind of comments a mass murderer might expect. The Brighton Evening Argus devoted a supplement to him headlined 'Goodbye … and good riddance'. The tabloids trumpeted the same feelings about Van Hoogstraten. The Sun's headline called him 'The Maniac in the Mink'.

Life imprisonment was staring Van Hoogstraten in the face. Amongst the crime reporters who had followed the case through three gruelling months, the concensus was that the judge would impose the maximum sentence. For manslaughter, that meant life. The tycoon would be in his late 60s by the time he was released … if he lived that long. As it was, under the strain of the trial, he'd aged visibly. Over the months he seemed to have shrunk. The expensive business suits hung loosely on him and looked a size too big. He'd lost weight. His face too had changed. The prison pallor emphasised the deepening lines around those vulpine features. A friend would later confirm that, at the end of the trial, he was far from well.

Yet, judging from the letters he wrote to the authors after the verdict, the inner man hadn't changed. Ill or not, he was as buoyant and venomous as ever. He blamed everyone except himself for what had happened. In his first letter, responding to a request to visit him, he wrote, 'I'm not sure that I should have any more to do with the media' as it is mainly media lies and distortion that have got me convicted along with the bent judge and police "investigation" that allowed the real culprit to get away.' Other letters were full of bile at the police, the lawyers, the Raja family and the judge. He was especially vitriolic about his highly respected lead counsel, Dick Ferguson, whose rows with him during the trial had become legend. The QC, he claimed, was incompetent and had been terrified of the judge.

'So much for a reputation,' he added. 'I should have known better than have someone with a reputation. After all look at mine!'

But, of course, Van Hoogstratan hadn't given up.

As his trial ended his fellow prisoners in Belmarsh high security prison in East London were agog over the story of how one of the biggest villains in the place had found a brilliant new lawyer who'd just saved him a cool £33 million. John 'Goldfinger' Palmer was a heavy duty crook who was serving eight years for masterminding a massive timeshare fraud in Spain. He was facing seizure of his ill gotten goods – £33 million – when an Italian born avvocato, called Giovanni Di Stefano, began acting for him. The Italian discovered that the Crown Prosecution Service had slipped up in the seizure order. It had quoted the wrong law. A tiny mistake. But such is the demand for precision under British law that the order had to be revoked. Palmer kept that £33 million. Di Stefano was on the way to gaining a reputation in the underworld as a lawyer who could work miracles. He'd eventually become known as 'the devil's advocate'. Van Hoogstraten put in a call to him.

Di Stefano would have appealed to the tycoon on several levels. Though raised and educated in England he was as unlike the bland lawyers who populate the English legal system as it's possible to imagine. Small, dark, bald and intense, he always wore the obligatory dark pin-stripe suit and impenetrable dark glasses. He talked endlessly about himself in a cockney accent and made no secret of his past. He'd been involved in the MGM takeover scandal of 1990, and been the business partner and friend of one of the most notorious killers in the world – Arkan, the Serbian warlord.

Van Hoogstraten signed up Di Stefano.

The Italian was hardly on board when there was a ham-fisted move from the authorities. Two weeks before Van Hoogstraten was due to be sentenced, the Governor of Belmarsh stopped Di Stefano visiting him. The Italian demanded a judicial review of the Governor's decision which meant an urgent hearing before a High Court judge . It was quickly over. Deaf to vague references about Di Stefano's character and to doubts about his legal qualifications, Mr Justice Jackson ruled that under EU law, the tycoon could have whichever lawyer he liked. That specifically included Italian avoccatos.

Whatever the Italian told Van Hoogstraten, the property magnate approached sentencing day in an optimistic frame of mind. He wrote to us claiming that the judge had misdirected the jury and the conviction would be overturned. He wrote that his enemies would all have 'egg on their faces when my wrongful conviction is quashed shortly, as it will have to be.' In an afterthought, Van Hoogstraten – who hates to be thought well of – crossed out 'egg' before 'on their faces' and substituted in capital letters 'SHIT'.

He also wrote to Mr Justice Newman. All that the judge

revealed about the contents was that they were 'characteristically forthright and direct'.

He wrote to the prosecutor, David Waters QC, as well. It was, characteristically, an abusive letter, but the details weren't released.

As he awaited sentencing in October 2002 Van Hoogstraten parted company with his counsel, Richard Ferguson QC. Not, one imagines, amicably.

Then he started work on his appeal. He also wrote a letter to Mr Justice Newman. All that the judge revealed about the contents was that they were 'characteristically forthright and direct'.

He wrote to the prosecutor, David Waters QC, as well. It was, characteristically, an abusive letter, but the details weren't released.

Sentencing was on 25 October.

The judge had the reports of the two psychiatrists. He also himself observed Van Hoogstraten for three months in various moods and under pressure.

He now summed up what he made of the man one newspaper had called the 'most evil millionaire' in the country.

Van Hoogstraten, said the judge, was 'almost self delusional' and 'incapable of accepting responsibility for anything'. He always believed that he was in the right and saw others as nonentities. His conduct was 'appalling' and provoked a similar reaction in others. Then he blamed them, seeing himself as the victim of their appalling conduct. 'The cyclical pattern appears to be that he never accepts responsibility for anything he has done.'

As Van Hoogstraten stood expressionless, the judge told him: 'You are not a victim. You are more often than not the author of your own misfortunes... At some point you will have to face reality and face up to the responsibility you have from your position.'

The judge announced that Van Hoogstraten's womenfolk and

children had written to him revealing that there was a generous side to the man. He didn't say whether that weighed with him.

He told the prisoner: 'I sentence you on the basis that you were the instigator of a terrifying piece of intimidation which necessarily was designed to convey a threat to Mr Raja that he would be caused really serious bodily harm or killed unless he desisted from the fraud claim.'

The sentence was ten years.

As he heard the sentence, newspapers reported that Van Hoogstraten 'smirked'. He did not. As sentence was passed he had his hands behind his back, clasping a pencil. It broke.

There was one last piece of defiance. Van Hoogstraten was ordered to pay a third of the prosecution costs, or £120,000. Looking up at the judge, he snapped: 'And you're suggesting I'm not the victim, I suppose?'

As far as the outside world was concerned that was the end of the story. Van Hoogstraten would, of course, appeal. But among hacks and lawyers at the Old Bailey the concensus was that he wouldn't stand a chance.

Van Hoogstraten's letters, though, remained upbeat. 'My leave to appeal will be granted shortly then the whole process starts to unravel,' he wrote on 30 December 2002.

The appeal was not his only concern. After his conviction the Raja family took up the fraud case which had begun the tragic saga.

This fight resumed a mile away from the Old Bailey, in the Law Courts. and very quickly Van Hoogstraten began to get the worst of it. Ordered by the court to disclose his worldwide assets, the tycoon claimed that he wasn't after all, mega rich. He didn't own the palace and that fabulous art collection was no longer his. Indeed the man who only months before let the Old Bailey believe he was worth £500 million now claimed to be worth only a few million pounds.

Judge Peter Smith, a no-nonsense, roly poly of a man with an Oliver Hardy moustache, made clear his disbelief. 'Charade' was one of the words he used to describe what he was hearing about the tycoon's finances. He fined Van Hoogstraten £200,000 for defying the court and told him that £50,000 would be added for every week in which he didn't come clean.

That didn't work and Judge Smith tightened the screws – or tried to. He ruled that because of Van Hoogstraten's actions – his involvement in the killing and his failure to disclose – the tycoon had forfeited the right to a defence against the fraud claim. The Rajas had won. Van Hoogstraten must pay their £5 million.

But it never happened. Everything began to change. Di Stefano had found the escape route Van Hoogstraten had prayed for.

18

FREEDOM

Whether fate has taken a hand in Hoogstraten's life is a moot point. If, as the ancient Greeks believed, we are the playthings of the gods, then fate surely took a hand in Nicholas van Hoogstraten's appeal against conviction.

The appeal came about because the judge who presided over the murder trial was not originally booked for the hearing. As we have seen, the original judge, Michael Hyams, had excused himself from hearing the case because he had previously been threatened by van Hoogstraten during a civil case. His withdrawal was to have far-reaching consequences that no one could have foreseen at the time.

The problem was his replacement's summing-up to the jury. While reviewing the case against van Hoogstraten, Judge Newman failed to mention one vital piece of information. Describing the tragic events that unfolded on that morning in July in 1999 at the home of Mohammed Raja, Newman did not mention that the assailants had carried a gun.

The judge's omission quickly became a focus for Hoogstaten and his new defence team. Even before he was sentenced he'd concluded that his sentence would be quashed on grounds of misdirection of the jury. He told the authors so in a letter from prison. Showing all the old bounce, he wrote, 'Don't forget that you heard it here first. And you should know that I'm very seldom wrong and I'm certainly not wrong on this.'

Thirty years earlier, Hoogstraten had successfully run his then much smaller empire from jail. Now he continued to run it through three people: the faithful Caroline Williams, the tough Greek Cypriot hotel owner, Andrew Emmanuel, and the secretive businessman David Martin. All kept their heads low, but the tycoon couldn't stay out of the headlines. From prison, he was said to be masterminding a plan to sell Mig fighter planes to the Mugabe regime in his beloved Zimbabwe. Then he and di Stefano were linked to a scheme to house a thousand asylum seekers in an old aircraft carrier, to be moored off the Kent coast.

The appeal began in the late spring of 2003 before Lord Justice Rose, Mr Justice McCombe and Mrs Justice Cox. It was time to see if Giovanni di Stefano's skills were as considerable as he claimed. Of course, Mr Stefano did not cast his legal spells alone; other top legal minds were also employed. Chief among them was Peter Kelson QC, who had acted for that other di Stefano client, John 'Goldfinger' Palmer, when a court order confiscating his millions was rescinded.

Kelson was a good choice. At the appeal, he carefully dissected the Crown's case against his client, paying particular attention to the judge's summing up. The hearing was technical, and hinged on minute points of law. Most of the attending journalists appeared lost in the complexities of the case for most of the time. But as Kelson developed the argument that the jury had been misdirected, the feeling grew in court that the verdict might indeed have to be quashed, just as Hoogstraten had earlier informed the authors. It began to look as if the man who, just a year before, had been jailed for ten years for manslaughter, might be about to get off.

Everything hinged on what Mr Justice Newman had said about manslaughter as an alternative verdict to murder. He had told the jury that a manslaughter verdict 'would come into play if you were sure that what Hoogstraten counselled Knapp to do was to frighten Mohammed Raja by, for example, threatening him with force, by assaulting him or kidnapping him ... and if you were sure he had not ordered any really serious bodily harm to be done to Mr Raja, but in the event things went wrong ... in that event Hoogstraten would be guilty of manslaughter.'

This direction was at the heart of the matter. For Hoogstraten, Peter Kelson argued that the jury could only reach a verdict of manslaughter if it was sure that Hoogstraten had contemplated the use of a lethal weapon. But in his summing up, Judge Newman had not mentioned the sawn-off shotgun used to kill Mr Raja. This was a serious omission.

For the prosecution, David Waters, QC, argued that everyone connected with the trial knew that the case centred around the use of a gun and that the judge's directions to the jury implied the use of a firearm. He was putting a good face on it, but his arguments sounded weak. Things were not going well for the Crown.

On 23rd July the appeal court gathered to give its verdict. The press benches were crowded, as were the public spaces. Members of both the Raja family and of Hoogstraten's were present in force. Lord Justice Rose quickly outlined the facts of the case, then moved on to his conclusions. Hoogstraten should only have been found guilty of manslaughter if the jury were sure he had contemplated the use of a lethal weapon – and the jury ought to have been directed of this. Lord Rose ruled that the trial judge's direction was too wide. It was flawed because it did not focus the jury's attention – in relation to any intention to frighten Mr Raja – on the use of a firearm.

'That being so,' said his lordship, 'There is no alternative but to allow this appeal and to quash the appellant's conviction.'

Throughout all this, Hoogstraten remained quiet and attentive. As he sensed victory his jaw took on a firmer set than usual and his eyes became more piercing than ever. But the court of appeal had not finished with him.

Lord Rose continued, 'The question which then arises is whether or not, in the interests of justice, there should be a retrial.' The gravity of the offence plainly pointed to the public interest lying in a retrial for manslaughter, he said.

Hoogstraten, it seemed, was not yet off the hook after all. A re-trial now faced him, and no one could tell what might happen with a new judge, a new jury, and maybe new evidence.

Kelson asked for bail, pointing out that his client had not absconded when on bail before the murder trial. But the Crown called Detective Inspector Andy Sladen, one of the police who had investigated Mohammed Raja's murder, as a witness. Sladen said there were grounds to fear that witnesses could be tampered with. Bail was refused.

An increasingly indignant Hoogstraten was to stay in prison until the retrial. It was set for February 2004. But there were hurdles in the way before it could start. One question hanging in the air was whether a fair trial was possible, given all the publicity surrounding the first trial and the vilification of Hoogstraten in the press. For the moment the appeal judges left that contentious issue hanging. It would, they said, be for another court to consider.

The second hurdle was a preliminary hearing which had to be held to ascertain whether there was a case to answer, i.e., whether there was evidence upon which a jury might conclude that Nicholas van Hoogstraten foresaw the act – the firing of a shotgun directly at the victim – which caused Mohammed Raja's death. Usually – if the prosecution has done its job thoroughly – such a hearing is a formality and the trail goes ahead. But, in the case of Regina versus Nicholas van Hoogstraten, nothing could be taken for granted.

The preliminary hearing took place at the Old Bailey before the High Court Judge, Sir Stephen Mitchell on 17th November 2003.

Hoogstraten was represented by another of his formidable new team of barristers, Geoffrey Cox, QC. Cox is a hugely experienced advocate whose expertise includes white collar crime and – of particular interest to Hoogstraten, given his concerns about a fair trial – human rights issues in criminal cases. He set out to persuade Sir Stephen that a retrial should not take place.

Once again, Judge Newman's summing up came into play. He had told the jury that manslaughter was an alternative verdict if they thought that, 'things went wrong, in the sense that Knapp and Croke ... went beyond what van Hoogstraten had ordered and killed Mohammed Raja, that would be a circumstance in which ... van Hoogstraten would be guilty of manslaughter.'

Cox advanced a new argument not used by the defence in the appeal. What really mattered was whether or not Hoogstraten could have foreseen that Knapp and Croke would go beyond the intention to frighten Mohammed Raja. If Hoogstraten could not have foreseen that the shotgun would be pointed at the victim and fired, then he was not guilty of manslaughter.

On 2nd December, Sir Stephen gave his judgement. He agreed with the defence that there was no case to answer. As the law stood, if a secondary party did not contemplate or foresee his accomplice departing from the intended plan to injure or frighten and instead committing murder, then he was not guilty of that action.

Hoogstraten had won. It was a stunning moment. But he wasn't quite off the hook just yet. Crown prosecutor David

Waters QC asked for leave to appeal. At this Hoogstraten betrayed the pressure he was under. He shouted, 'It's an absolute disgrace.'

Sir Stephen replied sternly, 'I know this is very difficult for you, but you must not interrupt Mr Waters.'

Events now gathered pace. Waters was granted his leave to appeal and six days later it was heard at the Royal Courts of Justice by three more judges under Lord Justice Kennedy. Four days after that, these three delivered the final verdict. They ruled that they had no jurisdiction over Sir Stephen's ruling and turned down the crown's appeal. Furthermore, the crown could make no further appeal.

Hoogstraten was finally a free man.

Outside the court he addressed a throng of reporters, television crews and jubilant friends and associates. Thirty years earlier he'd emerged from another period in jail boasting that he was more powerful and more dangerous than ever. There were no boasts this time. Twenty-two months in jail fighting his conviction while trying to keep his far-flung financial empire afloat had cost him physically. The dandy of the 1960s looked fully his 58 years now. But the venom was still there.

He told the cameras, 'This prosecution should never have been brought … I have suffered two years of legal incompetence and dishonesty.' He had been wrongly and vindictively charged and had sent in a dossier about the police handling of the case and would take legal action if it wasn't pursued. He made it clear that he wanted retribution.

A few yards away the shocked family of Mohammed Raja also faced the press. Amjad Raja said, 'Our family has now been deprived of an opportunity to have the case tried before a jury by what we see as a legal technicality.'

'The family are devastated that the extremely hard work of the police officers involved in the case has been totally undone by what we see as a catalogue of mistakes by the Crown Prosecution Service.'

Among the appeal court judges the unease at their ruling was palpable. In pronouncing that the lower court had been correct to stop the retrial, Lord Kennedy said that he nevertheless felt that it "thwarts the interests of justice."

The interests of justice, he said, required that Mr van Hoogstraten should be re-tried for his part in the death of Mr Raja. But under the present law it couldn't happen. He pondered the possibility of justice being better served in future if the prosecution were allowed to table a murder charge again when a retrial is ordered of someone acquitted of murder but found guilty of manslaughter. "But that is for parliament to decide, not this court," he said.

The Hoogstraten case had other consequences. A galaxy of convicted villains followed his lead and signed up with his colourful Italian lawyer, Giovanni di Stephano. They included the mass murdering GP, Harold Shipman, the fearsome underworld boss, Kenneth Noye, Jeremy Bamber, who slaughtered his whole family for an inheritence, the 'Railway' sex killer David Mulchy, and the 'Black Widow, Linda Calvey. Di Stephano was even engaged to try to clear two long-dead killers: the Kray twins. Hoogstraten had always relished the company of villains, but even he would recoil from many on this roll call of infamy.

Robert Knapp and David Croke protested their innocence as vehemently as Hoogstraten. Knapp argued in letters to the authors that there were flaws in the case that were not adequately examined – disputes over the DNA evidence, a phone call that, he alleges, alibis him on the morning of the murder, evidence that the payments to Hoogstraten made to him were indeed loans, and statements from witnesses who saw the killers. Knapp says that in all his years as an armed robber he never shot nor injured anyone, but now is cast as a 'hit man' in a murder he asserts he had nothing whatsoever to do with. In truth the case against him was always wafer thin. But on the day that Hoogstraten was given leave to appeal, both Knapp and Croke were denied it. Their one hope, perhaps, is Hoogstraten himself. During and after the trial the tycoon repeatedly dismissed the men who stood in the dock next to him as 'muppets'. But after his own release, Hoogstraten let it be known that he had high hopes of demolishing the case against his co-defendents just as the case against him was demolished. In July 2004 he claimed that he had evidence that would see them freed within months. Given the wonders he's worked on his own behalf no one is betting against it.

EPILOGUE

Even an age grown accustomed to the triumphs of lawyers was taken aback by Hoogstraten's emergence as a free man, legally exonerated of any connection to the Raja killing. The *Daily Mail* called it 'a mockery of justice'. The *Sunday Mirror* warned that the law was 'facing a crisis of confidence in its ability to dispense justice.' The *Mail on Sunday* proclaimed that, 'the smile on Nicholas van Hoogstraten's face outside the High Court ... should have sent a shiver through anyone who cares about Britain's judicial process.'

Hoogstraten remained impervious to it all. As was so often the case in the past, the demeanour of the man himself did not help his image. He expressed his gratitude gracefully to his latest team of lawyers, to the judges who'd freed him, and to the prison staff who'd kept him. But the familiar bile was still bubbling. He warned that he would sue 'just about everybody' responsible for what had happened to him.

'Be afraid. Be very afraid.' That, said the *Independent on*

Sunday, was Hoogstraten's message: 'Britain's most notorious landlord was back with a vengeance.'

There is no doubting his bitter sense of grievance. But the tycoon's first priority on release was to rescue his empire in Zimbabwe. He spent much of his first six months of freedom there trying to re-establish control where he could.

His next priority was to overturn the verdict in the fraud case in which Judge Peter Smith had ruled that by his actions the tycoon had forfeited the right of a defence.

He succeeded here thunderously. In July 2004 the appeal court decided that 'a serious injustice' had been done him. At a stroke the sequestration of his property world wide, £1 million in fines and the award of £5 million to the Rajas were all rescinded.

For the second time in 6 months Nicholas Van Hoogstraten faced the media in triumph. He issued a press release describing himself as the victim of a 'trail of dishonesty, incompetence, corruption and vindictiveness.'

The fight with Rajas wasn't finished. Amjad Raja vowed to continue with the fraud claim against Hoogstraten and Hoogstraten vowed to 'recover ... very substantial costs, damages and compensation' from the Rajas.

His third priority should be to build a new personal image. He has always insisted that he has such a terrible public persona because of media lies and distortion. But he remains his own worst PR man. At the end of an interview for the *Sunday Telegraph* in which his charm and cheek captivated the reporter, he couldn't resist this: 'I just hope the police and the judges or their families go to Zimbabwe or South Africa one day. My friends there would make sure they never got out again.'

There's a final, bizarre twist in the tale of Nicholas van Hoogstraten. During his time in prison he picked up a new qualification. Imagine the scene: a little old lady is terrified, her life a misery. Her landlord is trying to evict her and the new neighbours upstairs who have moved into the flat above her play loud music twenty-four hours a day. Becoming suicidal, she phones the Samaritans. A low, gravelly voice answers, 'Hello, Samaritans. Nick speaking. Can I help you?'

It may sound farfetched but it could happen. Whilst in prison, Hoogstraten picked up a qualification. Its nature is revealed in HM Prison Service document 10380, which reads, 'This is to certify that Nick van Hoogstraten has been trained by the Samaritans of Bexley/Bromley in listening and befriending skills.'

It will be interesting to see how he uses those new skills.